For Mrs Jane Waycott
With loving Greetings
from the
Womans Auxiliary
of Grace Church
March 22nd 1920.

The Optimist's Good Morning

The Optimist's Good Morning

Compiled by
Florence Hobart Perin

Boston
Little, Brown, and Company
1919

Printers
S. J. PARKHILL & CO., BOSTON, U.S.A.

TO
My Mother and Father

Acknowledgments

The compiler desires to make her grateful acknowledgments to the publishers and authors who have so generously given their permission to use selections from their copyrighted publications. She is especially indebted to Dodd, Mead & Co., Houghton, Mifflin & Co., The Century Co., The Outlook Co., Small, Maynard & Co., McClure, Phillips & Co., for extracts from "The Simple Life" by Charles Wagner and from "The Angelus" by Edwin Markham; G. P. Putnam's Sons for selections from "Christus Victor" by Henry Nehemiah Dodge; to Doubleday, Page & Co. for extracts from "The Story of My Life" by Helen Keller, copyright 1902, 1903; also for selections from "Afterwhiles," copyright 1887, "Riley Farm Rhymes," copyright 1885, "Riley Songs o' Cheer," copyright 1883, "Pipes o' Pan," copyright 1888, used by special permission of the publishers, The Bobbs-Merrill Co., to Charles Scribner's Sons for selections from "Fisherman's Luck," "The Lost Word," "Little Rivers," "The Story of the Psalms," "The Toiling of Felix and Other Poems," by Henry VanDyke, and a selection from "El Dorado" by Robert Louis Stevenson.

Preface

ONCE family devotions were general, now they are rare. There are reasons for the change. One reason is that the simplicity of the old family life is gone. It is not easy to get all the members of the family together at any one time in the day. A part of this is due to less leisure now than formerly. Men must catch trains in the morning. In the evening they are distracted by manifold social engagements.

Yet the need of spiritual adjustment is ever the same. Rapid transit, the telephone, the telegraph, do not take the place of God. Indeed the more rapid pace involved in these modern pace-makers, renders the more necessary some pause in the day for prayer, some upward look, when for a moment the soul may find an open way between itself and God. But how and when? Why not the breakfast table? Surely one or two minutes may be spared. Thirty seconds of silence, then the reading of a noble sentiment from some one who has been thinking for us, — another pause, — and a few words of prayer, framed by some one with more leisure than we have, but who puts us in the mood of prayer and so starts us right upon the duties of the day, — this will bring the needed readjustment.

Such is the plan and purpose of this little book. It is made for busy men and women, who *need* to begin the day with God. The quotations for each day are brief, but they are gleaned from the great Masters of thought. The prayers are from devout men of all the denominations.

As the title will have suggested, both quotations and prayers are generally in the spirit of a truly optimistic faith. However life may look in the middle of the night, it is a good thing to start out to do the work of the day with hope and courage. I shall be glad if I can feel that this little book has helped some busy people to begin the day in this spirit. I shall be particularly glad if I can feel that it has helped a little to keep the candles lighted on the family altar.

FLORENCE HOBART PERIN.

List of
Authors of Selections

xi

List of
Authors of Prayers

The Optimist's Good Morning

Throughout the year, why not keep sweet? No frown ever made a heart glad; no complaint ever made a dark day bright; no bitter word ever lightened a burden or made a rough road smooth; no grumbling ever introduced sunshine into a home. What the world needs is the resolute step, the look of cheer, the smiling countenance, and the kindly word. Keep sweet!

GEORGE L. PERIN.

God of the years, our Heavenly Father, whatever the message of the old year may have been, whether of darkness or light, joy or sorrow, — we stand this morning waiting expectantly and confidently for some message with glad tidings. May we therefore enter upon the New Year in the mood of hope and good cheer, — brushing from our faces every sign of care, let us go forth into the New Year with the spirit of a child who puts his hand into the hand of a Father to be led into a field where the flowers blossom and the birds sing. Not for to-day only do we pray for sweetness and light, but let us be glad and happy every day. Thou art with us today, — Thou wilt be with us through all the journey of the year. May our own daily gladness be born of the conviction that Thou art always near. Amen.

GEORGE L. PERIN.

To keep my health!
To do my work!
To live!
To see to it I grow and gain and give!
Never to look behind me for an hour!
To wait in weakness and to walk in power
But always fronting forward to the light,
Always, and always facing toward the right.
Robbed, starved, defeated, fallen, wide astray —
On, with what strength I have!
Back to the way!

CHARLOTTE PERKINS GILMAN.

With this new day, O God, let some new strength be mine, to walk in patience, the way appointed for me. Let me be strong to battle with the ills that shall beset me, to toil with faith and honest heart, to keep myself untainted and make my life helpful to my fellowmen. Help me to be forgetful of myself, but thoughtful to do no evil to any man. Thy hand is strong and mine is weak. I need Thy guidance, let Thy strength be mine, that though I stumble I may not fall nor fail. And when the day is done, may happy memories be mine. Amen.

ALMON GUNNISON.

Build on resolve, and not upon regret,
The structure of Thy future. Do not grope
Among the shadows of old sins, but let
Thine own soul's light shine on the path of hope
And dissipate the darkness. Waste no tears
Upon the blotted record of lost years,
But turn the leaf, and smile, oh, smile, to see
The fair white pages that remain to thee.

ELLA WHEELER WILCOX.

O Thou All-persuasive God, who dost speak within the souls of men in language which the heart interprets as its own! enlarge our trust in that better self which beckons us, that we may be led out of the lingering darkness of regret, out of the shadow of embittered memory into the brightness of a new resolve where we may see Thy face. Smile upon us in the smiling day; in the joy of strength renewed, and opportunity reborn; in the beauty of the promise each hour whispers to us as it passes by. So fill us with Thyself that each new day shall mean new life led by the glory of those hopes which do not fade at evening. Amen.

CHARLES A. KNICKERBOCKER.

We of our age are part, and every thrill that wakes
The tremulous air of Life its motion in us makes.

The imitative mass mere empty echo gives
As walls and rocks return the sound that they receive.

But as the bell, that high in some cathedral swings,
Stirred by whatever thrill, with its own music rings,

So finer souls give forth, to each vibrating tone
Impinging on their life, a music of their own.

W. W. STORY.

O living and loving One, brighter than the morning and fairer than the day, from Thee we come,
to Thee we turn, who art more than Father and
Mother to us all. Our times are in Thy hand. Thou,
who hast set the sun and stars in the sky, hast appointed our place and part in this human world.
May Thy light lead and Thy love win us into the
harmonies of law and grace, that we may become
responsive to every touch of nature, every whisper
of truth, every appeal of humanity. So prepare
us to serve our generation in the spirit of Him who
has taught us to do Thy will on earth as it is done
in heaven. Amen.

CHARLES G. AMES.

All such as worked for love, not wages — some
  Who, painting for a perfect tint did drain
  Their hearts, or some to save their country slain,
Or many who for truth braved martyrdom,
Or more who, in what common days may come,
  Have toiled in hope, beyond the hope of gain,
  Of doing something well, — all such would fain
Speak thus: These gifts more free than flowers from
The earth are given. Good world, if to our need
  Ye offer bread and shelt'ring roof unsought,
As guests our thanks we give, but not for greed,
  As if our gifts were bartered for and bought;
  And if, perchance, good world, ye offer nought,
Ah, well, that were of life the lesser meed.

J. S. JACKSON.

Father in Heaven, we thank Thee, as we enter upon another day, for strength with which to work. We thank Thee for our tasks; for our opportunities to work for Thee and for those we love, we thank Thee. May we know the joy, when night shall come, of having accomplished something worthy. Help us to see in that satisfaction a part of our pay. Make each of us faithful in his place; and help the humblest worker to understand that consecration and not rank is the all-important thing. Above all, may we not forget that living is giving, and may our desire either for rest or gain keep us from no helpful act. May we follow Him who came to minister, and live as sons and daughters of God. **Amen.**

FRANK W. WHIPPEN.

The sculptor moulds his clay with reverent hand,
That clay thro' which his fancy flashes free —
Quick with an answer to his soul's demand,
And pliant to his fingers' minstrelsy!
Could ever bronze or marble so respond
In wordless echo of the being's will?
Naught but the clay, as to a rapture fond
Could he with fire of genius thus infill!
And so the common people are the clay,
Swift moulded by Divine Deific hand,
Until transfigured, in the glorious day,
The statue of humanity shall stand!
It knows no tinsel crown, this masterpiece.
But all the sovereignty of God's release!

MARY HANAFORD FORD.

Heavenly Father, we are of Thy plain common people: we feel ourselves of very little worth. For what can we do of ourselves? But, if Thou wilt graciously use us, shaping us to Thine ends as the potter his clay, it may be that we shall serve some worthy purpose. We therefore yield ourselves to Thee, and beg Thee to use us this day. Make us pliant to Thy purposes, make us a help to someone who needs us today. So take us into partnership with Thyself, and so may this day be a day of delight, and our plain common lives be made rich with the Glory of service. Amen.

C. H. WHEELER.

And I, too, sing the song of all creation,
A brave sky and a glad wind blowing by,
A clear trail and an hour for meditation,
A long day and the joy to make it fly,
A hard task and the muscle to achieve it,
A fierce noon and a well-contented gloam,
A good strife and no great regret to leave it,
A still night — and the far red lights of home.

H. H. BASHFORD.

Almighty God, we thank Thee that Thou art our Father, and that Thou lovest us as though Thou hadst no other children; we adore Thee for the beautiful world in which Thou hast placed us; for trees and birds and flowers and sky, for friends and music and books and all the ten thousand mercies which crown our lives. We thank Thee too, for hard tasks and severe disciplines, for everything that is intended to make us strong and brave and true. Thou art the Lord of the day and of the night also. Give us grace to trust Thee and to believe in Thy motherly solicitude at all times. May Thy goodness lead us to repentance and to joyous unselfish living and may we so improve our opportunities for service that we shall make others think of Him who went about doing good and trusted in His Father with a perfect trust. **Amen.**

DILLON BRONSON.

Have we not all, amid life's petty strife,
Some pure ideal of a noble life
That once seemed possible? Did we not hear
The flutter of its wings and feel it near,
And just within our reach? It was. And yet
We lost it in this daily jar and fret.
But still our place is kept and it will wait,
Ready for us to fill it, soon or late.
No star is ever lost we once have seen:
We always may be what we might have been.

                             ADELAIDE A. PROCTER.

O Thou, whose goodness is new to us every morning and fresh every evening, we bless Thee for Thy patient and unforgetting care of all of us. Though we transgress Thy beneficent laws and frequently lose sight of our cherished ideals, our hunger and thirst for righteousness never dies, for we partake of Thy Divine Nature. O! that we might always be animated with Thy spirit of disinterested Love. We thank Thee this day for the inspiration of light and joy of our gifted poets and pray that we may meet the daily trials of life with a sweet and courageous spirit, remembering that "no star we have ever seen will cease to shine." Amen.

WILLIAM G. BABCOCK.

The future is lighted for us with the radiant colors of hope. Strife and sorrow shall disappear. Peace and love shall reign supreme. The dream of poets, the lesson of priest and prophet, the inspiration of the great musician, is confirmed in the light of modern knowledge; and, as we gird ourselves for the work of life, we may look forward to the time when in the truest sense the kingdoms of this world shall become the kingdom of Christ, and He shall reign forever and ever, King of Kings, and Lord of Lords.

JOHN FISKE.

All-wise and all-loving Father, we invoke Thy aid at the opening of a glad, new day. For the past we thank Thee, remembering that each day yielded its blessings. We rejoice that the victories of yesterday are the promise of larger successes today. Whenever during the day, we shall be conscious of our littleness, give us at that moment the vision of our possible largeness. Teach us, however tumultuous be the outward conditions, to maintain the inward calm. Today may Thy love work its miracle upon our pain and pleasure. So through faithful, hopeful work may we find Thy kingdom nearer at this day's close. Amen.

A. EUGENE BARTLETT.

Blessings on the man who smiles! I do not mean the man who smiles for effect, nor the one who smiles when the world smiles. I mean the man whose smile is born of an inner radiance, the man who smiles when the clouds lower, when fortune frowns, when the tides are adverse. Such a man not only makes a new world for himself, but he multiplies himself an hundred fold in the strength and courage of other men.

GEORGE L. PERIN.

Blessed art Thou, O Lord, our Father in heaven and on the earth! Give to us of Thy blessedness that all this day we may rejoice in Thee. Incline our hearts to see Thy goodness and wisdom. Make the gladness of our hearts constant that it may illumine our presence, so that those who walk with us may walk in Thy light and give Thee thanks. Make Thy joy our strength, whether expressed in storm or sunshine, that we may consent to Thy will cheerfully. We ask these and all gifts in the name of Him who would have His joy abide in us, that our joy may be fulfilled. Amen.

ALEXANDER McKENZIE.

Talk happiness! The world is sad enough,
Without your woes. No path is wholly rough;
Look for the places that are smooth and clear
And speak of those who rest the weary ear
Of earth, so hurt by one continuous strain
Of human discontent and grief and pain.

Talk health! The dreary, never changing tale
Of mortal maladies is worn and stale.
You cannot charm or interest or please,
By harping on that minor chord, disease.
Say you are well, or all is well with you,
And God shall hear your words and make them true.

ELLA WHEELER WILCOX.

Heavenly Father, by whose mercy we are permitted to greet another day, we offer Thee this morning our grateful praise for all the blessings of this life. We take from Thee with thankful heart the gift of health, conscious that we shall never know how rich the gift until we lose it. Now, while it is ours, may we use it with abounding joy for the good of those we may meet this day. To be able to bring light where there is darkness, hope where there is despair, comfort where there is sorrow, and so to be the children of our Father which is in Heaven, for this we pray, with the pardon of our sins, in Jesus' name. Amen.

FRANCIS H. ROWLEY.

The crest and crowning of all good,
Life's final star, is Brotherhood;
For it will bring again to Earth
Her long-lost Poesy and Mirth;
Will send new light on every face,
A kingly power upon the race,
And till it comes, we men are slaves,
And travel downward to the dust of graves.
Come clear the way, then, clear the way;
Blind creeds and kings have had their day,
Our hope is in the aftermath —
Our hope is in heroic men,
Star-led to build the world again.
To this event the ages ran;
Make way for Brotherhood — make way for Man.

EDWIN MARKHAM.

O Lord, make us like Thee. There can be no greater ambition, no loftier desire, no holier purpose, for Thou holdest the secret of Brotherhood. Like Thee, the only begotten of the Father, the essence of love, the joy of angels, the hope of the world, — make us like Thee, O Christ. Let Thy light be our light; thy service our joy; Thy peace our inheritance. Touch our lips that we may say no unkind word; touch our hearts that we may feel no wrong desires. May our living be for the world's good, our acts precious helps to Thy kingdom, our all consecrated to Thy blessed service. May we be satisfied when we awake with Thy likeness. Amen.

WILLIAM H. MAIN.

If there be some weaker one,
Give me strength to help him on;
If a blinder soul there be,
Let me guide him nearer Thee.
Make my mortal dreams come **true**
With the work I fain would do;
Clothe with life the weak intent,
Let me be the thing I meant;
Let me find in Thine employ
Peace *that dearer is than joy!*

JOHN GREENLEAF WHITTIER.

Heavenly Father! We humbly beseech Thee to breathe upon us Thy Holy Spirit, that we may be Thy true disciples, that we may be quick to see our brother's need, and quicker to relieve it. If he has lost his way, may we be aided to show it to him clearly. May we see our brother in the Master's " prodigal," and find in every needy soul our sphere of service. Forgive our weak excuses, and make the flickering embers burn to fervent heat, that the ideal Thou hast given in Thy Word may command every power of our lives. For Jesus' sake, Amen.

GEORGE WHITAKER.

A German allegory tells of two little girls. They had been playing together in a strange garden, and soon one ran in to her mother full of disappointment. "The garden's a sad place, mother." "Why, my child?" "I've been all around, and every rose-tree has cruel, long thorns upon it!" Then the second child came in breathless. "O Mother, the garden's a beautiful place!" "How so, my child?" "Why, I've been all around, and every thorn-bush has lovely roses growing on it!" And the mother wondered at the difference in the two children. Anonymous.

Divine Spirit and Soul of this day! We rejoice in its accomplished and its prophetic beauty and wealth which even our undisciplined hearts and minds may readily perceive, but may we increase the joy of its activities and its whole divine meaning by a deeper appreciation of its ministry to the disciplined life we bear. If there shall be fortunes in its passing which we would not choose, if there shall be encountered any experiences we would shun, may we remember that our reverses only emphasize our successes, that our sorrows intensify our joys, that even the humiliation and shame of the "far country" add divine meaning to the Father's House where wait the sandals and robes and rings for the comfort and beauty that are yet to be. May we learn that the thorn protects the rose, that the flaming sword turning in all directions protects the Tree of Life in every Eden of the world. May we remember that every great and good fortune of life is guarded by a seeming hostility which bears in its soul the secret of a lasting benevolence appointed for our own good. Amen.

E. L. Rexford.

*We are haunted by an ideal life, and it is because
we have within us the beginning and the possibility
of it. God is our continual incitement because we
are His children. So the ideal life is in our blood
and never will be still. We feel the thing we ought
to be beating beneath the thing we are. Every time
we see a man who has attained our ideal a little more
fully than we have it wakens our languid blood and
fills us with new longings.*

PHILLIPS BBOOKS.

O God, we thank Thee each morning for ideals
which appeal to us with such persistence that we have
no peace unless we pursue them. Even in our seeming indifference we are ill at ease, because Thy
voice calling to us disturbs our fancied content.
We are not satisfied with ourselves nor with our
attainments. "We shall be satisfied only when we
wake in Thy likeness." Weary though we often are
in our service yet we thank Thee that Thou relent-
lessly pursuest us with even greater and higher
demands. Help us in our onward and upward
plodding. Revive our failing spirits. Lead us ever
on. Help us to realize that "in our patience we
shall win our souls." We pray as followers of Jesus
Christ. Amen.

THEODORE A. FISCHER.

O Singer of today, this glorious hour
  Is all for you and me — what shall it give
To us, and ask of fate — what splendid power
  In brain and hand, what glorious right to live
Among our fellows and to war with sin?
  What quickening of the pulse as we aspire
To claim our right, and risk earth's joys to win,
  To conquer self, and force it through the fire!
Give us this force, dear God, and evermore
  Give us a deepening love of all our fellowmen;
Give us new insight — courage to explore
  With all the tenderness of human ken
The lowliest heart that beats in human kind,
  Its glory and its soul to seek and find!
                    WILLIAM ORDWAY PARTRIDGE.

O Soul of all souls! Baptize us afresh this morning into the lustral waters that we may devoutly thank Thee that Thou art and that Thou dost clearly reveal Thyself to Christian souls through Thy Son, as the Father of the great brotherhood of mankind. So wait upon us that we shall go forth to this day's duties resolved upon so living as to render the morning glad, the noon redolent with merciful activity, and the evening full of praise. Thus quickened and enlarged the night will afford rest and recuperation fitting us to welcome the morrow, still hoping, loving, progressing, obedient to the sainted call, "Up higher," being incessantly recompensed with the coveted refrain, "Well done." Amen.

S. H. McCOLLESTER.

There is one topic peremptorily forbidden to all well-bred, to all rational mortals, namely, their distempers. If you have not slept or if you have slept, or if you have headache, or sciatica, or leprosy or thunder stroke, I beseech you, by all angels, to hold your peace, and not pollute the morning, to which all the housemates bring serene and pleasant thoughts, by corruption and groans.

RALPH WALDO EMERSON.

Our Father, when we remember the multitude of Thy mercies our hearts are filled with peace and praise and we are ashamed to murmur and complain. Turn our thoughts toward the love and joy that this day holds for us; its opportunities, its privileges and victories. Let the morning light dispel the shadows on our faces and the fears in our hearts. Thou hast glorified us and will glorify us again. Help us to be grateful for the rose that smiles amidst the thorns and the light that ever shines behind the clouds. Grant that the spirit of trust may prevail in us and send us on our way with power to conquer. Amen.

ABRAM CONKLIN.

Simplicity is a state of mind. It dwells in the main intention of our lives. A man is simple when his chief care is the wish to be what he ought to be, that is, honestly and naturally human. And this is neither so easy nor so impossible as one might think. At bottom it consists in putting our acts and aspirations in accordance with the law of our being, and consequently with the Eternal Intention which willed that we should be at all. Let a flower be a flower, a swallow a swallow, a rock a rock, and let a man be a man, and not a fox, a hare, a hog, or a bird of prey: this is the sum of the whole matter.

CHARLES WAGNER.

Dear Heavenly Father, we rejoice in the awakening of body and soul to new activities. We thank Thee for the gift of divinity in the soul and for opportunity to give it expression. We would be true to ourselves, knowing we can thus alone be true to Thee. O God, hush the voice of evil passion. Quicken every noble aspiration. Grant the vision of Thy holy love that Thy image within us may remain clear in the turmoil of our life. We pray Thee stir the heart and mind that both may grow up to the full stature of man as it was in Jesus, our Saviour. Amen.

L. WARD BRIGHAM.

God has put the keys to His kingdom into your own hands. Your intelligence is a key, your affection is a key, your conscience is a key. With these keys you are to unlock the great doors of life, and gain access to its heavenly treasures.

JAMES M. PULLMAN.

Master of life, as Thou hast opened our eyes to see the sun, open the eyes of our hearts to see the splendor of Thy law. And even as Thou dost bring to birth, through the marriage of our eye and the sun, all the beauty of this visible world, so through the union between our hearts and Thy holy will, create a world rejoicing in the beauty of truth and justice and peace. Lead us this day deeper into the mystery of Thy life and our life and make us interpreters of life to our fellows, through Him who by His death opened for us the book of life, Jesus Christ our Lord. Amen.

HENRY S. NASH.

A noiseless, patient spider,
I mark'd how on a little promontory it stood isolated,
Mark'd how to explore the vacant, vast surrounding,
It launch'd forth filament, filament, filament, out of
*   itself,*
Ever unreeling them, ever tirelessly speeding them.

And you, O my soul, where you stand,
Surrounded, detached, in measureless oceans of space,
Ceaselessly musing, venturing, throwing, seeking
*   the spheres to connect them,*
Till the bridge you will need be form'd, till the ductile
*   anchor hold,*
Till the gossamer threads you fling catch somewhere
*   O my soul.*

WALT WHITMAN.

Thou Infinite Spirit, we are glad of all human relationships. We are thankful for all companionship with nature. We rejoice in the fellowship with books, yet like the child who grows tired with every plaything and every childish task and lonely for a mother's love, we look to Thee with an infinite longing. In our effort to solve the problems of life, we throw our web of life hither and thither, but it will not hold. Only when at last we have thrown the thread of faith to Thee, shall the ductile anchor hold. Our Heavenly Father, as we go forth into this day, may we not leave Thee for any dream or phantom, but may we walk with Thee all day long, and find in Thee the answer to every longing and the solution of every problem. Though we may not see, we may trust and wait. Amen.

GEORGE L. PERIN.

*Do not think of your faults, still less of others'
faults; in every person who comes near you, look
for what is good and strong; honor that; rejoice in
it; and as you can, try to imitate it; and your
faults will drop off like dead leaves when their
time comes.*

RUSKIN.

*With a clear sky, a bright sun, and a gentle
breeze, you will have friends in plenty; but let fortune frown, and the firmament be overcast, and then
your friends will prove like the strings of the lute,
of which you will tighten ten before you find one
that will bear the stretch and keep the pitch.*

GOTTHOLD.

Dear Father, may the new day bring some fresh
and inspiring thought of Thyself. May it give some
tender communion with the universe, kindling into
beauty as Thy smile shines through. May we make
and keep a few dear friends. May some good book
enrich the passing hours. May love flow through
all acts, and the star of hope shine in all shadows.
And trusting Thee supremely, may we humbly do
our best that good may abound on earth. Amen.

JOSEPH H. CROOKER.

The power of mere activity is often overrated. It is not what the best men do, but what they are, that constitutes their truest benefaction to their fellowmen. The things that men do get their value, after all, from the way in which they are able to show the existence of character which can comfort and help mankind. . . . It is the lives, like the stars, which simply pour down on us the calm light of their bright and faithful being, up to which we look and out of which we gather the deepest calm and courage.

PHILLIPS BROOKS.

Thou knowest, dear Father, how often we wish to do many things which are beyond our power. Help us to believe that Thou dost accept the wish when we cannot do the deed. But we thank Thee that we can do some things, though they are not large nor many. We know that as we grow in faith, in patience, in courage, in love, we radiate light and peace and power to those who are around us. As we begin a new day, we are uplifted by the thought that we have been called into being because Thou desirest the love of children, and because we are to co-work with Thee by loving and serving all whom we can reach. Always, we believe, art Thou ready to help us. Always art Thou brooding over us to draw us nearer to Thee, and to give us light and strength to be fellow-workers with Thee. In this new day, may we speak some word and do some work which shall please Thee and give us joy as we shall lie down to sleep. Amen.

HENRY BLANCHARD.

We pride ourselves, in weighing worth and merit,
Too much in virtues that we but inherit.
Some punctual grandsire makes us hate delay
And we are proud to keep our oath and day.
But our ancestral follies and abuses
We still indulge in, and make for them excuses.
Let him be proud, dared man be proud at all,
Who stands where all his fathers used to fall,
Holding their virtues fast and passing on
Still higher good through his own victories won.
                                   ISAAC OGDEN RANKIN.

This morning, the sun shines by his own inherent worth. The clouds often intercept his influence but he shines back of them and finds a way through the slightest cleft to tip them with glory. He always reveals himself — his inner self — and makes all purer and more beautiful. May we so shine! The world needs the divinity there is in us. We are a part of Thee. Thou art our deeper self. The Nazarean prophet relied entirely upon his inner life and found ancient good uncouth. Whatever clouds intercept our influence, teach us to reveal what conscience dictates, what intuition illumines, what reason shows, to purify our time, and all unrighteousness, wrong thinking and useless and hurtful custom. To this end, give us **purity, courage, and** nobility. Amen.

WILLIAM S. MORGAN.

My faith begins where your religion ends, —
In service to mankind. This single thread
Is given to guide us through the maze of life.
You start at one end, I the other; you,
With eyes fixed only upon God, begin
With lofty faith, and, seeking but to know
And do His will who guides the universe,
You find the slender and mysterious thread
Leads down to earth, with God's divine command
To help your fellowmen; but this to me
Is something strangely vague. I see alone
The fellowmen, the suffering fellowmen.
Yet, with a cup of water in my hand
For all who thirst, who knows but I one day,
Following faithfully the slender thread,
May reach its other end, and kneel at last
With you in heaven at the feet of God?

ALICE WELLINGTON ROLLINS.

Our Father in heaven, author of life and light, justice and mercy, liberty and love, we hail with joy and gratitude this new born day, token of Thy presence, good will and continued care. Help us with high ideals, pure thoughts and noble endeavors to hallow Thy name, trusting where we cannot prove, proving where we cannot trust, by a willing service to our fellowmen, ever advancing by faith, by works, with a strong heart, a firm step, a generous hand, a sunny smile, and a cheering voice, until we all come into the measure of the stature of the fulness of Christ; and Thy will be done on earth as it is in heaven. Amen.

HENRY N. COUDEN.

If you would have sunlight in your home, see that you have work in it: that you work yourself and set others to work. Nothing makes moroseness and heavy-heartedness in a house so fast as idleness. The very children gloom and sulk if they are left with nothing to do. Every day there is the light of something conquered in the eyes of those who work. In such a house, if there be also the good temper of love, sunshine never ceases. For in it the great law of humanity is obeyed, a law which is also God's law. For what said Christ, " My Father worketh hitherto and I work." Sunlight comes with work.

STOPFORD A. BROOKE.

O Thou, who art the source of light and life, we pause in Thy presence at the opening of the day, that in the light of thy countenance we may see ourselves as we are and as we ought to be, and receive the inspiration to consecrated effort and worthy achievement. We thank Thee that Thou hast done so much for us and yet left so much for us to do. May we think how important are these lives we are going to live today; that no matter how small we are, this universe in all its majesty can never be complete without our effort, and Thou, Almighty God, art waiting with infinite patience for us to do our part. Thus shall our work, however humble, be glorified by a Godlike temper and a Christlike faith. Amen.

FREDERICK A. BISBEE.

All that is, at all,
Lasts ever, past recall:
Earth changes, but thy soul and God stand sure;
What entered into thee,
That was, is and shall be.

. . . .

He fixed thee 'mid this dance
Of plastic circumstance,
This Present, thou, forsooth, wouldst fain arrest;
Machinery just meant
To give thy soul its bent,
Try thee, and turn thee forth, sufficiently impressed.
ROBERT BROWNING.

We thank Thee, O Father, for the yet unwrought possibilities of this day. Show us Thy purpose; or, if it please Thee, withhold the entire plan, yet may our faith claim a divine sanction for each hour's work as a part of the fulfilment of Thy purpose. We pray for strength and patience to have our souls rightly impressed by the cares, the joys, and disappointments of life. Make the things of the body only incidental to us. Save us from all but the best things. Give us the happiness of harmony with Thee. Wilt Thou grant these things through the power of Thy spirit, and in the name of Thy perfect Son, the vision of whom transforms our lives! Amen.

GEORGE W. OWEN.

Beloved, let us love so well,
Our work shall still be better for our love
And still our love be sweeter for our work.
             ELIZABETH BARRETT BROWNING.

If your name is to live at all, it is so much more to have it live in people's hearts than only in their brains! I don't know that one's eyes fill with tears when he thinks of the famous inventor of logarithms, but a song of Burns or a hymn of Charles Wesley goes straight to your heart and you can't help loving both of them, the sinner as well as the saint.
             OLIVER WENDELL HOLMES.

Our Father, who art in heaven, help us to hold Thee in our hearts this day, that we may live for Thee, from the love of Thee. Forgive us that we have not always a thankful spirit. Strengthen our wills to do good work, as in Thy sight, with clean hands and heart. Help us now as we pray, and flood the morning with the sunshine of Thy face, that we may be glad all the day long, and bring other lives into the brightness of Thy light. Save us from a partial mind, that we may love all Thy little ones with the same love of Him who said "Of such is the Kingdom of Heaven." Amen.

C. W. HOLDEN.

All thoughts of ill; all evil deeds,
That have their root in thoughts of ill;
Whatever hinders or impedes
The noble action of the will; —
All these must first be trampled down
Beneath our feet, if we would gain
In the bright fields of fair renown
The right of eminent domain.
We have not wings, we cannot soar;
But we have feet to scale and climb
By slow degrees, by more and more,
The cloudy summits of our time.

              HENRY W. LONGFELLOW.

We bless Thee, Lord, for the new day and for the new chance which it offers to our wayward lives. Forgive the evil in them, and make the good efficient. Let the tides of Thy spirit bring to us cleansing, refreshment and power. In the day's business may we be brave, cheerful and considerate. Grant us a clear vision of the path of honor and the will to choose it at whatever cost. We wait upon Thee for renewal of our strength; for uplift as on eagle's wings; for unwearied running upon Thy larger errands, if Thou shalt ordain us to such high employ; but most of all, for grace to walk life's common ways without fainting. So at evening wilt Thou send Thy peace. Amen.

EDWARD M. CHAPMAN.

*Don't you touch the edge of the great gladness that
is in the world, now and then, in spite of your own
little single worries? Well, that's what God means;
and the worry is the interruption. He never means
that. . . . If you are glad for one minute in the
day, that is His minute; the minute He means, and
works for.*

MRS. A. D. T. WHITNEY.

Dear Father, Thou hast made us fit for joy. Help
us today to grasp our birthright of gladness. For
those things which must be borne in sorrow give us
submission. Let us taste the salt tonic of our tears
and feel the strength born of struggle and the peace
wrested from trial. Make us glad that friendly hands
meet our own; that kindness is always sweet and
sympathy divine. Teach us to lay hold on the
radiance of each hour, that the morning bow of
promise may become our evening glory and prophesy
another glad new day. As children find content
and joy by looking into their father's face so we
turn to Thee. Amen.

EFFIE McCOLLUM JONES.

Still must I climb if I would rest;
The bird soars upward to his nest;
The young leaf on the tree-top high
Cradles itself within the sky.

I cannot in the valley stay:
The great horizons stretch away;
The very cliffs that wall me round
Are ladders unto higher ground.

I am not glad till I have known
Life that can lift me from mine own;
A loftier level must be won.
A mightier strength to lean upon.

LUCY LARCOM.

Heavenly Father, as the bird that soars first looks upward, we turn our souls to Thee, seeking inspiration that in the duties of today we may live to the full height of the faculties Thou hast given. Help us to know what is right and to follow it day by day continually. Grant that our toils this day may be acts of service as sacramental as our prayer. In our weakness, grant us of Thy strength that we may pass from glory to glory till we are transformed at last into the perfect image of Thy spirit. And when our work on earth is ended, when the clods of the valley are sweet to our weary frame, take us home to Thyself. Amen.

NATHANIEL S. SAGE.

Only a frown!   Yet it pressed a sting
  Into the day which had been so glad;
The red rose turned to a scentless thing:
  The bird-song ceased with discordant ring;
And a heart was heavy and sad.

Only a smile! yet it cast a spell
  Over the sky which had been so gray;
The rain made music wherever it fell;
  The wind sang the song of the marriage-bell;
And a heart was light and gay.

ANONYMOUS.

With our tribute of praise, O Father, we would begin this day; this day, which, with all its bounties, is Thy gift. Prepare us, we beseech Thee, for the experiences of the hours as they open before us. Gratefully remembering that we are Thy children, may our duties weigh with such sacredness upon our hearts that we may shun the evil way as unworthy those so richly endowed and blest. Write, we pray Thee, Thy law within us; and may our love of Thee make it so easy and so joyous to obey that we shall continually grow into the likeness of Him whose mission it is to fill the world with blessedness and peace. Amen.

CHARLES W. TOMLINSON.

Father, I will not ask for wealth or fame,
Though once they would have joyed my carnal sense.
I shudder not to bear a hated name,
Wanting all wealth, myself my sole defence.
But give me, Lord, eyes to behold the truth;
A seeing sense that knows the eternal right;
A heart with pity filled, and gentlest ruth;
A manly faith that makes all darkness light;
Give me the power to labor for mankind;
Make me the mouth of such as cannot speak;
Eyes let me be to groping man and blind;
A conscience to the base; and to the weak
Let me be hands and feet; and to the foolish, mind;
And lead still farther on such as Thy Kingdom seek.

THEODORE PARKER.

Heavenly Father, we speak to Thee this morning out of a sense of rest and trust. We would begin the day with Thee and keep in Thy company to its close. Whether we work or pray, wilt Thou rule our spirits? Conscious in this moment of freedom, that we shall soon be pressed and absorbed by our own cares, we pray, Father, that we may keep in mind the privilege and joy of bearing each other's burdens and so fulfilling the law of Christ. Nor ever permit us to fall away from perfect faith in Thy purpose. Work in us and through us to usher in the morning when Truth shall spring out of the earth and Righteousness shall come down from heaven. Amen.

ISAAC M. ATWOOD.

As when good news is come to one in grief, straightway he forgetteth his former grief, and no longer attendeth to anything except the good news which he hath heard, so do ye, also! having received a renewal of your soul through the beholding of these good things. Put on therefore gladness that hath always favor before God, and is acceptable unto Him, and delight thyself in it; for every man that is glad doeth the things that are good, and thinketh good thoughts, despising grief.

MARIUS THE EPICUREAN.

O Lord, we know there are a thousand reasons why we should be glad. We cannot always forget our sorrows and our failures; there are manifold sources of temporary vexation and annoyance and harassing care, but in the face of Thine overmastering Providence and Love we cannot long be vexed nor sad. If tears have dimmed our eyes let us brush away the tears. If troubles and cares have burdened our hearts let us rise triumphant over them all and for this day be glad; and in our gladness let us find our strength. Amen.

GEORGE L. PERIN.

Do not dare to be so absorbed in your own life, so wrapped up in listening to the sound of your own hurrying wheels, that all this vast pathetic music, made up of the mingled joy and sorrow of your fellow-men, shall not find out your heart and claim it and make you rejoice to give yourself for them. . . . Be sure that ambition and charity will both grow mean unless they are both inspired and exalted by religion. Energy, love, and faith, — these make the perfect man.   PHILLIPS BROOKS.

O Thou who art not far from any one of us, but art the Source and Sustainer of our life, gratefully do we acknowledge the Mercy that has given us this new day with its certain opportunity for living the glad, true life. Directed by Thee, may this be for us a day of progress. May its duties be performed with alacrity and cheerfulness, its lessons learned with humility, its temptations met with resolute will, its crosses with patient hope. We thank Thee for the life of the Master who has shown us that if we would live Thy divine life, ours must be one of continual service and constant progression. If, tried by the seeming drudgery of duties daily repeated, we long for the end of our labors or dream of an idle heaven, O forgive our weakness, and help us trustingly to obey Thy voice as it whispers, " Up and on, this is not thy rest." Thus let the day close on hours well spent, and Thy joy and peace fill our hearts. Amen.

JOHN MURRAY ATWOOD.

*Who art thou that complainest of thy life of toil?
Complain not. Look up, my wearied brother; see
thy fellow-workmen there, in God's eternity; surviving there, they alone surviving; sacred band of
the Immortals, celestial body-guard of the empire of
mankind. To thee, Heaven, though severe, is as
that Spartan mother, saying while she gave her son
his shield, "With it, my son, or upon it." Thou
too shalt return home in honor; to thy far distant
Home, in honor; doubt it not, — if in the battle thou
keep thy shield! Thou, in the Eternities, and deepest
death-kingdoms, art not an alien; thou everywhere
art a denizen. Complain not.*

THOMAS CARLYLE.

O Thou God of goodness and grace, who dost
turn Thy smiling countenance upon the upturned
faces of Thy children, help us to find in the light of
another day the continued proof of Thy fatherly
care and tender mercy. Since Thou art so well
disposed towards us, give us courage to attempt
anything which the duties of this day require, remembering that Thou canst not ask anything beyond
our strength, or withhold from us the blessing of
Thy Divine approval. Living under Thy smile help
us to be strong and calm and confident, delighting
Thy heart by our faith in Thee and our love for our
fellowmen. Amen.

SAMUEL C. BUSHNELL.

This goodly frame, the earth, seems to me a sterile promontory; this most excellent canopy, the air, look you, this brave o'er-hanging firmament, this majestical roof fretted with golden fire, why, it appears no other thing to me than a foul and pestilent congregation of vapors. What a piece of work is a man! how noble in reason! how infinite in faculty! in form and moving how express and admirable! in action how like an angel! in apprehension how like a god!

SHAKESPEARE.

Our Father in Heaven, we pray Thee that this may be a bright and happy day in each of our lives. May there be sunshine in our hearts because they are attuned to Thine. Going about our daily tasks, Thy spirit within us, may we make our little portion of the earth not a sterile promontory but a rich garden abounding in the fruits of the spirit, and may we, by Thy grace, be enabled to dispel some of the pestilent vapors of wordliness and doubt. In all things, may we remember our divine parentage and conform our lives more and more to the pattern shown us by Thy dear Son, Jesus Christ, in whose name we pray. Amen.

FRANCIS E. CLARK.

There was a merchant once, who on the way
Meeting one fatherless and lamed, did stay
To draw the thorn which pricked his foot, and passed
And 'twas forgot; and the man died at last.
But in a dream the Prince of Khojand spies
That man again, walking in Paradise.
Walking and talking in that blessed land,
And what he said the prince could understand;
For he said this, plucking the heavenly posies;
" Wonderful!   One thorn made me many roses! "
EDWIN ARNOLD.

Dear Father in Heaven, with our life refreshed and renewed by sleep, we would face the duties of the day with strong hope and a ready courage. Forbid that these shall in any degree be diminished by any difficulty or perplexity that may arise. We pray for wisdom and love. Grant us that interest in others that shall impel us to help those who are in need. And may our desire to minister move us not only to dress the wounds of those whom the thorns have injured, but to clear the paths, along which men must pass, of those conditions and influences which inevitably maim and blight. May we serve Thee faithfully and with gladness this day! Amen.

HARRY L. CANFIELD.

Quicksand years that whirl me I know not whither,
Your schemes, politics fail, lines give way, substances
　　mock and elude me,
Only the theme I sing, the great and strong-possess'd
　　soul, eludes not,
One's self must never give way — that is the final
　　substance — that out of all is sure,
Out of politics, triumphs, battles, life, what at last
　　finally remains?
When shows break up what but One's self is sure?
　　　　　　　　　　　　　WALT WHITMAN.

O Thou, who beholdest all the souls of men, in our vision of another new day, help us to see as Thou seest; to be conscious not of our own need and desert alone, but also of the deserts and needs of all those with whom we have to do; shaping our prayer and directing the effort that follows after all true prayer in accordance with this wider outlook. O Thou, who fashionest the hearts of all, who observest all their works, we would strengthen and purify our hearts that they may be fitted to be fashioned by Thee to noble ends, and set to some good service; and we would do our daily work as in the sight of one who knows and loves all honest, thorough workers, great or humble, wise or simple. Amen.

AUGUSTUS MENDON LORD.

Truth should be the first lesson of the child and the last aspiration of Manhood; for it has been well said that the inquiry of truth, which is the love-making of it, the knowledge of truth, which is the presence of it, and the belief of truth, which is the enjoying of it, is the sovereign good of human nature.

> *We search the world for truth; we cull*
> *The good, the pure, the beautiful,*
> *From graven stone and written scroll,*
> *From all old flower-fields of the soul.*
>   JOHN GREENLEAF WHITTIER.

Our Heavenly Father, we acknowledge Thee as the Author and Giver of all truth. We bless Thee that Thou hast attuned our souls to its music, and that when with conscious life we touch its strings covering the universe we feel harmony with the Divine. We thank Thee for the truths of our sonship in Thee and for the assurances of Thy Fatherhood. We bless Thee for Jesus who was the truth made life, and who is our daily guide to its blessings. We thank Thee for the truth of immortality, with its encouragement to eager life today and its assurances of endless joyful tomorrows. Make us seekers of truth, lovers of truth and examples of truth as it is in Jesus our Savior. Amen.

FRED A. DILLINGHAM.

All things are engaged in writing their history. The planet, the pebble, goes attended by its shadow. The rolling rock leaves its scratches on the mountain; the river, its channel in the soil; the animal, its bones in the stratum; the fern and leaf, their modest epitaph in the coal. The falling drop makes its sculpture in the sand or the stone. Not a foot steps into the snow or along the ground, but prints, in characters more or less lasting, a map of its march. Every act of the man inscribes itself in the memory of his fellows, and in his own manners and face. The air is full of sounds, the sky of tokens, the ground is all memoranda and signatures, and every object covered over with hints which speak to the intelligent.

RALPH WALDO EMERSON.

Our Father, who art in Heaven and in every manifestation of living nature, we turn our thoughts to Thee with the rising of each new sun. We hear Thy voice in the singing of every summer bird. We realize Thy presence in the shifting shadows of the clouds. In the arching blue above us we realize something of the depth and breadth of the love that arches over the horizon of our life and stretches like the radiant bow of promise from the green hills of childhood to the sombre mountains of old age. We beseech Thee to give us thoughts so beautiful and ennobling that even amid the sods and clods of life's daily drudgery we can always face the morning light of some new hope which comes like the old song sung in the new land. Amen.

JOHN KIMBALL.

First, when I feel that I am become cold and indisposed to prayer, by reason of other business and thoughts, I take my psalter and run into my chamber, or, if day and season serve, into the church to the multitude, and begin to repeat to myself — just as children used — the ten commandments, the creed, and, according as I have time, some sayings of Christ or of Paul, or some Psalms. Therefore it is well to let prayer be the first employment in the early morning, and the last in the evening. Avoid diligently those false and deceptive thoughts which say, Wait a little, I will pray an hour hence; I must first perform this or that. For with such thoughts a man quits prayer for business that lays hold of and entangles him, so that he comes not to pray the whole day long.

MARTIN LUTHER.

O Lord, our Heavenly Father, who keepest covenant and loving kindness with Thy servants, who walk humbly with Thee, and who hast been attentive to the prayers of our fathers when they lifted up their hearts and their hands to Thee, teach us to pray, and to love to pray. Visit us in the night season and before the morning watch. Touch our spirits with the flame of Thy Spirit, before the day's business lays hold upon us and entangles us, through Jesus Christ, our Lord. Amen.

REUBEN KIDNER.

In one of Dean Stanley's sermons to children, preached at Westminster Abbey, he told the following story: "There was a little girl living with her grandfather. She was a good child, but he was not a very good man; and one day, when the little child came back from school, he had put in writing over the bed, 'God is nowhere,' for he did not believe in the good God, and he tried to make the little child believe the same. What did the little girl do? She had no eyes to see, no ears to hear, what her grandfather tried to teach her. She was very small. She could only read words of one syllable at a time; she rose above the bad meaning which he tried to put in her mind: she rose, as we all ought to rise, above the temptation of our time; she rose into a higher and better world; she rose because her little mind could not do otherwise, and she read the words, not 'God is nowhere,' but 'God is now here.' That is what we all should strive to do. Out of words which have no sense or which have bad sense, our eyes, our minds, ought to be able to read a better sense."

WILLIAM MOODIE.

O Thou, Invisible Presence, there can be no place where Thou art not. Thou, our Father, art in heaven and on earth and everywhere. Thou art in the order of the rock, the beauty of the flower, the light of the sun and stars, and goodness in the human soul. Teach us to be conscious of Thy nearness to us, and so may we never be afraid. In the light of Thy countenance, may we see duty and truth, and recognize more easily the good in one another.

Amen.

ALVA ROY SCOTT.

ABRAHAM LINCOLN BORN 1809

Chosen for large designs, he had the art
  Of winning with his humour, and he went
Straight to his mark, which was the human heart;
  Wise, too, for what he could not break he bent.

Upon his back a more than Atlas-load —
  The burden of the Commonwealth was laid;
He stooped, and rose up to it, though the road
  Shot suddenly downwards: not a whit dismayed.

Hold, warriors, counsellors, kings! all now give place
To this dear benefactor of the race.
RICHARD H. STODDARD.

Almighty Father, we thank **Thee today** for the gracious memory of Thy servant who lived and died for the sake of a free and united nation. We thank Thee more that we have his life inwrought into the very fabric of the life of the nation. We had in him "a hiding place from the wind and a covert from the tempest, a river of water in a dry place and the shadow of a great rock in a weary land." We gratefully join in praise with the thousands who found help and cheer in the shadow of his strength. And now we humbly beseech Thee, help us in some small way this day to be a helper to the helpless, a friend to the needy, sunshine to those whose day will be gray and gloomy, the shadow of a great rock to those who are buffeted by the world's storms. Thus shall we prove our gratitude to Thee for the gift of Thy servant whom we honor today, and thus shall we honor Thee. We ask and **offer** all in the name of **Thy Son Jesus Christ. Amen.**

AVERY A. SHAW.

Let us learn to be content with what we have. Let us get rid of our false estimates, set up all the higher ideals — a quiet home; vines of our own planting; a few books full of the inspiration of a genius; a few friends worthy of being loved, and able to love us in return; a hundred innocent pleasures that bring no pain or remorse; a devotion to the right that will never swerve; a simple religion empty of all bigotry, full of trust and hope and love — and to such a philosophy this world will give up all the empty joy it has.

DAVID SWING.

Thou gracious Spirit of Life, our Father, at the beginning of this new day we wait for a moment before Thee with uncovered heads and with reverent spirits; Thou knowest us through and through, whatever man may think of us Thou knowest just what we are. In Thy sight we need not pretend; we need not make believe, we need only be simple and genuine and brave and earnest. We need be glad in the possession of what we have. Help us this day to rightly value that which is good and honest. Let us for this day at least, put away all vanity and give ourselves unreservedly to Thy service and the love of our fellow men. To this high end, may we have the sweet companionship of Jesus. Amen.

GEORGE L. PERIN.

We go through life as some tourists go through Europe, — so anxious to see the next sight, the next cathedral, the next picture, the next mountain peak, that we never stop to fill our sense with the beauty of the present one. Along all our pathways sweet flowers are blossoming, if we will only stop to pluck them and smell their fragrance. In every meadow, birds are warbling, calling to their mates, and soaring into the blue, if we will only stop our grumbling long enough to hear them.

MINOT J. SAVAGE.

Give us, O God, the vision to see the way where duty lies and strength to walk in it, to ever keep the forward look and never to lose heart today because of the stumblings and fallings in the yesterdays that are forever gone. Let us remember that we are in Thy hands and we are faithless to Thee and to ourselves if knowingly we fail to do Thy work. Though we cannot see Thee, we now see our fellow men and we shall best serve Thee if, in love and patience, we help our fellows. Amen.

ALMON GUNNISON.

> *May I reach*
> *That purest Heaven — be to other souls*
> *The cup of strength in some great agony,*
> *Enkindle generous ardor, feed pure love,*
> *Beget the smiles that have no cruelty,*
> *Be that sweet presence of a good diffused,*
> *And in diffusion ever more intense!*
> *So shall I join the choir invisible,*
> *Whose music is the gladness of the world.*
>
> GEORGE ELIOT.

Our heavenly Father, we bless Thee for the gift of another day with all its opportunities for service. And we pray that our hearts may respond in sympathy with the heartbeats of those who love and toil and suffer around us today. May we learn to make their joys and sorrows our own. Do not let our unfeeling hands strike the heart-strings of others harshly, nor allow our feet to go crushing roses of love, without thought. Help us, we pray Thee, to walk tenderly and reverently among our fellow men. May their hopes and noble endeavors ring within us the prayer bells of the soul. Make us thus to grow large and tender and noble through our helpful ministries. Amen.

JOHN WESLEY CARTER.

Ah, love and love alone at last will solve
All the vast, threatening questions that distract
Mankind; that fellow-men in strife array,
And the whole world with fierce contentions rend.
Still keep your idle millions under arms —
Fed on the hard-earned substance of the poor —
Still watch each other with keen jealousy,
Still slaughter thousands on the field of war,
Or strive with statesman's craft to arbitrate ;
Thread the sly mazes of diplomacy,
Try communistic cures for every ill,
And when all fails at last, for lack of love,
Try love — the mightiest of them all — and win !

HENRY NEHEMIAH DODGE.

God of the light, — within, without, who hast lifted the curtain of night from our abodes, perfect now Thy blessing unto us, and take the veil from all our hearts, and make clear to us Thy holy presence. Filled with the everlasting light, may we look on each other, and on our work here below, and on the strifes and conditions of humanity, with a love and hope that are not of this world. May Faith, Hope and Love abide with us — and may we realize that the greatest of these is Love. Hasten Thou the time when by love alone Thy kingdom shall come, and Thy will be done on earth as it is in heaven. Amen.

WILLIAM B. EDDY.

*If the day and night are such that you greet them
with joy, and life emits a fragrance like flowers and
sweet-scented herbs, is more starry, more immortal, —
that is your success.   All nature is your congratula-
tion and you have cause momentarily to bless yourself.*
                                    HENRY DAVID THOREAU.

Father, I have found Thy gift of life, a sweet
and beautiful thing. It has known cloud and rain,
but these have nourished it, and the darkness has
sheltered it. It has felt driving storms, but these
have strengthened it. It has known sunshine too.
And now every day is a transfiguration and every
night a benediction. Let thanksgiving be my prayer.
What I need Thou wilt give. My hands Thou wilt
touch with the soft petals of Thy flowers; and the
arms of Thy strong care shall be about me. By
the voices of brooks and rivers and winds and birds
and little children Thou wilt speak to me, and
in the deeper silences I shall hear Thy still small
voice. Father, I thank Thee. Amen.
    O. C. S. WALLACE.

Let us not care too much for what happens: Let us not leave our peace of mind at the mercy of events.
CHARLES G. AMES.

Let us lay hold of the happiness of today. Do we not go through life blindly, thinking that some fair tomorrow will bring us the gift we miss today? . . . Know thou, my heart, if thou art not happy today, thou shalt never be happy.
ANNA ROBERTSON BROWN.

We thank Thee, our Father, that the Satisfaction of righteousness is present as well as future. Help us, we beseech Thee, to live this day so that earth shall seem like heaven. In the proof of our adequacy to the demands of duty may we find a delight that shall more than compensate us for any pleasure or profit surrendered for its sake. May the sense of Thine approval sanctify our joys and comfort our sorrows. May we win love by deserving it, and find happiness in bestowing it. Through obedience to Thy will may we add strength and spiritual beauty to our own character and carry into the evening shadows the sweet assurance that other lives have been enriched by our kind words and helpful deeds. We ask it as Thy children. Amen.

J. FRANK THOMPSON.

'Tis always morning somewhere, and above
The awakening continents from shore to shore,
Somewhere the birds are singing evermore.
                                    HENRY W. LONGFELLOW.

The inconveniences and the petty annoyances, the
pains and the sorrows, do we ever forget them? In-
deed, no; we grumble and groan continually. The
blue sky and the sunshine, the everyday mercies and
the wonderful blessings that we accept as a matter
of course, do we remember to rejoice because of them?
Only too seldom. On this one day, do let us be sin-
cerely and expressedly thankful.

                                    ANONYMOUS.

Our Father, we rejoice to believe that Thy love
is the eternal sun which knows no eclipse and that
in its pure shining, we Thy children can go forward
with brave hearts and radiant hopes, assured that
Thy wisdom hath left nothing unfinished and that
" Thy goodness faileth never." We greet this new
day with newness of joy in Thy Fatherhood as
our personal right, and with ascending ideals of a
service whose gracious light shall kindle other souls
into a larger hopefulness and a deeper tenderness.
We would fill this day with all sunny thoughts, with
all cheering words and with all generous deeds,
and thus the more effectually bring the divine light
into the human and make clearer the outlines of a
heaven on earth. Amen.

ARNOLD S. YANTIS.

No blast of air or fire of sun
Puts out the light whereby we run
With girdled loins our lamplit race,
    And each from each takes heart of grace
And spirit till his turn be done,
    And light of face from each man's face
In whom the light of trust is one;
    Since only souls that keep their place
By their own light, and watch things roll,
And stand, have light for any soul.
           ALGERNON CHARLES SWINBURNE.

O Thou, Who coverest Thyself with light as with a garment, even the true light which lighteth every man coming into the world, shine Thou in us, putting to flight all the powers of darkness, and guilt of sin, and selfishness. Shine also through us to any that live in the shadow; and so fill us with Thy radiant Spirit, that we may be a lamp unto a neighbor's feet and a light unto his path. And when this day is done may every face we have met be the brighter for our meeting, and every heart braver with new joy and cheer and grace and strength. For in Thee O Lord, is life, and Thy life is the light of men. Amen.

THEODORE PARKER.

The longer on this earth we live
And weigh the various qualities of men
The more we feel the high, stern-featured beauty
Of plain devotedness to duty,
Steadfast and still, nor paid with mortal praise,
But finding amplest recompense
For life's ungarlanded expense
In work done squarely and unwasted days.

JAMES RUSSELL LOWELL.

Our dear Heavenly Father, we would greet Thee
as this morning greets us. We thank Thee for the
daily duty; that, amid this wondrous world, Thou
hast set somewhat for our doing. May we appreciate
the honor. May we not grudge our best, even in
the humblest tasks, since Thou appointest them.
Strengthen us, we beseech Thee, if sometimes the
heart fails, and the tired hands get laggard. Show
us how the lowliest service becomes loftiest if done
with the glorifying motive of pleasing Thee. Make
us this day blithe in duty. When our heads find
pillow may Thy peace enfold us; forgive our failures;
and, for Jesus' sake, may we never cease endeavor.
Amen.

WAYLAND HOYT.

George Washington. Born 1732.

Welcome to the day returning,
   Dearer still as ages flow,
While the torch of faith is burning,
   Long as Freedom's altars glow!
See the hero whom it gave us
   Slumbering on a mother's breast;
For the arm he stretched to save us,
   Be its morn forever blest.

                   Oliver Wendell Holmes.

Father of life, we thank Thee that Thou hast been with the Fathers; that Thou hast been with him whose birth this day we celebrate. Thou wert willing to speak to them, and they were willing to hear Thee and answer Thee, "Lo, here am I; send me." We thank Thee that the memory of this great man has come down to us; of him who was first in war, first in peace, and first in the hearts of his countrymen; and we ask Thee that Thou wilt be with our countrymen today; that Thou wilt teach us Thy law, that we may walk in Thy ways; that this may be that happy nation whose God is the Lord. In all time of our trial, if we have sought Thee we have found Thee, — in all time of our success Thou hast won for us our victories, — Thou hast been with our counsellors. Father, today, tomorrow, and in days to come, in our memories and in our hopes be with us still, Our Father, Who art in Heaven. Amen.

Edward Everett Hale.

If you always remember that in all you do in soul or body God stands by as a witness, in all your prayers and your actions you will not err; and you shall have God dwelling with you.

EPICTETUS.

Faith acts on our souls as a moral tonic; it takes the fret and fever out of our lives; it gives the appetite and desire for noble living; it removes despondency; it gives energy, courage, hope, patience, and persistence; and in its highest manifestations it makes our lives a blending of power, sweetness, and peace.

JAMES M. PULLMAN.

Father of spirits! We yield ourselves to Thee. We will be afraid of neither sorrow nor death in a world where many saintly souls have sanctified them by a divine patience, and amid a Providence wherein no evil thing can dwell. Clinging unto Thee, we shall not perish with the fashion of this world that passeth away. As sparks falling on the river, so shall the glories of our strength go out. But the graces of the holy soul shall be as the brightness of the firmament, and as the stars forever and ever. In Thee, O Lord, is our undying trust. Amen.

JAMES MARTINEAU.

Be of good cheer, brave spirit; steadfastly serve that low whisper thou hast served; for know, God hath a select family of sons now scattered wide thro' earth, and each alone, who are thy spiritual kindred, and each one by constant service to that inward law, is weaving the sublime proportions of a true monarch's soul. Beauty and strength, the riches of a spotless memory, the eloquence of truth, the wisdom got by searching of a clear and loving eye that seeth as God seeth. These are their gifts, and time, who keeps God's word, brings on the day to seal the marriage of these minds with thine, thy everlasting lovers.

RALPH WALDO EMERSON.

O Thou, who makest the outgoings of the morning and evening to rejoice, help us to welcome this new day as Thy gift, to take up its duties with courage, and to follow the light which Thou shalt give. Conscious of the meaning and purpose of life, undismayed by the failures of past days, and ever remembering that Thy strength is made perfect in human weakness, may we consecrate ourselves anew to the glad service of life, knowing that in so doing we enter into fellowship with all who have been workers together with Thee, and into increasing likeness of soul to Thy holy Son. May the beauty of the Lord our God be upon us, and may life become stronger and sweeter and richer, until at last we receive through grace the "well done!" of the Master. Amen.

HENRY M. KING.

There is no music in a rest, but there is the making of music in it. In our whole life melody, the music is broken off here and there by "rests," and we foolishly think we have come to the end of time. God sends a time of forced leisure — sickness, disappointed plans, frustrated efforts — and makes a sudden pause in the choral hymn of our lives, and we lament that our voices must be silent, and our part missing in the music which ever goes up to the ear of the Creator. How does the musician read the rest? See him beat time with unvarying count and catch up the next note true and steady, as if no breaking place had come in between. Not without design does God write the music of our lives. But be it ours to learn the time, and not be dismayed at the "rests." They are not to be slurred over, nor to be omitted, nor to destroy the melody, nor to change the key-note. If we look up, God Himself will beat the time for us. With the eye on Him we shall strike the next note full and clear.

JOHN RUSKIN.

O God, help us to trust where we cannot see, and to feel that life is not necessarily a failure because we are shut out from its activities. Grant us in sickness such visions and such communion with Thee that disease of the body shall be transformed into a healer of the soul; and, as the crushed rose the sweeter fragrance emits, so may our sorrows chasten and refine us.

O Heavenly Father, grant that all our sickness and pain and disappointment may so sweeten our dispositions, purify our character and strengthen our souls that we shall bring heaven's sunlight into the lives of all whom we meet. Amen.

MYRON W. HAYNES.

Love is the greatest thing that God can give us, for Himself is love; and it is the greatest thing we can give to God, for it will also give ourselves, and carry with it all that is ours.

JEREMY TAYLOR.

High thoughts and noble in all lands
   Help me, my soul is fed by such;
But ah, the touch of lips and hands,
   The human touch!
Warm, vital, close, life's symbols dear,
   These need I most and now and here.

RICHARD BURTON.

Our Father in Heaven, we bless Thee this morning for all Thy care and love; Thou hast made our houses homes, sweet, quiet dwelling-places. We thank Thee for sleep, for communion with one another in all holy and tender speech. We thank Thee for all our hopes; the worlds are nearer than we thought, heaven's fragrance attempers the winds of earth, we almost hear the upper song: may we listen for it, may our souls delight in sweet anticipations of immortal fellowship, and may we come out of these high reveries determined to work more, suffer more patiently, to accept every discipline more willingly, and to do all our little day's work as men whose citizenship is in heaven. Amen.

JOSEPH PARKER.

Flame of the spirit, and dust of the earth, —
This is the making of man,
This is his problem of birth;
Born to all holiness, born to all crime,
Heir of both worlds, on the long slope of time
Climbing the path of God's plan;
Dust of the earth in his error and fear,
Weakness and malice and lust;
Yet, quivering up from the dust,
Flame of the spirit, unleaping and clear,
Yearning to God, since from God is its birth —
This is man's portion, to shape as he can,
Flame of the spirit, and dust of the earth —
This is the making of man.

PRISCILLA LEONARD.

O God, Thou art the Father of our spirits, but our spirits have come to us through ways of flesh. We are both spiritual and carnal. Our spirits seek Thee evermore, but our flesh turns away from Thee and strives to drag us down. Between our best and our worst is bitter conflict. Help us to the discovery that all that lives is in like conflict, and that there can be no virtue and no glory except in overcoming. Make us see that the spirit is stronger than the flesh because it is of God, and that in the obedience and inspiration of Jesus, Thy Son and our Brother, we may at last be enthroned with Him. Amen.

CEPHAS B. CRANE.

Neither let mistakes nor wrong directions, of which every man, in his studies and elsewhere, falls into many, discourage you. There is precious instruction to be got by finding we were wrong. Let a man try faithfully, manfully, to be right; he will grow daily more and more right. It is at bottom the condition on which all men have to cultivate themselves.

Thomas Carlyle.

Almighty God, our heavenly Father, — in Thine own loving way Thou dost bless us when we do the right; when we fall into mistakes so teach us by Thy judgments that we become wise unto salvation. Help Thy children to recognize their proneness to blunder, that they learn to walk circumspectly. When we fall into the wrong, grant that we lie prone not long but arise undismayed to greater effort. Bring to bear upon us the influences of the Holy Spirit, that we strive earnestly and devoutly to be right at the centre of our being; that rightness be the fabric of our life. To Thee be all glory evermore. Amen.

Edward A. Perry.

Henceforth I learn that to obey is best,
And love with fear the only God, to walk
As in His presence, ever to observe
His providence, and on Him sole depend,
Merciful over all His works, with good
Still overcoming evil, and by small
Accomplishing great things — by things deemed weak
Subverting worldly strong, and worldly wise
By simply meek, that suffering for Truth's sake
Is fortitude to highest victory,
And to the faithful death the gate of life —
Taught this by His example whom I now
Acknowledge my Redeemer ever blest.

JOHN MILTON.

O Thou Eternal One before whom from day to day we walk and on whom we ever depend, help us to-day to love whatever is good and beautiful and to follow obediently the behests of Thy Spirit. May we overcome evil with good; and may we accomplish whatever tasks the hours as they pass demand of us, whether small or great, with such strength as may be vouchsafed us and with a wisdom begotten of meekness. If we must suffer for truth's sake may we manifest such humility and fortitude as shall be conducive to the highest success. Open for us hourly the gates of life, as those who endeavor to be faithful to their high calling. These favors we ask in the name of Him who redeems our lives from all evil and crowns us daily with His loving kindness. Amen.

EDWARD DAY.

All the strength of the world and all its beauty, all true joy, everything that consoles, that feeds hope, or throws a ray of light along our dark paths, everything that makes us see across our poor lives a splendid goal and a boundless future, comes to us from people of simplicity, those who have made another object of their desires than the passing satisfaction of selfishness and vanity, and have understood that the art of living is to know how to give one's life.

CHARLES WAGNER.

Heavenly Father, help us to be like Thyself, as manifested in the person of Jesus Christ, Thy Son! It was His will to do the will of His Father by living and dying for others. Teach us so to live. Help us to learn by positive personal experience that supremest joy comes only "in ministering unto others." Teach us what Jesus meant when He said: "I am among you as he that serveth." Plant deeply within us His passion for a life of service. May our morning hours be gladdened and inspired by this divine purpose. Let Thy holy will be done in us this day. Amen.

CHARLES PARKHURST.

The year's at the spring
And day's at the morn;
Morning's at seven;
The hill-side's dew-pearled;
The lark's on the wing;
The snail's on the thorn;
God's in His heaven —
All's right with the world!

ROBERT BROWNING.

Father in Heaven, refreshed and heartened by the night, we begin again with Thee the high adventure of our life. Add to the beauty of the world about us a finer spiritual beauty in our souls. Save us from our own undoing. If our thoughts are dark, shine in upon them with Thy glory; if they be bright, make them to light the pathway of another. Have us wholesomely to forget ourselves, in the joy of Thy good world, the promise of our imperfection and the trust in God that maketh not afraid. And when the duties of the day are done, dismiss us, Thy well-meaning children, with a quiet mind to rest. Amen.

ALBERT WELLMAN HITCHCOCK.

We will do something worth doing — that is the resolution for you and me.
EDWARD EVERETT HALE.

We admire the man who embodies victorious efforts, the man who never wrongs his neighbor, who is prompt to help a friend, but who has those virile qualities necessary to win in the stern strife of actual life.
THEODORE ROOSEVELT.

Father of Lights in whom is no darkness at all, and in whose light we see light, help us to clearly see and never forget that only right deeds are worthy of a child of Thine. May we in no moment forget that to yield to the wrong is to bring upon us Thy just condemnation and sow for us a sure reaping of sorrowful repentance. By doing the things we know to be right and worth doing, the things worthy of our true selves and of our Father and of our Master whose we are, may this day, through us, yield some benefit to other children of Thine, and bring to us the sweet reward of Thine approval. Amen.

OSCAR F. SAFFORD.

It is worth a thousand pounds a year to have the habit of looking on the bright side of things.

SAMUEL JOHNSON.

Not by appointment do we meet delight and joy;
They wait not our expectancy;
But round some corner in the street of life,
They, on a sudden, greet us with a smile.

GERALD MASSEY.

Our Father, at the beginning of a new day, refreshed by the night's rest, we turn to Thee for strength for the day's task. We know not what the hours hold for us, but this we do know, that come what may, Thou wilt go with us to bless, to cheer; we shall not walk or work alone. As we faithfully and cheerfully perform our work, conscious of Thy presence, there will come joys and smiles unexpected and unsought. This is Thy way of teaching us faithfulness and endurance. May we soon learn, that if we would make the day happy and worth while, we must not seek our own pleasure and good, but that of our brethren. May we so live that when the night shadows are again upon us, there shall be no cause for shame or regret. In the Master's spirit! Amen.

O. HOWARD PERKINS.

Not in dumb resignation we lift our hands on high;
Not like the nerveless fatalist, content to do and die.
Our faith springs, like the eagle's, who soars to meet
   the sun,
And cries exulting unto Thee, " Oh, Lord, Thy will
   be done."

Thy will! It bids the weak be strong; it bids the
   strong be just;
No lips to fawn, no hand to beg, no brow to seek the
   dust,
Wherever man oppresses men beneath the liberal sun,
O Lord, be there, Thine arm made bare, Thy righteous
   will be done.   JOHN HAY.

It is with the beautiful assurance of Thy love and
kindness, our Father, that we draw nigh unto Thee.
It is Faith that seems to give us wings by which we
rise above the darkness, into Thy Presence of light
and love. We feel our divine relationship to Thee,
so that we lift up our hands to Thee, as the child
to the parent. We are content to do Thy will, because we know then just what it is to love Thee.
Our Master taught us this great lesson by His own
faith in Thee. To do Thy will means strength to
the weak, hope to the hopeless. To the sorrowing
there can be seen, beyond the tear, the rainbow of
Thy promise. Thus, as we realize our sonship will
we work to make all men feel their own power,
and all become one in Thy great love. May
Thy Kingdom come and Thy will be done, in Christ
our Lord. Amen.

C. E. FISHER.

If you are my friend you cannot be indifferent to my faults of character, any more than you can be indifferent to my sickness or suffering. But, if you care to help me cure these faults, please let them alone! Please make much of my good qualities if you can discover any. And especially bless me with the encouraging sight of a better man than myself, and cheer me with a high example. I know that there are times when a sharp or gentle rebuke is in order, and that "faithful are the wounds of a friend." But the wiser doctors have lost their faith in blood-letting; and they know that clumsy surgery kills more than it cures. CHARLES G. AMES.

In our prayer, our Heavenly Father, we desire to be consciously grateful for the opportunities this new day affords us of being helpful to each other. The inspiration so to act comes from Thee. Thou art the constant and never-failing Helper of Thy children. May we be mindful of the fact that our noblest service to another may not be an alms, but a look of encouragement, a word of cheer. Enable us to be not too sensible of others' faults and failings. Assist us to see and magnify the good in other lives. To this end may we be to others such examples in conduct and character as we would have them be to us. We offer and ask all in the spirit of Jesus. Amen.

LEROY W. COONS.

The mariner of old said to Neptune in a great tempest, "O God! Thou mayest save me if Thou wilt, and if Thou wilt Thou mayest destroy me; but whether or no, I will steer my rudder true."

                MONTAIGNE.

I go to prove my soul
I see my way as birds their trackless way.
I shall arrive! what time, what circuit first,
I ask not; but unless God send His hail
Or blinding fire-balls, sleet or stifling snow,
In some time, His good time, I shall arrive;
He guides me and the bird. In His good time!

                ROBERT BROWNING.

Once more we face the day that can be dreadful only to our poor sight and trembling faith. For Thou hast made flame and pain, the hurricane and quaking earth to be Thy ministers of grace. Shall trust depart when shadows fall? Thou art "in the shadow keeping watch above Thine own." As truly in severity as in gentleness, Thou art the All-Loving and All-Wise. Shall we fear to go anywhere? Lord, Thou art everywhere! Defend us only from the blindness and fear of ignorance and sin. Draw us nearer to Thee, this day, by any means in Thy good pleasure, so that at last, truly knowing Thy way, we shall rise above the worst that circumstances may do into joy unspeakable and peace unbroken. In the name of Him made perfect through suffering. Amen.

HENRY B. TAYLOR.

We complain of the slow, dull life we are forced to lead, of our humble sphere of action, of our low position in the scale of society, of our having no room to make ourselves known, of our wasted energies, of our years of patience. So do we say that we have no Father who is directing our life, so do we say that God has forgotten us, so do we boldly judge what life is best for us, and so by our complaining do we lose the use and profit of the quiet years.

BISHOP HUNTINGTON.

Infinite and Holy One, by the tender mercies of Thy great love show us this day the true life that is hid in Thee. Feed us with Thy spirit that we hunger not. Make us strong and merciful in Thee. Help us to be simple, brave, and true. Give us to speak and live the truth. Make us content with life while ever dreaming of the more perfect day. Fix our lives in a great and brave integrity. Humble us in our pride, lift us from our despondency. Keep our hearts pure and our lips from speaking guile. Send us forth in perfect faith that here and now our lives may be patterned after that of Jesus without loss of influence over men. Make us not ashamed to be good and forgiving and gentle in all our ways. Amen.

FREDERICK W. BETTS.

Count each affliction, whether light or grave,
God's messenger sent down to thee; do thou
With courtesy receive him; rise and bow;
And, ere his shadow pass thy threshold, crave
Permission first his heavenly foot to lave.

. . . .

Grief should be
Like joy, majestic, equable, sedate,
Confirming, cleansing, raising, making free.
Strong to consume small troubles; to commend
Great thoughts, grave thoughts, thoughts lasting to
*   the end.*   AUBREY DeVERE.

Our Father, we would learn to trust Thy love, to live so that Thy grace shall have in us its perfect work. Not the easy thing is what we ask, but strength for duty. Give us the confidence that Thou art by our side. Let Thy strong touch be felt, Thy blessed presence seen. In all the turmoil that rages within, without, grant us Thy peace. In childish helplessness, grant us the Father's help. To grow like Jesus is our heart's desire. All things that Thy great heart permits or sends, we would receive with gratitude, that so our wills and lives may be in harmony with Thine. And so day by day may something of the Saviour's glory shine through us and bless and brighten other lives in need. Amen.

FRANK M. HOLT.

Dawn and its silence draw a silver sigh
Far in the east where early shadows lie
All flocked and folded like soft peaceful sheep.
The spirit of the spring stirs in its sleep,
Breathes into life a misty floating sheen;
The willows dreamy drip of constant green;
Exultant beats a bird-heart o'er a nest,
Where dim, vague stirrings 'neath the tiny breast
Spell fresh the miracle of motherhood.
Ah, how the world is young! ah, how 'tis good!
To feel the new life flutter mystic wing;
Like to a lark to feel one's soul upspring,
Transpierce the very limit of the sky,
And toss its challenge to Eternity!

MARY BALDWIN.

O God, our heavenly Father, make our hearts exultant, as the earth in the spring morning, with the radiance of Thy Presence. Fill them with the joy and hopefulness of eternal youth, and cause them to be uplifted in gratitude and thankfulness to Thee. We have seen earthly faces so beaming with the light of love that we never shall forget them. We have spoken names that are so endeared to us that they will linger in our memory as long as we live. So, O Father, may it be with Thy face and Thy name. May Thy face beaming upon us as the sun of righteousness win our love to holiness and virtue, making us fruitful of good works, and Thy name be so woven in our affections that we shall cherish and hallow it forever. Amen.

EDGAR W. PREBLE.

You must be serving something, some one, that needs your help in order to really appreciate the Divine care. It may be the parents' care of their children; the teacher and her scholars; the charity-worker and the poor, the friendless, the benighted; it may be friend helping friend — in some way the life of loving service must be there as something out of which God can help us think of and value the care which infinite love bestows upon us.

JULIAN K. SMYTH.

Heavenly Father, with the opening of a new day we thank Thee for father love and mother love, for love of patriot and philanthropist, and for the love which that has called into being in our own hearts. Through this love and the service of mutual helpfulness to which we have been led thereby, Thou openest our eyes to behold the world pervaded and overruled by a spirit of infinite goodness, society resting upon mutual services, and through that service mankind rising to a nobler and diviner civilization. Help us to be mindful of this heavenly vision, and so make our feet swift to run and our hands eager to work in the service of righteousness and mutual helpfulness. We ask in His name, who loving us, has taught us the divinity of service. Amen.

LeGrand Powers.

Far better is it to dare mighty things, to win glorious triumphs even though checkered by failure, than to rank with those poor spirits who neither enjoy nor suffer much because they live in the gray twilight that knows neither victory nor defeat.

THEODORE ROOSEVELT.

But only he whose judgment never strays
Beyond the threshold of the right, learns this —
Not always is it good to have one's wish;
What seemeth sweet full oft to bitter turns;
Fulfilled desire hath made mine eyes to weep.
Therefore, O reader of these lines, if thou
Would'st virtuous be, and held by others dear
Will ever for the power to do aright.

LEONARDO DA VINCI.

God of the morning light, with the dawn of another day we come to Thee with prayer for help in the steadfastness of our manifold duties. The cares that oppress us, the burdens we carry, the obligations that fall upon us, are too much for our little strength without Thy help. That help we crave from Thee, the only source of all-availing strength. Let us not be dismayed by the powers of this world or busy ourselves in vain ambitions seeking the praise of men, but may we seek that Divine approval which is of more worth than all the favors of earth. Make us brave and strong to follow in the way of Thine appointment, and grant that we may so sincerely feel and act in the busy times of this day that when the evening comes no wasted hours may be laid to our charge. Amen.

EDWARD M. BARNEY.

*You are in God's world; you are God's child.
Those things you cannot change; the only peace
and rest and happiness for you is to accept them and
rejoice in them. When God speaks to you, you must
not believe that it is the wind blowing or the torrent
falling from the hill. You must know that it is God.
You must gather up the whole power of meeting
Him. You must be thankful that life is great and
not little. You must listen as if listening were your
life. And then, then only can come peace. All other
sounds will be caught up into the prevailing richness
of that voice of God. The lost proportions will be
perfectly restored. Discord will cease; harmony will
be complete.*

PHILLIPS BROOKS.

Almighty God! We thank Thee for the peace
and comfort of the night; for the new day and all
the hope and peace and promise that it brings to us.
Help us that with glad faces and joyous hearts we
may take up its every privilege and duty, doing, in
the spirit of the Master every good and helpful thing
our hands find to do. And when the evening shall
have come may we look back on a day of plenty,
service, and peace, retiring to our rest with songs
in our hearts and thanksgiving on our lips because
Thy blessings have been on this, as on all other days
new every morning and fresh every evening. Amen.

GEORGE MAYO GERRISH.

It is the first mild day of March:
Each minute sweeter than before,
The red-breast sings from the tall larch
That stands beside our door.

There is a blessing in the air,
Which seems a sense of joy to yield,
To the bare trees and mountain bare,
And grass in the green fields.

WILLIAM WORDSWORTH.

Our Father, we wake each morning refreshed and thankful for the joy of living; for the air we breathe, the things we see, the sounds of nature's sweetest harmonies and all the beauty which surrounds our earthly life. May the wonders of the earth speak to us in witness of Thy love. Let springing-grass and opening flower remind us of the new life which is ours through the resurrection of our Lord. His blessing like the light of the sun runs everywhere, carrying with it morning and hope, springtime and gladness. The joy is in the song of the birds, the murmur of the waters, the children's laughter and the song of happy hearts. Attune our hearts to notes of praise and make us glad upon the earth until Thou bringest us to perfect and un-shadowed joys where we shall see Thee as Thou art and be like Thee. Amen.

J. W. STEPHAN.

As to equality and inequality, all the beauty and glory of life come from inequalities. If we were all Beethovens or Shakespeares or marvelous in any one direction, life would be unbearable. Who shall tell me if an Easter lily is the equal of a rose, or if either is equal to an oak or a pine? The question of equality is out of the court. The one thing we need to do is to cultivate the finest and sweetest things in us; and then, whether we are one of the California big trees or the violet in a valley, we shall help on the beauty and glory of the earth.

ROBERT COLLYER.

Our Heavenly Father, we thank Thee for the manifold beauties of Thy universe, the revelations of Thyself to Thy children. For those large wonders which stir men's minds and rouse their souls to awe, we thank Thee, but not less for the little things of life, filling their places well, and showing daily to the seeing eye that without them Thy universe could not be complete. Help us to grasp the lesson that they teach. If Thou hast given to us the great place, we thank Thee, but we thank Thee not less for the homely task, the humble duty, for it is all necessary to Thy plan. Help us, day by day, with stronger purpose, larger consecration, to fill our place, to do Thy will, in His name. Amen.

GEORGE F. FORTIER.

There must be a way of taking worry rightly, so that it shall do us good and not harm. Worry, rightly taken, should train to quietness, humility, patience, gentleness, sympathy. It ought not to eventuate (though it naturally does) in making others suffer because we are uncomfortable; in making us a source of painful worry to others because we are worried ourselves.

A. H. K. BOYD.

Father of Love, Thy blessing it is which gives us another day. Help us to put before its cares the spirit that will banish care, to find in its beginning the power that will make labors happy and its ending sweet, and so to open our hearts to Thy light that no gloom of night shall linger round our way. If heaviness there be in ours or others' lives may every wholesome cheer make it less sore. If remembered faults and follies quench a better hope, send Thy patience and Thy will to be our courage and fresh resolve. Through all the noisy world may the secret music of Thy law swell in our breasts and every step keep time with its glorious march. Amen.

JOHN DAY.

Therefore to whom turn I but to Thee, the ineffable
    Name?
  Builder and maker, Thou, of houses not made
    with hands!
What, have fear of change from Thee who art ever
    the same!
  Doubt that Thy power can fill the heart that Thy
    power expands!
There shall never be one lost good! What was, shall
    live as before;
  The evil is null, is nought, is silence implying
    sound;
What was good, shall be good, with, for evil, so much
    good more;
  On the earth the broken arcs; in the heaven, a
    perfect round.

ROBERT BROWNING.

We thank Thee, O God, that each morning brings us fresh assurance of Thy wisdom and goodness— that the days have taught us to believe in Thee and to trust Thee as our perfect Friend. We are glad that we can face the day in the faith that Thou art sufficient to the needs of the day — to all the needs of all Thy children. In this trust, we beseech Thee, make us more and more to rejoice in life and its high privileges. Help us to go on our way with gladness and peace in our hearts — to worship Thee hourly by honest work, by faithful service, by kind words, by helpful deeds, and so, to find life good by doing something to make it good. **Amen.**

FLINT M. BISSELL.

" If I were you," she said, " I should not worry. Just make up your mind to do better when you get another chance. One can't do more than that. That is what I shall think of: that God will give each of us another chance, and that each one of us will take it and do better — I and you and everyone. So there is no need to fret over failure, when one hopes one may be allowed to redeem that failure later on. Besides which life is very hard. Why, we ourselves recognize that. If there be a God, some intelligence greater than human intelligence, He will understand better than ourselves that life is very hard and difficult, and He will be astonished not because we are not better, but because we are not worse. At least, that would be my notion of a God. I should not worry if I were you. Just make up your mind to do better if you get the chance and be content with that."

BEATRICE HARRADEN.

O Lord, how often we have failed — how weak and frail we are — we have groped and stumbled along the pathway of life and have been defeated over and over again. Yet in the light of Thy providence and Thy love in spite of all defeats, we take heart and face the day with hope. In Thine economy no failure is ever final — we rejoice that Thou openest before us another opportunity. Let us be brave and earnest to seize the opportunities of these passing hours. Amen.

GEORGE L. PERIN.

To every life there comes a time supreme:
One day, one night, one morning, or one noon,
One freighted hour — one moment opportune,
One rift through which sublime fulfilments gleam;
One time when fate goes tiding with the stream,
One Once in balance 'twixt Too Late, Too Soon —
And ready for the passing instant's boon
That shall in favor tip the wavering beam.
Ah! happy he who, knowing how to wait,
Knows also how to watch and how to stand
On life's broad deck alert, and at the prow,
To seize the happy moment big with fate
From Opportunity's extended hand
When the great clock of Destiny strikes Now!

MARY ASHLEY TOWNSEND.

Our heavenly Father! Thou art the Author of all our days, and all our times and seasons are hid in the unfolding mystery of Thy Thought and Purpose. It is not given to us to know what a day or an hour may bring forth, but the opportune moments come, ways are opened before us to larger life and usefulness and privilege and duty. May we, by faithfulness, and watchfulness, and the readiness of those on duty, be prepared for each divinely offered opportunity. Surrounded by blessings, may we live to bless. Ministered unto, may we minister. Grateful to Thee, may we show our gratitude by service. In Thy name, Amen.

DWIGHT M. HODGE.

Put out of your thought the past whatever it may be; let go even the future with its golden dream and its high ideal; and concentrate your soul in this burning, present moment. For the man who is true to the present is true to his best; and the soul that wins the ground immediately before it, makes life a triumph.

OZORA STEARNS DAVIS.

Almighty Giver of every good, we come to Thee amid the joys of a new morning, with its new blessings and opportunities. We would dedicate this day to Thy service. We would forget the past and waste not our time in idle dreaming of to-morrow, but with consecrated zeal we would apply ourselves to the tasks Thou hast appointed us for this present hour. Thy hand is ever opened to let down the tokens of Thy love. May all that is best within us rise up in answer, and may we be dedicated anew to our upbuilding in righteousness and the fulfilment of our duties to one another. May we this day follow the footsteps of the Christ and prove ourselves His faithful disciples! Amen.

R. PERRY BUSH.

I believe that today is better than yesterday, and that tomorrow will be better than today.

GEORGE F. HOAR.

Make yourselves nests of pleasant thoughts, bright fancies, faithful sayings; treasure-houses of precious and restful thoughts, which care cannot disturb nor poverty take away from you, — houses built without hands for your souls to live in.

JOHN RUSKIN.

Dear Father in heaven, around Thy name cluster the most sacred and holy affections. Thy name, indeed, is above every name infinite in love, and awakening in each heart a sense of filial gratitude. At this morning hour, therefore, we are mindful of the tie that binds us to Thee, that provides a nesting-place for pleasant and restful thoughts, that makes duty less irksome, home-love more tender, sacrifice more willing, and character more noble. In this spirit we pray Thee, O Father, send us forth to the labor which awaits us, only to realize, under Thy Providence, that this is the best day of our life, and full of assurance and rejoicing for a still better tomorrow. In the light of faith, hope and love do we ask and offer all. Amen.

WILBURN D. POTTER.

Scarce tangible may be the first glad sign,
  Yet how it shakes us with a vernal thrill!
  The voice of the south wind behind the hill;
Or an elusive bird-note faint and fine;
A flush at dawn along the wan sky-line;
  A lyrical exuberance in the rill;
  A something working its mysterious will
Both in majestic bole and tenuous vine!

It is the vernal spirit.   In the earth
  It throbs and pulses; quickens in the air;
    And permeates all nature thro' and thro'.
In the expectant poignancy of birth
  What raptures, what rare ecstasies we share —
    Old, — ah, how old! — and yet forever new!
                                    CLINTON SCOLLARD.

O God, how good Thou art! All Thy works
praise Thee. The world is filled with Thy glory.
This dawning Springtime brings Thee very near
every responsive heart. Thou art the fountain of
life. We see Thee in bursting bud and incipient
bloom. We hear Thee in the rapture of birds and
in the new-found gladness of sun-kissed rivulets.
May we, the children of Thy love, be new born
into a deeper spirituality, — a richer life! May
the beauty of the Spirit breathing through our hearts
call forth the latent goodness that slumbers there!
Speak through us the music of Thy love. Perfume
us with the odors of Thy heavenly grace, and may
we walk this day in tune with Thee! Amen.

JOSEPH COOPER.

Work is the grand cure of all the maladies and miseries that ever beset mankind — honest work, which you intend getting done.

THOMAS CARLYLE.

Thank God every morning when you get up that you have something to do which must be done whether you like it or not. Being forced to work and forced to do your best will breed in you temperance, self-control, diligence, strength of will, content and a hundred virtues which the idle will never know.

CHARLES KINGSLEY.

Kind Father and Friend, Thy presence has watched over us all our days and has been a comfort in all our labors. We thank Thee for Thy unwearied watching over us. May we at the dawn of this new day, come to our tasks with thanks in our hearts and a song on our lips. May all life's stern duties and its perplexities get grace and beauty from our hallowed thoughts and sanctified resolves. We would ask that Thy free spirit be with us this day to give us hope and joy in our several tasks. May the sweet peace of mind of those who learn to labor and to wait crown all our efforts. Dear Father, forgive our failures and keep us ever Thine. **Amen.**

CHARLES E. PETTY.

Ah, the mis-takings and the mis-leavings; and all the ignorant beginning, when we can only lay up things for late wisdom to repent of!

Nothing really bad can ever happen. . . . I've meant right, — and I mean right now. I'll do the best I can, and the Lord will take care of everybody.

Mrs. A. D. T. Whitney.

Lord, Thou comest to us with light and life, forgive us for coming to Thee as aliens and beggars; daily Thou art our refuge and strength, and this should subtract our fear and multiply our confidence, comfort and consecration. Our needs are Thy opportunity; we have more sunshine than we can use, more love than we can repay and more revelation than we can translate. O may this satisfy us early and strengthen us through all our days. Alone we are very weak, but we are never alone; all of life is a company affair, for Thou art with us; help us to be as truly Thy children as Thou art our Father and Mother. Through our thinking, working and waiting may men see Thee and glorify Thee. O teach us to abide ever in Thy love, and help us to work some helpful miracle by the gates of need, and to see the rainbow of prophecy through earth's tears and over its years. **Amen.**

Alan R. Tillinghast.

'Tis the fine souls who serve us, and not what is called fine society.

RALPH WALDO EMERSON.

We find what we look for in the world. I have always been looking for the nobler qualities in human beings, and I have always found them. There are great souls all along the highway of life, and there are great qualities even in the people who seem common and weak to us ordinarily.

ELLA WHEELER WILCOX.

Gracious Father, we thank Thee for the power Thou hast given us to labor for our own and others' advancement and happiness. As we begin this new day we trust in Thy bounty and would draw on Thy strength to sustain us in our toil. We thank Thee for the brave souls in every walk of life who have set us an example worthy to be followed. Many have been or are notable in the world for their fortitude, honor and achievements; many others have been known to us but have been unheralded by men, and from all these we have ourselves been made more capable and faithful. By Thy grace may we be aided in emulating the good we see in others, and be able to make the world a little brighter because of Thy gift to us of this day. Amen.

FRANK S. RICE.

An old, worn Harp that had been played
Till all its strings were loose and frayed,
Joy, Hate, and Fear, each one, assayed
To play.   But each in turn had found
No sweet responsiveness of sound.

Then Love the Master-player came
With heaving breast and eyes aflame;
The Harp he took all undismayed,
Smote on its strings, still strange to song,
And brought forth music sweet and strong.
PAUL LAURENCE DUNBAR.

Heavenly Father, I pray Thee that Thou wilt help me to love to-day.   Thou art Love and if Thou shalt fill my life there will be no room for hate and no room for fear, for " Perfect Love casteth out fear." As the Master stilled the waves in Galilee, so speak Thou peace to my soul, and bid all discord cease, that my whole life may be in tune with heaven, and may be one happy song.   Love alone can bring harmony out of discord, love out of hate, trust out of fear, and music out of a worn-out, or a long un-used or misused life.   So let Love control the whole of my life for Jesus' sake.   Amen.

B. L. JENNINGS.

> *No stream from its source*
> *Flows seaward, how lonely soever its course,*
> *But some land is gladdened. No star ever rose*
> *Or set without influence somewhere. Who knows*
> *What earth needs from earth's lowliest creature? No*
>   *life*
> *Can be pure in its purpose and strong in its strife,*
> *And all life not be purer and stronger thereby.*
>   OWEN MEREDITH.

If I am this day to touch other lives helpfully so that they may be gladdened and strengthened for truer and nobler living, I shall need, my Father, not only a clear perception of myself in relation to that to which Thou dost call me, but also a clear vision of the Christ who would be felt through me, not only the impulse of a strong purpose but also the endowment of power by Thy spirit of power. That this may be, do Thou test my purpose by that of Thy son and fashion my life by His teaching, keeping my heart open always toward Thee. Amen.

F. H. WHEELER.

*I but open my eyes, — and perfection, no more and
    no less,*
*In the kind I imagined, full-fronts me, and God is
    seen God,*
*In the star, in the stone, in the flesh, in the soul and
    the clod.*
And thus looking within and around me, I ever renew
*(With that stoop of the soul which in bending up-
    raises it too)*
*The submission of man's nothing-perfect to God's
    all-complete,*
*And by each new obeisance in spirit, I climb to His
    feet.*

ROBERT BROWNING.

Thou Infinite Spirit, we cannot understand Thee,
yet we feel Thy presence within us and about us.
We cannot unravel the mystery of Thy life, not even
of our own lives, yet we feel ourselves linked as by
chains of steel to Thyself. We are poor and ignorant
and little and finite; Thou art great and strong
and infinite, yet we cling to the thought that we
are Thy children. Even in Thine infinity Thou
stoopest to listen to us. Thou carest for us, lovest
us. O Thou Father of our Souls, may we cling to
Thee to-day and every day. We do not ask Thee
to explain Thyself, but we do ask that in storm
and sunshine, in adversity and in prosperity, and
in every emergency we may keep our anchorage to
Thee unbroken, and feel Thy presence with us. Amen.

GEORGE L. PERIN.

I wonder why it is that we are not all kinder to each other than we are. How much the world needs it! How easily it is done!

HENRY DRUMMOND.

Let us awaken to the divine privilege of sharing the heartaches of our friends; of the meaning of good fellowship; of that independence of spirit that does not imitate; of courage and pride that can endure adversity with dignity, and without fear.

ANONYMOUS.

Our Heavenly Father, help us through this new day to allow the impulses of our hearts to have fullest play. Help us to help each other, Lord, and of whatever grace or influence we have to bless and uplift our fellowmen to give generously and gladly. Help us scatter sunshine along our pathway, to speak the cheering word to discouraged hearts and to lend the helping hand to feeble or halting ones along the way. May we find our greatest happiness following in the footsteps of our Master, humbly serving our neighbor's needs, and doing good even at every wayside opportunity. Amen.

JAMES F. ALBION.

*Once to every man and nation comes the moment to
    decide,
In the strife of Truth with Falsehood, for the good
    or evil side;
Some great cause, God's new Messiah, offering each
    the bloom or blight,
Parts the goats upon the left hand, and the sheep
    upon the right,
And the choice goes by forever 'twixt that darkness
    and that light.*

JAMES RUSSELL LOWELL.

Almighty Father, we are before Thee, asking
for strength this day, that for today's duty we may
have the help of Thy Infinite wisdom, as we know
we have Thy love, Our Father with His Children.
Father, help us to look to Thee for strength and
wisdom in every moment of doubt. We are not
afraid, because we can come to Thee for counsel,
and companionship. We can come to Thee for
everything, and we find everything if we seek for it
with all our heart and soul and strength. So today,
Father, be with us to show each one of us here, the
youngest or the oldest, the weakest or the strongest,
what is the duty next his hand today, that we may
enter into that work and go about our Father's
business. Go with us and be with us as with Thine
own children. Amen.

EDWARD EVERETT HALE.

I long to accomplish great and noble tasks, but it is my duty and joy to accomplish humble tasks as though they were great and noble.

HELEN KELLER.

It is a fine notion of life to liken it to the loom. God puts on the warp in those circumstances in which we find ourselves, and which we cannot change. The woof is wrought by the shuttle of everyday life. It is made of very homely threads sometimes, common duties, unpromising and unwelcome tasks. But whoever tries to do each day's work in the spirit of patient loyalty to God is weaving the texture whose other side is fairer than the one he sees.

ANONYMOUS.

Our Father in heaven, grant that we may be "faithful in that which is least," leaving to Thy will whether we have the opportunity of being "faithful in much." May we understand that the value of our service is not so much in what we do as the spirit in which we do it. Help us to remember that no service is common in Thy sight, if it is done for Thy glory and the betterment of humanity; that in blessing others, we ourselves are blessed; that life is mostly made up of little things, but a character which is perfected by Thy grace and humble service is not a little thing, but a jewel to shine in Thy crown forever. Amen.

E. T. CURNICK.

April is here!
There's a song in the maple, thrilling and new;
There's a flash of wings of heaven's own hue;
There's a veil of green on the nearer hills;
There's a burst of rapture in woodland rills;
There are stars in the meadow dropped here and there;
There's a breath of arbutus in the air;
There's a dash of rain, as if flung in jest;
There's an arch of color spanning the west;
April is here!

EBEN E. REXFORD.

O God, ever-living and ever-acting, all Thy works praise Thee, and Thy saints bless Thee! We rejoice that Thou art bringing in this new springtime, and art preparing to pour out Thy summer glory and bounty in garden and field and wood, that Thy children may be richly blessed. As Thou art working mightily in nature today so wilt Thou work in us, Thy children, that the blessed fruits of the Spirit may appear in all that we think and do and are? And may the spontaneous spring song of the woods find its counterpart in the perpetual gladness of our souls sunk deep in the love of Christ! Amen.

HENRY IRVING CUSHMAN.

The sweetest sound our whole year round
 'Tis the first robin of the spring!
The song of the full orchard choir,
 Is not so fine a thing.
                    EDMUND CLARENCE STEDMAN.

The grass comes, the flower laughs where lately lay
   the snow,
O'er the breezy hill top hoarsely calls the crow,
 By the flowing river the alder catkins swing
 And the sweet song sparrow cries, " Spring, it is
   Spring! "
                          CELIA THAXTER.

Accept from a heart of gratitude, O God, thanks-giving and praises for the glad anticipation of the coming days of spring. May the awakening of nature, this living garment in which Thou hast robed Thy mysterious loveliness, be to each of Thy children symbol of the new life which comes to those who put their trust in the risen Christ and of the higher life beyond where shadows are no more and light and gladness bless an eternity of joy. O, Thou Father of lights, make every hour of this opening day rich and radiant with Thy effulgent presence through Jesus Christ.   Amen.

KERR BOYCE TUPPER.

Within my earthly temple there's a crowd;
There's one of us that's humble, one that's proud,
There's one that's broken-hearted for his sins,
There's one that unrepentant sits and grins;
There's one that loves his neighbor as himself,
And one that cares for naught but fame and pelf.
From much corroding care I should be free
If I could once determine which is me.

THEODORE MARTIN.

Our Heavenly Father, we thank Thee for our multiform life. Thou hast made us a little lower than the angels and hast crowned us with glory and honor, yet how little we know ourselves! We go astray; we fall from our high estate; like the moth we flutter around the blaze that burns us. When we would do good, evil is present with us. Yet through all complexity of thought and feeling, of passion and appetite, through all our wanderings and all our sins we thank Thee that there shines clearly the light of our own Divinity. We are Thy children. Help us, we pray Thee, to know ourselves at our best. May we not be betrayed in this day's journey by any siren voice. Let us go forth to the tasks of the day with the consciousness that until the evening shadows fall Thou wilt be with us. Amen.

GEORGE L. PERIN.

If we but knew the secret of that power
That opes the bud in early days of spring,
If we but knew what makes the robin sing
His wondrous song just at the matin hour,
If we but knew the priceless boon and dower
Of human life when man is truly king.
If we but understood the little thing
That vexes us just at the present hour,
If we but knew — ah, well, 'tis vain to sigh
And speculate on things beyond our ken!
We know that earth is fair and life is sweet,
And something tells us that we cannot die.
And if we live and love the good, ah! then
We face to face with truth some day must meet.

                       CLARENCE HAWKES.

O Lord, we thank Thee for a day so sweet and fair as this, when the trees lift up their hands in a psalm of gratitude to Thee, and every little flower that opens its cup and every wandering bird seem filled by Thy spirit, and grateful to Thee. We thank Thee for all thine handwritings of revelation on the walls of the world, on the heavens above us and the ground beneath, and all the testimonies recorded there of Thy presence, Thy power, Thy justice, and Thy love. Amen.

    THEODORE PARKER.

Yet we must give the children leave to use
Our garden tools, though they spoil tool and plant
In learning. So the Master may not scorn
Our awkwardness, as with these bungling hands
We try to unroot the ill, and plant with good
Life's barren soil: the child is learning use.
Perhaps the angels even are forbid
To laugh at us, or may not care to laugh,
With kind eyes pitying our little hurts.

EDWARD ROWLAND SILL.

Our Father: Thou knowest how unskilled are
these hands and hearts of ours. Thou knowest
how much that we do, think, and speak often tends
to retard the progress of that which we would pro-
mote. Give us, then, this day that wisdom which
is from above, that no touch of our hand may mar
the beauty of one of Thy creations: no thought nor
word wrong one of Thy creatures. Help us to know
that we are workers with God, and in this knowledge
may we strive for that excellence of service that
shall hasten the coming of that kingdom of peace,
joy and righteousness which is life eternal. Amen.

FLORENCE KOLLOCK CROOKER.

Plant flowers in the soul's front yard,
  Set out new shade and blossom trees,
An' let the soul once froze an' hard,
  Sprout crocuses of new idees.

Yes, clean yer house, an' clean yer shed,
  An' clean yer barn in ev'ry part;
But brush the cobwebs from yer head,
  An' sweep the snow banks from yer heart.

SAM WALTER FOSS.

Gracious Father, help us gratefully to begin this day with Thee. We expect the day to bring its accustomed routine of cares and duties, and its round of petty irritations, but we confidently believe that Thou wilt help us in all our experiences. Let this morning's freshness, hope and vigor be ours through the whole day. Help us to put faith in the place of fear that all our efforts may be crowned with the success of helpfulness. May we go blithely about our business with kind words and cheerful faces that our day's work may be our day's worship. Amen.

AUGUSTUS B. CHURCH.

Ye seek for happiness — alas the day!
Ye find it not in luxury nor in gold,
Not in the fame nor in the envied sway,
For which O willing slaves to custom old,
Severe taskmistress, ye your hearts have sold.
Ye seek for peace, and, when ye die, to dream
No evil dreams; all mortal things are cold
And senseless then; if aught survive, I deem
It must be love and joy, for they immortal seem.

SHELLEY.

O Thou Eternal God who hast given us life, help us to love Thy will and to walk in Thy way this day. If flowers chance to grow beside our path we would pluck them, but most of all would we rejoice in Thee alone, knowing that in Thy will is perfect peace. Fill our souls with Thy joy and strengthen us in the spirit of self-forgetfulness to spill it out into the lives of others. Give us hearts " roomy, radiant, and full of laughter," learned of " Jesus Christ, whom not having seen we love; on whom though now we see Him not, yet believing, we rejoice greatly with joy unspeakable and full of glory, receiving the end of our faith, even the salvation of our souls." Amen.

WALTER HEALY.

A gush of bird song, a patter of dew,
  A cloud and a rainbow's warning,
Suddenly sunshine and perfect blue —
  An April day in the morning.
                              HARRIET P. SPOFFORD.

There is something in the air
  That's new and sweet and rare —
There's something too that's new,
  In the color of the blue
That's in the morning sky,
  Before the sun is high.

                              NORA PERRY.

Infinite and Holy One, be with us in the beauty of this new day. May the dewy sweetness of the dawn Thou hast given to us be regarded as a token of Thy love for Thy children. As an atmosphere of joy and peace may be the thought of Thy consolation and Thy care. The delicate tints of Thy sky arching over us may we compare to the blue of a constancy that is divine, and which is freely shown to even the humblest and more erring of Thy flock. Bless us and guide us on our pilgrim way, and inspire our hearts and our hands to perform well their daily task. In His name do we ask it. Amen.

EDMUND Q. S. OSGOOD.

As I have walked in Alabama my morning walk,
I have seen where the she-bird — the mocking-bird
*   sat on her nest in the briers hatching her brood,*
I have seen the he-bird also,
I have paused to hear him near at hand inflating
*   his throat and joyfully singing,*
And while I paused it came to me that what he really
*   sang for was not there only,*
Nor for his mate nor for himself only, nor
All sent back by the echoes,
But subtle, clandestine, away beyond,
A charge transmitted and gift occult for those being
*   born.*

WALT WHITMAN.

Thou great Spirit of Life, Our Father in heaven, and in the earth, with what myriad voices dost Thou speak to us, sometimes with the voice of thunder and sometimes with the voice of bird. Even the rocks and hills have their language. With every manifold voice Thou tellest us that we do not live nor work for a day only. The song and the word and the work of today have larger relations. They pass over into other days. We pray this morning that the thoughts we think, the words we speak, and the work we do may be so true that they may be fit for another day. So may we begin *now* to realize the meaning of Eternal Life. Amen.

GEORGE L. PERIN.

If the stream had no quiet eddying place, could we so admire its cascade over the rocks? Were there no clouds, could we so hail the sky shining through them in its still calm purity?

The night is mother of the Day
The Winter of the Spring,
And ever upon old Decay
The greenest mosses cling.
Behind the cloud the starlight lurks,
Through showers the sunbeams fall:
For God, who loveth all His works,
Has left His Hope with all!
JOHN GREENLEAF WHITTIER.

Our Father, with childhood's glowing morning face we would turn to Thee and be conscious that the brightness of life comes only to those upon whom the sun of righteousness shines with clear light. Full of trust, full of joy, we turn our faces towards the light and take up the labors of life with entire confidence in the Divine care and guidance that blesses the open vision, the faithful hand and the loving heart. We would follow our Master, feeling that we could choose no better way, and content if we be not called to suffer more than He in His life of service and sacrifice, while our hearts praise the giver of spiritual things with unceasing happy songs. Amen.

RALPH EDWIN HORNE.

*Oh, the little birds sang east, and the little birds sang
      west,
And I smiled to think God's greatness flowed around
      our incompleteness, —
Round our restlessness, his rest.*

ELIZABETH BARRETT BROWNING.

*And I saw that there was an Ocean of Darkness
and Death; but an infinite Ocean of Light and Love
flowed over the Ocean of Darkness; and in that I
saw the infinite Love of God.*

GEORGE FOX.

Father of Light, in whom is no darkness at all,
to Thee we lift our longing eyes again. Shine away
the darkness of our minds by the light of Thy presence.
Complete our incompleteness. Bring us out of our
restlessness into Thy rest. We thank Thee for our
daily gifts, — bread to feed the body, strength to
sustain the soul, light to guide the feet. Help us
to put away the mistakes of the past, remembering
them only with the penitence that shall cause Thee
to remember them no more. Help us all through
this day to know ourselves surrounded by Thine
Infinite Love. Amen.

A. GERTRUDE EARLE.

Just as you now play a piece without the music and do not think what notes you strike, though once you picked them out by slow and patient toil, so, if you begin of set purpose, you will learn the law of kindness in utterance so perfectly that it will be second nature to you and make more music in your heart than all the songs the sweetest voice has ever sung.

FRANCES E. WILLARD.

Father, we rejoice and will be glad all the day that Thou hast made it possible for us and all Thy children to learn the sweet song of true life and that Thou dost give us so many opportunities for its practice. O Lord, give us patience and kindness toward our fellowmen and trust in Thee, so that whether the lessons be easy or hard we may take them cheerfully, believing that Thou dost give us only that which is best. Grant that we may be earnest and faithful until our souls can sing the highest, purest and sweetest notes, until we are in harmony with All Good. Amen.

ABBIE E. DANFORTH.

So many little faults we find:
We see them, for not blind
  Is love — we see them; but if you and I
  Remember them, perhaps, some by and by
They will not be
Faults then, grave faults to you and me,
  But just odd ways, mistakes, or even less —
  Remembrances to bless.

GEORGE KLINGLE.

Our dear Father in Heaven: for this day help us to be good. All through the long night Thou hast watched over us. Under Thy wing have we been sheltered as the chickens under the wing of the mother. Now that light has come we will help Thee to keep this world sweet and bright and clean. Help us to be true to this our promise; we resolve to be patient, steadfast, cheerful, kindly, sturdy, and good. Our Father, we need Thee. We want to walk in Thy way. Help us, for we are Thy children. Amen.

WILLIAM CHANNING BROWN.

The man without a purpose is like a ship without a rudder; a waif, a nothing, no man. Have a purpose in life, if it is only to kill and divide and sell oxen well, but have a purpose; and having it, throw such strength of mind and muscle into your work as God has given you.

THOMAS CARLYLE.

Neither a borrower nor a lender be;
For loan oft loses both itself and friend,
And borrowing dulls the edge of husbandry.
This above all: to thine own self be true
And it must follow, as the night the day,
Thou canst not then be false to any man.

SHAKESPEARE.

Almighty God, at the commencement of this day's work may we look on high, and measure everything we are about to do by the scale of eternity. Keep us from all littleness; may we not be turned aside by things that are insignificant and unworthy. Help us, we beseech Thee, to make the glory of our life commensurate with the splendors of our privileges. May we live life in a great spirit, realizing that there is no duty so simple, no position so humble, but that we may show forth the grandeur of trust, and obedience toward Thee. May the great and holy purpose we cherish find its expression as we cooperate with the divine purpose. Amen.

J. H. BARKER.

'*Twas one of those charmed days*
When the genius of God doth flow,
The wind may alter twenty ways,
A tempest cannot blow;
It may blow north, it still is warm;
Or south, it still is clear;
Or east, it smells like a clover farm;
Or west, no thunder fear.
RALPH WALDO EMERSON.

Father of Lights, from whom cometh every good and perfect gift, we thank Thee for the morning and for the sunshine. We rejoice in the light, but when it is hidden from us, we are thankful that in the upper air above our clouded morning it still fills Thy heavens. Thou gavest us good things while we slept, and now, refreshed by Thy Spirit, may we go forth to our appointed tasks with cheerful obedience and joyful expectation. If trial and trouble await us, or if, in the heat of the day the burden seems too great, may we still be comforted, because we put our trust in Thee. Amen.

GEORGE BATCHELOR.

But spring-wind, like a dancing psaltress, passes
Over its breast, to waken it, rare verdure
Buds tenderly upon rough banks between
The withered tree-roots and the cracks of frost,
Like a smile striving with a wrinkled face;
The grass grows bright, the boughs are swol'n with
   blooms
Like chrysalids impatient for the air,
The shining dors are busy, beetles run
Along the furrows; ants make their ado;
Above, birds fly in merry flocks, the lark
Soars up and up, shivering for very joy;
Afar the ocean sleeps; white fishing gulls
Flit where the sand is purple with its tribe
Of nested limpits; savage creatures seek
Their loves in wood and plain — and God renews
His ancient rapture.

                              ROBERT BROWNING.

O Lord, who givest to mankind liberally, and upbraidest not, we thank Thee for the blessings Thou bestowest from day to day. We thank Thee for this material world, now clad in its garment of Northern beauty, for the great sun which all day pours down his light upon the waiting and the grateful world, and for the earth underneath our feet. We bless Thee for the grass, bread for the cattle, its harvest of use spread everywhere, and for the various beauty which here and there spangles all useful things which Thine eye looks down upon. May we use this world of matter to build up the being that we are to a nobler stature of strength and of beauty. Amen.

   THEODORE PARKER.

O brothers all! come near
    And hear
    A bird's
Melodious dreaming set to words, and flung
The spring's new leaves and tender buds among,
    For very joy of life, and hope, and love
In a world made broad enough
    For all God's creatures to be merry in,
    With joyous clash and din,
    And yet too small
    For any greed at all!
    Lo! deep and sure
Is cut this truth in heaven's book of gold:
Out of one mother in the garden old
    Were born the rich and poor.

                                        MAURICE THOMPSON.

Our Father, may we begin this day with a song
in our hearts, — a song as rich and full and free
as the bird sings at the earliest dawning of the
sun's light, — a song so attuned with infinite life
and hope and love that it must be sung. Thou
giver of abundance unto the rich and poor alike,
help our souls to mount unto the highest reaches of
living thoughts and generous deeds, that we may
give unto others as Thou givest. Unfettered by
unholy passions and freed from the spirit of greed,
may we feel the unity of the bonds of a universal
brotherhood, and be just and true, honest, and
helpful in all our dealings with all men this
day. Amen.

HENRIETTA G. MOORE.

O spring, of hope and love and youth and gladness
  Wing-winged emblem! Brightest, best and fairest!
Whence comest thou when with dark Winter's sadness
  The tears that fade in sunny smiles thou sharest?
Sister of Joy! thou art the child who wearest
  Thy mother's dying smile, tender and sweet:
  Thy mother Autumn, for whose grave thou bearest
Fresh flowers, and beams like flowers,
Disturbing not the leaves which are her winding-sheet.
                                           SHELLEY.

God unchanging, and still the creator of the seasons, we look up to Thee, as the springtide works out the miracle of the resurrection from the sleeping forms of the past season, in confidence and in trust that ever Thou wilt bless us with a nobler, holier, sweeter, more wholesome life, as the seasons come and go. The resources of trusting hearts are always reinforced and reinvigorated by contact with Thy life, Thy power, Thy goodness and Thy love. Out of the winter of our discontent, we enter the springtime of love, that leads us forward in confidence through the glad summer of growth to the soul's fruition and the place of rest and peace in our Father's Home beneath Thine everlasting Love. Amen.

FRANCIS A. GRAY.

*One sound always comes to the ear that is open;
it is the steady drum-beat of Duty. No music in it,
perhaps, — only a dry rub-a-dub. Ah, but that
steady beat marks the time for the whole orchestra
of earth and heaven! It says to you: "Do your
work, — do the duty nearest you!" Keep step to
that drum-beat, and the dullest march is taking you
home.*

GEORGE S. MERRIAM.

O Thou great impelling Spirit, whom we see manifest in all the world, as we open our eyes to the
light of another morning, may we be as responsive
to Thy influence as the sun and the flowers which
brighten our way. May we be very sensitive to Thy
promptings as we go about our day's work. May
we be very quick to do the things Thou wouldst
have us do. May we give ourselves to Thy service
without reserve. When again the night shades draw
about us, may our hearts be filled with deepest
gratitude for all the experiences of the day, and,
deep within, may our spirits be conscious of Thy
approving benediction, "Well done, good and
faithful servant; enter Thou into the joy of Thy
Lord." Amen.

FRANK LINCOLN MASSECK.

Thyself and thy belongings
Are not thine own so proper as to waste
Thyself upon thy virtues, they on thee.
Heaven doth with us as we with torches do
Not light them for themselves; for if our virtues
Did not go forth of us, 'twere all alike
As if we had them not. Spirits are not finely touched
But to fine issues, nor Nature never lends
The smallest scruple of her excellence
But like a thrifty goddess, she determines
Herself the glory of a creditor,
Both thanks and use.

               SHAKESPEARE.

Father, with faith and confidence in Thee we begin the day's duties, with a blithe song upon our lips, expressing the melody of our souls, thanking Thee for opportunities for work, and thought and love. We ask not for more blessings but to be more worthy of those we have, using and not abusing them. May our minds be open to Thy truth, and hearts to Thy love, and when received may we be almoners of both to the waiting world. May we keep by giving Thy love abundantly, and grow through the glory of self-sacrifice. Give us the heart, O God, to sanctify our work and to lift it above drudgery into the divinest service, and give us strength to perform it. Amen.

U. S. MILBURN.

_A man is simple where his chief care is the wish
to be what he ought to be; that is honestly and naturally
human. We may compare existence to raw material.
What it is matters less than what it is made of; as
the value of a work of art lies in the flowering of a
workman's skill. True life is possible in social conditions the most diverse and with natural gifts the
most unequal. It is not fortune or personal advantage,
but our training them to account, that constitutes the
value of life. Fame adds no more than does length
of days; quality is the thing._

CHARLES WAGNER.

Heavenly Father, our eyes are ever toward Thee.
We do not pray for the things of the world. Teach
us to walk in Thy truth. Though our days be few,
may our lives be hopeful and cheerful. Though
our bodies be frail, may we be invincible in spirit.
All Thy children are immortal, but it is for us to
attain the eternal life. May we know Thee through
Jesus. Then days and hours and minutes will
disappear in the liberty and glory and peace of the
life eternal. Then poverty of worldly goods will be
forgotten in the riches of the Spirit. Then the cares
of the world that now is will be lost in the joy of
the life that is to be. Amen.

REIGNOLD K. MARVIN.

A little sun, a little rain,
  A soft wind blowing from the west —
And woods and fields are sweet again
  And warmth within the mountain's breast.

So simple is the earth we tread,
  So quick with love and life her frame,
Ten thousand years have dawned and fled,
  And still her magic is the same.
                                    STOPFORD A. BROOKE.

Gracious God, we thank Thee for the gift of sight whereby we behold the marvels of the outer world. But greater is our gratitude for the inner sight, the power to see things as they ought to be. If we but look deep enough, we find Thy central laws ever at the heart of all life. With such insight, apparent confusion shall not bewilder us, life's cares shall not harden us, the world's show cannot dazzle us. Give us, we pray Thee, unceasing ability to wonder and admire, which brings perpetual youth; to hope, to believe, to trust; to rest content in working with Thee, the Eternal One, Lord of the seasons, this is our heart's desire. Amen.

EDWARD A. HORTON.

*"What is the secret of your life?" asked Mrs.
Browning of Charles Kingsley; "tell me, that I
may make mine beautiful too." He replied, "I had
a friend." Somewhere in her "Middlemarch,"
George Eliot puts it well: "There are natures in
which, if they love us, we are conscious of having a
sort of baptism and consecration; they bind us over
to rectitude and purity by their pure belief about us;
and our sins become the worst kind of sacrilege, which
tears down the invisible altar of trust."*

WILLIAM C. GANNETT.

Our Heavenly Father, we thank Thee for all the
sweet and sacred influences of life. Music comes
with its invisible fingers to weave a magic charm
around our souls; — the home with its love is ours, —
but we thank Thee to-day for the sweet and saving
influence of friendship, — for the counsel and fellowship of those who are wise and good and faithful to
us. We would not walk alone — we would find
strength in the strength of others, and faith in other's
faith. Let us cherish such fellowships and give
back to those, who love us, love again. Amen.

GEORGE L. PERIN.

Live in the sunshine, don't live in the gloom,
Carry some gladness the world to illume.
Live in the brightness, and take this to heart;
The world will seem gayer if you'll do your part.
Live on the housetop, not down in the cell;
Open air Christians live nobly and well.
Live where the joys are, and, scorning defeat,
Have a good-morrow for all whom you meet.
Live as a victor, and triumphing go
Through this queer world, beating down every foe.
Live in the sunshine, God meant it for you!
Live as the robins, and sing the day through.

MARGARET SANGSTER.

O God, our heavenly Father, Thou who givest us the sunshine of this new day, Thou who art the God of life and light, we ask Thy help and Thy strength as we again go out to our separate duties and cares. Help us to fill this day with good deeds, to give cheer and comfort to all we meet. May our lips be clean. May our hearts be pure. And when the even time comes, may it find us conscious that we have put no cloud upon the day, that we have walked through its hours true disciples of the Master who went about doing good. Amen.

WILLIAM H. MORRISON.

To weigh the material in the scales of the personal, and measure life by the standard of love; to prize health as contagious happiness, wealth as potential service, reputation as latent influence, learning for the light it can shed, power for the help it can give, station for the good it can do — to choose in each case what is best on the whole, and accept cheerfully incidental evils involved; to put my whole self into all that I do, and indulge no single desire at the expense of myself as a whole; to crowd out fear by devotion to duty, and see present and future as one; to treat others as I would be treated, and myself as I would my best friend; and to recognize God's coming kingdom in every institution and person that helps men to love one another.   WILLIAM DeWITT HYDE.

For the dear love that kept us through the night,
   And gave our senses to sleep's gentle sway,
For the new miracle of dawning light,
    Flushing the east with prophecies of day,
      We thank Thee, O, our God!

For the fresh life that through our being flows,
   With its full tide to strengthen and to bless,
For calm, sweet thoughts, upspringing from repose,
    To bear to Thee their song of thankfulness,
      We praise Thee, O, our God!

Thou knowest our needs, Thy fulness will supply
   Our blindness — let Thy hand still lead us on,
Till, visited by the dayspring from on high,
    Our prayer, one only, " Let Thy will be done,"
      We breathe to Thee, O, God!
               Amen.

W. H. BURLEIGH.

Is it not possible, then, that the hindrances which arrest our progress, and the obstacles that lie broadly in our path, are the divinest agents of help which our Creator could give us? The painful struggles to overcome and remove them develop in us strength, courage, self-reliance, and heroism. They are the hammer and chisel that release the statue from the imprisoning marble,— the plow and the harrow that break up the soil, and mellow it for the reception of the seed that shall yield an abundant harvest. Perfection lies that way.

MARY A. LIVERMORE.

We seek Thy face anew this day, O our Father, and ask Thee that Thou wilt help us to live our lives in constant communion with Thee. Let us see Thee at every turn in the way. Let us find Thy hand in all our duties, all our meditations, all our intercourse with men, all our doings and all our deeds. Help us to make Thee our counsellor every hour. Help us to undertake nought without Thy blessings, to finish nought without Thy benediction. Morning and evening may we turn in prayer to Thy throne. At every meal may we seek Thy grace and give Thee thanks. So may we find the blessing of them that abide in Thy house. Amen.

J. COLEMAN ADAMS.

*I think the sweetest thought, the very central idea,
of the revelation of the character of God to me, is this:
that He does everything out of His supreme will.
There is no one thing that I can say with more hearti-
ness, or that has in it more echoes of joy, than " Thy
will be done." If anything works righteousness in
me or in you, it is God. The nature of God is fruitful
in generosity. He is so good that He loves to do
good, and loves to make men good, and loves to make
them happy by making them good. He loves to be
patient with them, and to wait for them, and to pour
benevolence upon them, because that is His nature.*

HENRY WARD BEECHER.

Father, we thank Thee for the blessing. We
know what are our privileges, we know what are
our duties, and we are before Thee again to consecrate this day in all its glory and beauty to Thee,
the Father of perfect Love. Thou wilt be with us
as we strive to be with Thee. Thou wilt make us
strong when we are weak. Thou wilt make us see
where we are in darkness. Thou wilt send us forth
on Thine infinite mission to the world. Boys or
girls, men or women, here we are, the living children
of the living God, sent forward by Thee to proclaim
it that all may be one as Christ Jesus with Thee
and Thou with Him, that this world may be perfected into one, that men may know that Thou art
Father and what the Father has given us to do,
that each one of us may lift up what has fallen down,
that each one may open the eyes that are blind and
the ears that are deaf, that each one of us may proclaim the gospel of Thy perfect love. This is our
prayer and our hope, in Christ Jesus. Amen.

EDWARD EVERETT HALE.

With every rising of the sun,
Think of your life as just begun.

The past has shrived and buried deep,
All yesterdays; there let them sleep.

Nor seek to summon back one ghost
Of that innumerable host.

Concern yourself with but today.
Woo it, and teach it to obey

Your will and wish. Since time began
Today has been the friend of man;

But in his blindness and his sorrow,
He looks to yesterday and tomorrow.

You, and today! a soul sublime,
And the great pregnant hour of time,

With God himself to bind the twain!
Go forth, I say, attain, attain!

ELLA WHEELER WILCOX.

Infinitely wise and loving Father, our minds and hearts reach out to Thee in this morning hour thankful that the rest of the night has prepared us for the work of the new day, and that the light brings the call to service. The past cannot be recalled, but today is ours. I and today, with God and in the Spirit of Jesus! Priceless privilege! Grant us, O Father, to use it for Thee, for humanity and " In His name." Amen.

SAMUEL GILBERT AYERS.

Life is full of new beginnings. Some change may come, something is sure to come, to close one chapter and begin another. Life is planned just so, . . . that there should be a break from former link and habit, often from imperfection and mistake, and a clear, clean start for the fulfilment of the best one has grown to, even in desire, unhampered by the poorest one has ever happened to be, or to get credit for.

MRS. A. D. T. WHITNEY.

O, Thou who dwellest in the light, help Thy children this morning to see the light of Thy truth and feel the warmth of Thy love. We thank Thee for the open doors of opportunity for helpful service; for the exhibition of kindness and for growth in the kingdom of Heaven. May we clearly see the way to the Eternal life and have strength to walk therein. May we so welcome Thy truth that we shall be free from error and sin. May Thy wisdom so guide our energies that we shall reach after greater perfection. May the evening of this day find us more in harmony with God than we now are. And may the evening of life find us rich in the treasures of heaven. Amen.

ANDREW WILLSON.

True worth is in being, not seeming;
In doing each day that goes by,
Some little good — not in the dreaming
Of great things to do by and by,
For whatever men say in blindness,
And spite of the fancies of youth,
There's nothing so kingly as kindness,
And nothing so royal as truth.

We get back our mete as we measure:
We cannot do wrong and feel right;
Nor can we give pain and gain pleasure,
For justice avenges each slight.
The air for the wing of the sparrow,
The bush for the robin and wren,
But always the path that is narrow
And straight for the children of men.

ALICE CARY.

Almighty Father, who with every morning dost give us a new day and with each day some fresh duty, mercifully equip us for every task that awaits us! Give us eyes to see, and hearts to love the truth and right, and the disposition that makes every duty a delight, and the doing of good to others a sacred privilege. Save us this day from angry passions and low desires. Forgive us when we are selfish; recall us when we go astray; save us from wronging ourselves by thinking ill of others, and in all places and to all people give us the mind which was in Christ Jesus. Amen.

JOHN CUCKSON.

To the Woods:— Whoso goeth in your paths readeth the same cheerful lesson, whether he be a young child or a hundred years old, comes he in good fortune or in bad, ye say the same things, and from age to age. Ever the needles of the pine grow and fall, the acorns on the oak, the maples redden in autumn and at all times of the year the ground pine and the pyrola bud and root under foot. What is called fortune and what is called time by men, ye know them not. Men have not language to describe one moment of your life.

RALPH WALDO EMERSON.

Thou God of Nature and of the human heart, we thank Thee for our human relations, but we thank Thee also for our kinship with the birds. We thank Thee for that instinct which makes us to sympathize with the mating of the bird lovers and for that music of the heart which makes us to love the song of the birds. We pray this morning for a life so simple and natural that we shall be able to enter into sympathetic relations with everything that lives — the flowers of the garden, and the field — the bees that sip the flowers' honey, and the bird that makes her nest among the trees. If Thou speakest to men in the glory of the heavens, Thou speakest also in the manifold voices of all Thy loving creatures. May our ears be trained to hear Thee when Thou speakest thus. Amen.

GEORGE L. PERIN.

Hail bounteous May, that doth inspire
Mirth and youth, and warm desire;
Woods and groves are of thy dressing,
Hill and dale doth boast thy blessing,
Thus we salute thee with our early song,
And welcome thee and wish thee long.

JOHN MILTON.

Almighty and All-loving Father, who dost make all the earth to rejoice in the brightness of returning springtime, fill our hearts with like joy and renewal. Graciously awaken in us the life that the cold or care or trouble or sorrow of the world often has caused to fade and go out. As our eyes behold all this outward beauty and glory, give unto us that spiritual vision by which we behold the beauty and glory of divine things. Then when the springtime of our life passes with the summer and the summer ripens into the autumn, and our work is done, may we bring unto Thee the harvest of spiritual riches. Amen.

JAMES DeNORMANDIE.

Success! It is won by a patient endeavor,
  Energy's fire, and the flame-glow of Will;
By grasping the chance with a " Now, now or never!"
  Urging on, on! while the laggard stands still.

Success! It is facing life's trials, undaunted;
  Fighting the present — forgetting the past:
By trusting to Fate, though for years she has taunted,
  And bearing Time's scars; facing front, to the last!

Success! Would you win it and wear its bright token?
  Smile and step out to the drummer's light lilt;
Fight on till the last inch of sword-blade is broken.
  Then do not say die. Fight on with the hilt!
                                        MARY MARKWELL.

We thank Thee, Our Father, that Thou hast enriched our being with those faculties which prompt to noble endeavor. We rejoice in our power, guided by Thy free Spirit, both to overcome evil and to do good. Help us, dear Father, to recognize the great incentives of conscience and of duty, assured that in cheerful conformity thereto we shall find the sweetest zest of life. Increase our faith in Thee, O Lord. Enable us more clearly to realize that in the end truth and right will gain the victory. Thus may we be inspired to live brave, true and wholesome lives. May we fight the good fight of faith and win the crown of life promised to all those who follow the conquering Christ. In His name. Amen.

HENRY W. RUGG.

The green grass is bowing;
The morning wind is in it;
'Tis a tune worth the knowing,
Though it change every minute.
'Tis a tune of the Spring;
Every year plays it over.
           RALPH WALDO EMERSON.

God does not send strange flowers every year.
   When the spring winds blow o'er the pleasant places
   The same dear things lift up the same fair faces.
The violet is here.
           MRS. A. D. T. WHITNEY.

O God, Father Almighty, who bringest light out of darkness and at whose word night yields to day, we offer Thee glad worship and praise. We thank Thee for Thy gifts which are beautiful and good: for flowers which renew old friendships and awaken new affections; for songs in which voices of all yesterdays sound through today's melodies; for rich memories of the past; for the joy of living now; for the hope of better days; for new expressions of abiding truth and fresh breathings of eternal love; for courage to do right and for confidence in righteousness. May we this day, mindful of earthly duty and of heavenly promise, humbly follow Him " who went about doing good " and " gave Himself a ransom for many." Amen.

W. I. WARD.

*Bishop Brooks taught me no special creed or dogma;
but he impressed upon my mind two great ideas —
the fatherhood of God and the brotherhood of man,
and made me feel that these truths underlie all creeds
and forms of worship. God is love, God is our Father,
we are His children; therefore the darken clouds
will break, and though right be worsted, wrong shall
not triumph. He said: " There is one universal
religion, Helen — the religion of love. Love your
Heavenly Father with your whole heart and soul,
love every child of God as much as ever you can, and
remember that the possibilities of good are greater
than the possibilities of evil; and you have the key
to Heaven."* HELEN KELLER.

Infinite Spirit! We shall not look upon Thee as
a friend looketh upon the face of his friend, but
may we learn to see Thee in every form of life and
beauty and service here in this great world of Nature
and of Man. May we discover Thee in the midst
of common things and then they shall no more be
common, but all things shall be sacred and divine.
May we see Thy face in all human faces, clasp Thy
hand in all human hands, and when we have walked
with a friend, or talked with those we love, may it
be as a walk with Thee and a communion with Thee.
May we not think of Thee as afar off but always
near, making all things holy. May we realize that
it is a diviner thing to serve the lowly who need our
help than to praise the Infinite who needeth not.
May the sense of Thy presence in all things be the inspiration and interpretation of all days for us. Amen.

E. L. REXFORD.

The brown, brown woods of March
Are the green, green woods of May,
And they lift their arms with a freer swing
And shake out their pennons gay.
And the brown, dead world of March,
Is the living world of today;
Life throbs and flushes and flashes out
In the color and fragrance of May.

ANONYMOUS.

Infinite Spirit of the winter and the summer and of the night and the morning, Thou hast watched over and guarded, during its winter sleep and rest, this earth which Thou hast made, and which Thou hast made for a purpose — to be beautiful and fruitful in its season, to be a humble and obedient servant of Thy will of goodness. And now, as the woods of May are radiant in the beauty of springtime, and ready to do Thy will; so as we wake to the opportunity of this new day, may we rejoice in the privilege of living to Thee and doing Thy will in the glad service of lives lived as the Master lived. Amen.

GEORGE WALLACE PENNIMAN.

*One who never turned his back, but marched breast
    forward,*
Never doubted clouds would break,
*Never dreamed, though right were worsted, — wrong
    would triumph,*
Held we fall to rise, are baffled to fight better,
Sleep to wake.

ROBERT BROWNING.

Our Father, in the heaven, we thank Thee for
the birth of a new day. May we be full of gladness
during its golden hours, may our hearts be tranquil
with God's peace. A day is a part of Thy eternity.
Thou hast set us in the battle, Thou art watching
us in the fight; Thou art training us by well-accepted
controversy. May nothing of Thy purpose be lost
because of the blinding details of the conflict.
Strengthen our hearts to do the work of this day.
Help us to be as grateful as we are dependent upon
God. Inspire our whole life; help us quickly to
learn why we are here, what we are to do while here,
and the path that leads home when the work-day
is over. In the name of the Christ! Amen.

W. A. WOOD.

Then sing, ye birds, sing, sing a joyous song!
  And let the young lambs bound
As to the tabor's sound!
We in thought will join your throng,
  Ye that pipe and ye that play,
Ye that through your hearts today
  Feel the gladness of the May!

                    WILLIAM WORDSWORTH.

God of the morning, Father of the Soul, we bless Thee for the light, for it is pleasant to behold the world made beautiful by the King of day, and sweet with the melody of the song of bird, and cheerful with the promise of hope in the swelling buds of spring. We join with Thy faithful ones in ascriptions of praise to Thee for the depth of the riches both of the wisdom and the knowledge of God. Help us to look upon our every faculty of soul, and power of body, as gifts from Thee, to be used for the advancement of love, truth and beauty, in our own hearts, and in the world. Give us Thine own help to bear every burden cheerfully, to stand erect before every responsibility, and if in our efforts to do much good for this day we seem to fail, may we look to Jesus and learn of Him that in a conscience void of offence there is no such thing as failure. Help us to strive with the evil of the world and sin not, that at the close of the day we may look back and say, we have kept ourselves unspotted from the world. **Amen.**

L. L. GREENE.

Fairer grows the earth each morning
  To the eyes that watch aright;
Every dew-drop sparkles warning
  Of a miracle in sight;
Of some unexpected glory
  Waiting in the old and plain;
Poet's dream nor traveller's story
  Words such wonders as remain.

WILLIAM C. GANNETT.

O Thou, who makest things seen and temporal quiver and flash with Thine own informing spirit, so illumine our pathways that the Luz where we meet our duties may become the Bethel where we meet our God. As Thou dost clothe the lily with beauty and inspire the bird with song help us to grow into the beauty of holiness, and to know the joy of Thy salvation. Whatever our past, open our eyes this day to some better thing which Thou hast always in reserve. Teach us what hinders our attainment and help us burst through the barrier. Make us so conscious of Thy indwelling spirit that we may yield to its gracious impellings toward righteousness and peace and joy. Amen.

THOMAS D. ANDERSON.

Listen to the exhortation of the dawn!

Look to this day!
For it is life, the very life of life.
In its brief course lie all the
Varieties and realities of your existence;
The bliss of growth,
The glory of action,
The splendor of beauty:
For yesterday is but a dream,
And tomorrow is only a vision,
But to-day well-lived makes
Every yesterday a dream of happiness,
And every tomorrow a vision of hope.
Look well, therefore to this day!

Such is the salutation of the dawn.

FROM THE SANSKRIT.

Dear God, in Thy loving kindness, Thou hast brought us to the opening of another day; from darkness to light, from sleep to wakefulness, from rest to labor. We thank Thee for its opening glory and its coming opportunities; but above all, for the new strength we feel within ourselves to do its work and live its life. As radiant dawn climbs to full-orbed day and glides to setting sun, may we come to this day's close with the consciousness that we have lived a little closer to the great heart of the Eternal in every thought, word and deed, that we have woven into the texture of our lives, and gently as twilight enfolds the fruitful earth, shall " peace that passeth understanding " enfold **our souls.** Amen.

THOMAS B. PAYNE.

As the insect from the rock
  Takes the color of its wing;
As the boulder from the shock
  Of the ocean's rhythmic swing
Makes itself a perfect form,
  Learns a calmer front to raise;
As the shell, enameled warm
  With the prism's mystic rays,
Praises wind and wave that make
  All its chambers fair and strong;
As the mighty poets take
  Grief and pain to build their song;
Even so for every soul,
  Whatsoe'er its lot may be —
Building, as the heavens roll,
  Something large and strong and free —
Things that hurt and things that mar
  Shape the man for perfect praise;
Shock and strain and ruin are
  Friendlier than the smiling days.

JOHN WHITE CHADWICK.

Dear Father, as the light of this morning follows the darkness of the night, may we devoutly believe that the light of Thy love shall dispel all darkness and bring us into the morning of eternal peace. May we learn each day that our trials and sorrows are but stepping-stones in Thy divine economy, to bring us up into the clearer atmosphere of heavenly thought and life. Help us to live closer to Jesus, to understand how even He was made glorious through suffering, and ever learn to conquer in His name. Amen.

ELMER F. PEMBER.

I live for those that love me
For those that know me true,
For the heaven that smiles above me,
  And waits my coming, too;
For the cause that lacks assistance,
For the wrongs that need resistance,
For the future in the distance,
  For the good that I can do.

G. L. BANKS

Father, we bless Thee for such as love us and those whom we love in the varying forms of affection, thanking Thee for the sacramental cup of joy in which Thou givest the wine of life to all of Thy children, humble or high. We thank thee for that love which setteth the solitary in families at the beginning, and then reaches wide arms all around, and will not stay its hold till it joins all nations and kindreds and tongues and people into one great family of love. We bless Thee for the noble men and women whose generous heart has lit the altar fire of philanthropy in many a dark and else benighted place. We thank Thee for the unbidden faith which springs up in our hearts, impelling us to trust Thee and love Thee and keep every commandment of Thine, and that while we know not what a day shall bring forth, we are sure of everlasting life. **Amen.**

THEODORE PARKER.

Gladness of morning —
To hear the lark begin his flight,
And singing, startle the dull Night
From his watch-tower in the skies,
Till the dappled Dawn doth rise;
Then to come in spite of sorrow,
And at my window bid good-morrow
Through the sweetbrier, or the vine,
Or the twisted eglantine.

JOHN MILTON.

O Thou, in whose light we see light, who hast lifted the shadows of night from our dwellings, complete now in our behalf Thy ministry of light, we beseech Thee, and let the day star arise in our hearts. Make clear Thy face unto us. Rise with Thy morning upon our souls. May the light which envelops us throughout the day be the radiance of Thy presence. May our eyes behold only what Thou revealest and our lives be warmed with the glow of Thy love. O, that we may be new-born like the day and live a new life in Thy mercies which are new every morning; that our love may rise fresh as the dawn and our obedience be as sure as the path of the law. Let no shadow from the past dim the joy of Thy presence. Scatter the darkness of sense and self within us. As the morning reveals, interprets and fulfils the beauties of a world which was wrapped in night, may the mystery of our lives unfold, our latent forces be summoned to service, and our hearts find fulness of joy because we live in Thee. **Amen.**

EVERETT D. BURR.

It may be truly said that no man does any work perfectly who does not enjoy his work. Joy in one's work is the consummate tool without which the work may be done indeed, but without its finest perfectness. Men who do their work without enjoying it are like men carving statues with hatchets. A man who does his work with thorough enjoyment of it is like an artist who holds an exquisite tool which is almost as obedient to him as his own hand, and almost works intelligently with him.

PHILLIPS BROOKS.

O Heavenly Father, we thank Thee that Thou hast placed us where we are and hast given us the work we have to do. We would not seek far and wide for some better place or more honourable task. We pray today for the spirit that shall make us glad in our common toil. We need not to fly away to find enjoyment; we have only to feel that in the duties of this day we are in partnership with Thee, — then shall we be happy that Thou hast called us to so divine a fellowship. Make us strong and earnest and brave — that when the evening shadows fall we shall not look regretfully back because we have been unfaithful, — but that we may be satisfied and happy in the memory that we have been serving with Thee. Amen.

ANONYMOUS.

I love the flowers that come about with spring,
  And whether they be scarlet, white or blue,
It mattereth to me not anything,
  For when I see them full of sun and dew,
My heart doth get so full with its delight,
  I know not blue from red, nor red from white.
                                        ALICE CARY.

Father Divine, we remember Thee at the beginning of another day, and the obedience to Thy laws of life which Thou dost require. About us is Thy beautiful world, thrilling with new life. We would that our lives today may be likewise beautiful, restrained from sin against body and spirit. As there is now in the earth, so there is always in human souls a springtide ready to burst forth into beautiful living. In our hearts there is always the stirring energy of a spiritual spring that needs but the warmth of Thy heavenly sunshine. Let that warmth now stream into our hearts that our lives today may show forth Thy praise. Amen.

MINOT O. SIMONS.

Violet: "*Well, but surely at least one ought to be afraid of displeasing God; and one's desire to please Him should be one's first motive.*"

Lecturer: "*He never would be pleased with us, if it were, my dear. When a father sends his son out into the world — suppose as an apprentice — fancy the boy's coming home at night, and saying, 'Father, I could have robbed the till to-day; but I didn't because I thought you wouldn't like it.' Do you think the father would be particularly pleased?*" (*Violet is silent*). "*He would answer, would he not, if he were wise and good, 'My boy, though you had no father, you must not rob tills.' And nothing is ever done so as really to please our Great Father, unless we would also have done it, though we had had no Father to know of it.*"

JOHN RUSKIN.

Father of Life, Thy children raise their thoughts in prayer to Thee at the dawning of each day. Their prayer asserts love, trust and conformity to Thy will. May the spirit of prayer abide with us the day through, that we may be dutiful and worthy. The moral law is Thy way of life, may we make it our way by intelligent obedience. To know Thee aright and to find our joy in Thy life is to have fullness of being through purity and strength. O Father, may we be as those who broaden and deepen and purify life by word and deed that none may suffer loss through us, but find aid to reach the perfect life in Thee. Amen.

WILSON M. BACKUS.

Through the harsh noises of our day
A low sweet prelude finds its way:
Through clouds of doubt and creeds of fear
A light is breaking, calm and clear.

Henceforth my heart shall sigh no more
For olden time and holier shore:
God's love and blessing, then and there
Are now and here and everywhere.

JOHN GREENLEAF WHITTIER.

Our Father, as we enter upon the duties of this new day, incline our minds and hearts unto Thee. May we feel, amid its harsh noises, the assurance of Thy love and care. If doubt or fear assail us may we turn unto Thee who art the source of life, love and light, and find calm and peace. We would forget the things behind and make the most of the present. We rejoice that today is better than yesterday and that tomorrow will be better than today. Thou art here now, as Thou art everywhere always, to bless us with Thy love and care. Direct us through the hours of this day and may its close find us better children of Thine. Amen.

JOHN B. REARDON.

The sun does not shine for a few trees and flowers, but for the wide world's joy. The lonely pine of the mountain top waves its sombre boughs, and cries, "Thou art my sun!" And the little meadow violet lifts its cup of blue, and whispers with its perfumed breath, "Thou art my sun!" And the grain in a thousand fields rustles in the wind, and makes answer, "Thou art my sun!" So God sits, effulgent, in heaven, not for a favored few, but for the universe of life; and there is no creature so poor or so low that he may not look up with child-like confidence, and say, "My Father, Thou art mine!"

HENRY WARD BEECHER.

O God, the Eternal Source of all life, we rejoice that there are no bounds to Thy love. We thank Thee that Thou givest us all things richly to enjoy. May we learn that Thy bounties are for all human beings. Make the hearts of men eager that the ignorant, the lowly, the poor, the wayward, may come into the full estate of knowing that they are children of God. Let them in no way be denied the joy of unfolding the divinity within them. Lead us all into those fields of labor where we can be our best selves and develop our lives by what we do to meet the growing demands of truth and love and goodness. Wherever the morning breaks and the sunshine falls upon human faces, may its cheer make homes happy and true, men and women good, and little children joyous. Amen.

ALVA ROY SCOTT.

Hear the Master's risen word!
   Delving spades have set it free,
Wake! the world has need of thee,
   Rise and let thy voice be heard,
Like a fountain disinterred,
   Upward springing, singing, sparkling;
   Through the doubtful shadows darkling;
   Till the clouds of pain and rage
   Brooding o'er the toiling age,
As with rifts of light are stirred
By the music of the Word;
Gospel for the heavy-laden, answer to the labourer's
   cry;
"Raise the stone, and thou shalt find Me: cleave the
   wood, and there am I."

                           HENRY VanDYKE.

God of light and strength and beauty, for this day we thank Thee. The morning hours come to us freighted with messages of gladness. Thou, our Father, art refreshing our spirits, and home seems dearer, love more sacred and the way of duty clearer before our waiting feet. We thank Thee for life as it is given us, day by day. Help us to fill it with honest, cheerful, fruitful service. May we realize and rejoice in the nobility of labor, and may we learn how it is that a child of Thine, standing in his own place, giving himself to the tasks of the hour, imparts strength and courage to his fellow-worker, and helps the world forward in the path of righteousness and peace. So may Thy will be done in and through us. Amen.

   JOHN P. FORBES.

O the green things growing, the green things growing
The faint sweet smell of the green things growing!
I should like to live, whether I smile or grieve,
Just to watch the happy life of my green things
*   growing.*

DINAH MULOCK CRAIG.

Not all these sweets, these sounds, this vernal blaze,
Is but one joy, express'd a thousand ways;
And honey from the flowers, and song of birds,
Are from the poet's pen, his overflowing words.

LEIGH HUNT.

O Thou who art the Creator of life in every form
in which it is expressed in the earth, we thank Thee
for the grass and the flowers, the trees and the shrubs,
the music of the streams and the melody of the
birds. As nature is ever vocal with Thy praise, so
may our hearts be attuned to deepest joy that we are
a part of Thy creation and made capable of constant
exultation in the beauty and the beneficence of Thy
purpose therein displayed. In this spirit may we
rejoice and be glad in this new day which Thou
hast made for us. Amen.

I. J. MEAD.

*As one familiar with the sonatas and the symphonies
of Beethoven, while passing along the street in summer,
gets, from out of the open window, a snatch of a song
or a piece that is being played, catching a strain here
and another there — and says to himself, " Ah,
that is Beethoven. I recognize that: it is from such
and such a movement of the Pastoral," or whatever
it may be; — so men in life catch strains of God in
the mother's disinterested and self-denying love, in
the lover's glow, in the little child's innocent affections. Where did this thing come from? No plant
ever brought out such fruit as this?*

HENRY WARD BEECHER.

Father of all and giver of every good thing, to Thee
we pray; to Thee we look for light, for truth, for
beauty. In the travail of thought may there come
only the highest and best good. Where there is
division we ask for unity; where there is confusion
we ask for serenity; where there is discord, we ask
for harmony. May divergent paths lead to the
larger way of widening vision, distinctive service,
unstinted love. Hasten the day when Thy purpose
shall be accomplished in us, and when that which
is now imperfect shall become the perfected whole.
Grant to us wisdom to pursue noble ends with intelligent zeal, and patient effort, and in a charitable
and hopeful spirit. Amen.

C. C. CLARK.

*It is very interesting to watch a plant grow, it is
like taking part in creation. When all outside is
cold and white, when the little children of the woodland
are gone to their nurseries in the warm earth and the
empty nests on the bare trees filled with snow, my
window-garden glows and smiles, making summer
within while it is winter without. It is wonderful
to see flowers bloom in the midst of a snow-storm! I
have felt a bud " shyly doff her green hood and blossom
with a silken burst of sound," while the icy fingers of
the snow beat against the window panes. What secret
power, I wonder, caused this blossoming miracle?
What mysterious force guided the seedling from the
dark earth up to the light, through leaf and stem and
bud, to glorious fulfilment in the perfect flower? Who
could have dreamed that such beauty lurked in the
dark earth, was latent in the tiny seed we planted?
Beautiful flower, you have taught me to see a little
way into the hidden heart of things. Now I understand that the darkness everywhere may hold possibilities better than even my hopes.*

HELEN KELLER.

Grant us, O God, this day, vitality of brain and
heart, to lay hold on the ordinary events and experiences of life, and transmute them into beautiful
and permanent values for ourselves and others.
May we have courage, love and faithfulness, to
conquer adversities and fulfil our duties. And
should the winter of discontent and disappointment
beat without against our souls, even so may Thy
Kingdom come. Amen.

JULIUS P. WEST.

Brother — there is no payment in the world!
We work and pour our labor at the feet
Of those who are around us and to come.
We live and take our living at the hands
Of those who are around us and have been.
No one is paid. No person can have more
Than he can hold. And none can do beyond
The power that's in him. To each child that's born
Belongs as much of all our human good
As he can take and use to make him strong.

And from each man, debtor to all the world,
Is due the fullest fruit of all his powers,
His whole life's labor, proudly rendered up,
Not as return — can moments pay an age?
But as the simple duty of a man.
Can he do less — receiving everything?

CHARLOTTE PERKINS GILMAN.

O, Thou Most Bountiful Giver! We thank Thee
this morning for all the conveniences and comforts,
the stored knowledge and acquired wisdom, the
inspirations and encouragements of our daily life.
Truly others have lived as Thy children and
labored as Thy servants, by mind and hand
and heart, and we are wondrously permitted to
enter into the fruits of their labours. Grant unto
us this day, O Father, so to strive and so to live
that some other life may be cheered and blessed
by the spirit and by the fruit of our day's service.
May our thoughts and words and deeds somehow
express our gratitude for the blessings which we are
constantly receiving. Amen.

WILLLIAM H. GOULD.

What a wonderful thing it is to meet a man or woman whose manners are instantly open and free — opening up a direct road between him or her and yourself!

EDWARD CARPENTER.

There is a world in us that God keeps to himself, except when He calls some few souls, with special errand for us, to receive a glimpse. It is full of life, and growths, and wonders, that are to be developed and revealed. We ourselves know not what we shall be; but He knows that we shall be like Him. . . . It is the world of the spiritual microscope.

MRS. A. D. T. WHITNEY.

Our Father and Mother God, — we have cried for Thee as little children cry for parental love to wait upon their wants, and, like babes that cry, we have looked for Thee in nothing else. We would be now Thy sons and daughters of a larger growth, who learn to find Thee in a more complete and blessed fellowship of service and sacrifice with Thee, of united thought and will with Thine, of such living as shares in Thy perfect and eternal life. Help us so to be and so to live that even in ourselves we may get glimpses of Thine infinite good will and faithfulness, and show in our human lives, that God is in His world and all is well. **Amen.**

GEORGE W. KENT.

What are we set on earth for? Say to toil:
Nor to seek to leave the tending of thy vines,
For all the heat of the day, till it declines,
And death's mild curfew shall from work assoil.
God did anoint thee with His odorous oil
To wrestle, not to reign; and he assigns
All thy tears over, like pure crystallines,
For younger fellow-workers of the soil
To wear for amulets. So others shall
Take patience, labor, to their heart and hand,
From thy hand, and thy heart, and thy brave cheer,
And God's grace fructify through thee to all.
The least flower with a brimming cup may stand,
And share its dewdrop with another near.

ELIZABETH BARRETT BROWNING.

Our Father in Heaven, we devoutly thank Thee for that ceaseless and refreshing tide of blessing that, from the reservoir of Thine exhaustless goodness, flows into our hearts and lives. And we further thank Thee that among the choicest of those blessings, is the one of being, not merely the receptacles of this inflow, but also co-workers with Thee, and with Thy Son, our Saviour, Jesus Christ, in carrying forward to successful issue Thy beneficent purposes of grace and salvation. Grant us, we beseech Thee, day by day, such an infusion of Thy Holy Spirit as shall fittingly equip us for the gladsome and effective discharge of the duties of this divine relation, and its exalted privileges. All of which grant for Thy mercy's sake. Amen.

CHARLES P. NASH.

The deepest secret of life is love. Without love there is no enthusiasm, and without ideals there is no enthusiasm. We freeze our hearts by selfishness, and stifle them by sordidness. We fix our eyes upon the little field circumscribed by our day's activities and ends. With no wide-reaching affection and no uplifting ideal, we make of our life a treadmill and of our duty an unwelcome drudgery. We disclaim the highest endowment of the soul and deny our sonship to God. Narrow faiths and narrow hopes put fetters on the spirit, and small affections keep small the heart.

PHILIP S. MOXOM.

Our Father, every morning is a fresh witness of Thy loving kindness. When we sleep the vigils of Thy love are round about us. At the threshold of this new day, may it please Thee to inspire us with lofty aims, so that we may rise out of our selfish selves into conscious kinship with Thee. Help us to know the mystery of love, how limitless and all-conquering it is. Animated by its sweet law, may we go out into this great, needy world with hearts to sympathize and words to cheer and hands to minister. Then we shall know the divine sweetness of our Christian faith, the joy of Christlike living; we shall know that love is the fulfilling of the law. Amen.

Q. H. SHINN.

Every day is a fresh beginning,
  Every morn is the world made new.
You who are weary of sorrow and sinning,
  Here is a beautiful hope for you,
  A hope for me and a hope for you.

Every day is a fresh beginning;
  Listen, my soul, to the glad refrain,
And, spite of old sorrow and older sinning,
  And puzzles forecasted and possible pain,
  Take heart with the day, and begin again.
                                    SUSAN COOLIDGE.

O Thou, who makest all things new, we are glad each day is not only a new day but one unlike any before it. Everything breathes freshness and newness of life; a new heaven is over our heads, a new earth beneath our feet. We know this day will be full of new opportunities for work, new scenes for pleasure, new chances to make better our lives. If yesterday was not all we could wish, if there were failures in duty, or loss of faith in ourselves, and Thy great love, may this be filled with larger faith, greater hope, complete love. May we so take heart in this quiet morning hour, that we may be brave and faithful all the day, so that in spite of old sorrows and older sins, the memory of which may now and then shadow our way, we may find ourselves when the evening shall come, nearer heaven in heart and life, and more worthy to be called Thy children. Amen.

WILLIAM F. POTTER.

O friend, never strike sail to a fear! Come into
port greatly, or sail with God the seas. . . . He
has not learned the lesson of life who does not every
day surmount a fear.

RALPH WALDO EMERSON.

There is no storm but this
Of your own cowardice
    That braves you out;
You are the storm that mocks
Yourself; you are the rocks
    Of your own doubt;
Besides this fear of danger there's no danger here
And he that here fears danger does deserve his fear.

RICHARD CRASHAW.

Thou knowest, O Lord, the weakness of our human
nature, and how prone we are not only to shrink
from the difficulties and to tremble at the dangers
which lie in our way, but to allow imaginary difficulties and dangers to hinder us from living as Thy
children should. Help us, we pray Thee, to be free
from all such fear today. Be Thou our refuge from
whatsoever may threaten us, either without or within.
Deliver us from faint-heartedness and enable us to
stand fast in the glorious liberty of those who fear
nothing but to offend against Thee and to wrong
their own immortal souls. We ask it as disciples of
Christ. Amen.

EDWIN C. SWEETSER.

Whichever way the wind doth blow,
Some heart is glad to have it so;
Then blow it east or blow it west,
The wind that blows, that wind is best

My little craft sails not alone:
A thousand fleets from every zone
Are out upon a thousand seas;
And what for me were favoring breeze
Might dash another, with the shock
Of doom, upon some hidden rock.
And so I do not dare to pray
For winds to waft me on my way,
But leave it to a Higher Will
To stay or speed me; trusting still
That all is well, and sure that He
Who launched my bark will sail with me
Through storm and calm, and will not fail,
Whatever breezes may prevail,
To land me, every peril past,
Within His sheltering heaven at last.

CAROLINE ATWATER MASON.

O Lord let us know that we do not sail life's seas alone. Thou art the God of the storms. Thou goest with us whithersoever we go. Grant us, our Heavenly Father, that we may not suffer shipwreck of our faith. Grant us that the voyage of our lives may be prosperous, and that at last, whether soon or late we shall find some harbor of rest and peace. Amen.

GEORGE L. PERIN.

Our Memorial Day celebrations will be but a hypocritical play-acting unless they shall remind us of the cause and the country for which our brave soldiers gave their lives. It is not enough for us to recall their names and sing their praises. We must love the country they loved and in our turn be ready to do the hero's part.

GEORGE L. PERIN.

But what is it to love one's country? Is it to carry a banner in a procession? Is it to shout as we see the flag? Is it to fling bunting from the tops of the buildings, and send off sky-rockets in the evenings? Vastly deeper than that is love of country, deeper than any soldier's uniform, deeper than any pictures of battleships with which we adorn our walls.

W. H. P. FAUNCE.

God of the Nations, we thank Thee today for every heroic deed of every heroic soul. We rejoice that in every hour of real emergency there have ever been men who were ready to die for their country. O Lord, may the memory of their sacrifice ever remain to us and to the children of coming generations a sacred heritage. Yet, O Lord, let us not be satisfied to glorify their deeds with a memory. Let us do them the higher honor of consecrating our lives to the service of the country they loved. So shall we, in the honor we render them find the title to our honor. Thus in *our* land and in *our* time may Thy Kingdom come and Thy will be done. Amen.

GEORGE L. PERIN.

To be glad of life because it gives you the chance to love and to work and to play and to look up at the stars; to be satisfied with your possessions, but not contented with yourself until you have made the best of them; to despise nothing in the world except falsehood and meanness, and to fear nothing except cowardice; to be governed by your admirations rather than your dislikes; to covet nothing that is your neighbor's except his kindness of heart and gentleness of manners; to think seldom of your enemies, often of your friends, and every day of Christ; and to spend as much time as you can, with body and with spirit in God's out-of-doors — these are little guide-posts on the footpath to **peace.** HENRY VANDYKE.

O Thou God of peace and of love. How shall we come to Thee? How shall we share Thy strength and know Thy life? Let us commune with Thy gracious spirit and so learn Thy way. How beautiful the vision which prayer unfolds to us when we worship in spirit and truth! We see the virtues which ennoble and sanctify other lives. Sweet and tender patience appears and in her light ruffled and distorted tempers are subdued and clothed in their right mind. Faith is seen and as irresolution and doubt take their flight, confident trust and cherished conviction appear in magnetic power. So, O Lord, would we read the signs which other lives present. So would we strengthen our own aspirations and make real the vision. So, O Father, would we find Thy peace. Amen.

AUGUSTINE N. FOSTER.

*A season for simple living with the kindly sun
and the blue sky, days of keen delight in little things,
of joyous questing after beauty, days for the making
of true friends by being a true friend to others, days
when we may enlarge our little lives by excursions
to strange places, by friendly association, by the companionship of great thoughts, days that may teach
us to live nobly, to work joyously, to play harder, to
do our labor better. So should each June bring us
indeed a golden summer.*

EDWIN OSGOOD GROVER.

Heavenly Father, Thou givest all good things. We
thank Thee for life and hope and cheer. In gratitude
we consecrate this day to blessing Thy children, and
so to serving Thee who hast said, "Inasmuch as
ye have done it unto these, ye have done it unto Me."
Teach us the gladness of a life responsive to Thy
messages through Nature. Grant us the joy of
making friends by being friendly with our fellow
men. Whatsoever we may do, at work or at play,
may it be in the spirit of the Saviour. We begin
this day with Thee. By its ministries may our com-
rades be helped and our lives together be made
nobler, stronger, and well-pleasing in Thy sight.
Amen.

MAURICE A. LEVY.

Over the shoulders and slopes of the dune,
  I saw the white daisies go down to the sea,
A host in the sunshine, an army in June,
  The people God sends us to set our hearts free.

The bobolinks rallied them up from the dell,
  The orioles whistled them out of the wood,
And all of their singing was "Earth, it is well,"
  And all of their dancing was, "Life, Thou art good!"
                                    BLISS CARMAN.

O Thou, who art the Father of Light and Love, from whom cometh down every good and perfect gift, we thank Thee for this new born day, which Thou sendest us, for the splendor of Thy presence in the sunlit sky above us and the blossoming earth beneath; for spring-time flowers that border our paths with loveliness and happy bird song, lifting our hearts to responsive joy and praise. We thank Thee for life and health, for home and friends, for opportunities and duties, for temptations and trials, yea, for the very sorrows and bereavements which bring us to ourselves in penitence, to others in sympathy, and to Thee in faith and adoration. Thy will be done! Thy kingdom come! Amen.

CHARLES W. WENDTE.

One small life in God's great plan,
How futile it seems as the ages roll,
Do what it may, or strive how it can,
To alter the sweep of the infinite whole!
A single stitch in an endless web,
A drop in the ocean's flow and ebb!
But the pattern is rent where the stitch is lost,
Or marred where the tangled threads have crossed;
And each life that fails of its true intent
Mars the perfect plan that its Maker meant.

SUSAN COOLIDGE.

O Thou, the heavenly Father, in whom we live and move, whose life-giving spirit is ever around us like the air we breathe, — we lift our thoughts to Thee in reverence and gladness at the coming of the new day. We are glad for the quiet hours of the night, while the stars shine over us. May we be ready now, with willing and obedient hearts, for the work, the cares, the joys and the friendly converse of the day. We know how small our lives are; may we share the thoughts of Thy infinite mind, may Thy power and beauty, Thy justice and goodness possess us. May our feeble wills be strong to carry the current of the one Good Will that sways the universe. Amen.

CHARLES F. DOLE.

I have lived, sir, a long time; and the longer I live, the more convincing proofs I see of this truth, that God governs in the affairs of men.

BENJAMIN FRANKLIN.

All I have seen teaches me to trust the Creator for all I have not seen. Whatever it be which the great Providence prepares for us, it must be something large and generous; and in the great style of His works. The future must be up to the style of our faculties, of memory, of hope, of imagination, of reason.

RALPH WALDO EMERSON.

O Thou, who in Thy greatness holds the planets on their way, and in Thy providence guides the sparrow's flight, and in Thy tenderness marks the sparrow's fall, may we not be blind to Thy footprints in the events of every day, but see them guiding our way and feel more and more Thy love. Father, we ask not for great things, but we ask Thee to help us in the little needs and longings that fill our every day, to be the strength of our every endeavor, that in our daily walk, we may feel that the earth is warm with life and joy, that the air is full of strength, that there comes to us from every side some message, sweet and tender, if only we can be patient, trustful, believing that all things work together for good to them who seek to do Thy will. Amen.

JOSHUA YOUNG.

And do not fear to hope. Can poet's brain
More than the Father's heart rich good invent?
Each time we smell the autumn's dying scent,
We know the primrose time will come again;
Not more we hope, nor less would soothe our pain.
Be bounteous in our faith, for not misspent
Is confidence unto the Father lent:
Thy need is sown and rooted for his rain,
His thoughts are as thine own; nor are his ways
Other than thine, but by their loftier sense
Of beauty infinite and love intense.
Work on! One day, beyond all thought of praise
A sunny joy will crown thee with its rays;
Nor other than thy need, thy recompense.

GEORGE MacDONALD.

Our Father, in the gratitude of loved and loving children we thank Thee for life and all the faith and hope and love Thy goodness has awakened in our souls. For the splendors of the world and the greater splendor of the mind radiant with Thy love, we bow in rapture and adoration. Overwhelmed at times by the mysteries and vicissitudes of life, we will trust Thy will to lead us out of darkness into the light of Thine informing spirit of truth and wisdom. Conscious of our weakness and needs, we rejoice that strength and supply are assured to us in the permanence of Thy Fatherhood. Lead us more and ever more to realize that in Thee we live and move and have our being. Amen.

RICHMOND FISK.

When a feller goes a-huntin' for a rose
He shouldn't be a-thinkin' of the thorn;
He must woo it, he must win it —
Where his heart beats he must pin it
An' breathe the breath that's in it
　　　　Every morn!

When a feller goes a-huntin' for a rose
He shouldn't see the thorn beneath its breast,
But for all its thorny foes,
Red and reckless, — one poor rose
Is sweet enough, God knows,
　　　　For the best.

　　　　　　　　　FRANK L. STANTON.

O Lord, our God, so great is our life we may find that for which we look, — the good or the bad. Send us into this day with eyes searching for the good. Beholding it may we admire it and admiring it we shall become like it changed into the same image from character to character by the Spirit. May we be more concerned to do right than not to do wrong. Save us from a humility that is weakness and give us largeness of life without pride. May we want nothing so much as opportunity, — opportunity to be, to do, to suffer. May we not strive for bigness but for fitness and may our reception of the Christ be our forgiveness and our salvation for His name's sake. Amen.

　　T. C. MARTIN.

The beauty of work depends upon the way we meet it, — whether we arm ourselves each morning to attack it as an enemy that must be vanquished before night comes, or whether we open our eyes with the sunrise to welcome it as an approaching friend who will keep us delightful company all day, and who will make us feel at evening, that the day was well worth its fatigues.

LUCY LARCOM.

Our Heavenly Father, Thou givest us light for the hours of labor and darkness for the hours of slumber. We toil and then we rest. We sleep and then we arise, to perform the tasks which await us. Convince us, O God, that the life which Thou hast given us to live is more than working that we may rest, and resting that we may work. Persuade us that it is for some great and good end. Help us to understand that even as we live in Thee so Thou dost fulfil Thine eternal purposes in and through us. Teach us that our smallest effort is important to Thee. So may we dread no duty. So may every moment of every day be precious in our sight. Amen.

ROGER S. FORBES.

And those who heard the Singers three
Disputed which the best might be;
For still their music seemed to start
Discordant echoes in each heart.

But the great Master said, "I see
No best in kind, but in degree;
I gave a various gift to each,
To charm, to strengthen, and to teach.

"These are the three great chords of might,
And he whose ear is tuned aright,
Will hear no discord in the three,
But the most perfect harmony."
                              HENRY W. LONGFELLOW.

O God, our Heavenly Father, we thank Thee for
all Thy mercies new every morning, and fresh every
evening, but especially we bless Thee that Thou
callest us to Thy service and kingdom by Jesus
Christ, our Lord, and hast vouchsafed to each of
us some gracious gift whereby we may accomplish
Thy holy will concerning us. Grant that we may
so improve and use that pearl of price as to enhance
greatly the welfare of Thy children. Help each to
see the good in all, and all to see the good in each,
that all may strive together in sinless and sweet
accord for the common weal and thus for the glory
of Thy name, and so hasten the happy day when
all souls shall be one, as prayed the Saviour of the
world. Amen.
ALFRED P. PUTNAM.

Men talk sometimes as if the passage of a ship through the sea or a bird through the air is a fit symbol of man's passage through this world. I do not think so. A better symbol would be the passage of a plough through the soil leaving a furrow behind. What does the furrow include? All the memory of every beautiful picture and landscape you have ever seen. It includes the memory of every experience, every sweet association, every tie of love, whether of father, mother, wife or children. All these, whether living or dead, speak to you. They have a voice, a language that you will understand.

GEORGE L. PERIN.

We thank Thee, O God, for the many influences past and present which have had a share in the moulding of our lives and characters toward a larger usefulness and a more perfect realization of the Christian ideal. We thank Thee for the mother's love which watched over us through years of helplessness; for the father's love which made provision for our wants, for the human sympathy which has everywhere blessed and strengthened us and made life brighter; for the friends of youth and age who have helped us to better things. Grant, O God, that a memory of these blessings may abide with us so long as life may last, and that as we have been helped by others to walk the way of life we may not forget to extend a helping hand to those who may need our comfort and our sympathy.

ORIN EDSON CROOKER.

It is not to taste sweet things, but to do noble and true things, and vindicate himself under God's heaven, as a God-made man, that the poorest son of Adam dimly longs. This dim longing for what is noble and true, the still small voice which calls to one imperatively in moments of temptation, is the safeguard which, if hearkened to, not only protects one in severe trials of manliness and womanliness, but also incites to the formation of a fine character, without which all acquisitions, all graces and accomplishments, all talents and all learning, are but as sounding brass and a tinkling cymbal.

THOMAS CARLYLE.

Almighty God, our heavenly Father, in grateful recognition of Thy love and watchful care, we thank Thee for the repose of the night and the promise of the day. Our desire is to do Thy will, and we ask for the guidance and inspiration of Thy spirit. Enable us to perform faithfully all the work that Thou hast given us to do. Grant us a sufficiency of Thy grace to treat all our fellowmen as children of Thine, and when night comes may we have the blessed assurance that through the experiences of this day we have become a little more like Thine own glorious self in love and holiness. We ask it in the name of Jesus, our example, and Saviour. Amen.

WARREN S. PERKINS.

Now it is June, and the secret is told;
Flashed from the buttercup's glory of gold;
Hummed in the bumblebee's gladness, and sung
New from each bough where a bird's nest is swung;
Breathed from the clover-beds, when the winds pass;
Chirped in small psalms, through the aisles of the
  grass.

HENRY JAMES, SR.

Dear Father, in the morning hour of this new day, we thank Thee for the glorious revelation of Thyself in the open Book of Nature. May we love the beautiful and therein love Thee, with a true and abiding affection. Grant unto us the understanding that it is only as we have the spirit of the beautiful in our lives that we can appreciate the beautiful without us. So may we value this life, which is from Thee, as a means of attaining a larger usefulness and for realizing that goodness which is ever heavenly. In simply trying to be nobler, more unselfish, like unto Christ, we pray, that we may learn how good is life. Amen.

THOMAS EDWARD POTTERTON.

Methinks I love all common things,
The common air, the common flower,
The dear, kind, common thought that springs
From hearts that have no other dower,
No other wealth, no other power,
Save love; and will not that repay
For all else fortune tears away?

BRYAN WALLER PROCTER.

We thank God for the beauty of the world. We thank God that it is good to be alive. We thank God for the joy that joins us to Thy world in gladness, and makes it seem to be the open book of Thy graciousness and tenderness and compassion. We thank Thee also for the ministry of those days that were not bright, but that were full of comfort, even in their darkness, into which God came shrouded, only to reveal Himself more clearly as the light. We thank Thee for the intervening by the hand of love and tenderness that is human, so that our best nature was called out for love's sake, and all the lower forces of our lives led in the leash of that sweet attraction. We thank God for everything for which our life is better, and pray Thee to help us to use Thy mercies to turn them into strength, not the strength of praise alone, but the strength of service also. Amen.

THOMAS R. SLICER.

A creed is a rod,
And a crown is of night;
But this thing is God,
To be man with thy might,
To grow straight in the strength of thy spirit, and
live out thy life as the light.

ALGERNON CHARLES SWINBURNE.

Life is fuller and sweeter for every fulness and
sweetness that we take knowledge of. And to him that
hath, cannot help being given from everything.

MRS. A. D. T. WHITNEY.

Infinite Love and Beauty, who stirrest in the tiniest
seed that breaks its earthly shell to greet the light
and warmth of thy beneficence and round its life
in blade and flower and ripened fruit, — awake in
us, we pray, that we may burst the casements of our
dead selves and live to bear the fruits of completed
lives. Be love alone our creed and service our crown;
and in the sweetness and light of these twin
ministers draw Thou us on, until having taken
full knowledge of the fulness and sweetness of
our Lord the Christ, we shall have measured
in our spiritual stature, His perfect manliness and
strength. Thus shall we have indeed and to us
shall be given from everything. Amen.

ALBERT C. WHITE.

He fails who climbs to power and place
Up the pathway of disgrace.
He fails not who makes truth his cause,
Nor bends to win the crowd's applause.
He fails not, he who stakes his all
Upon the right and dares to fall.
What though the living bless or blame,
For him the long success of fame!

RICHARD WATSON GILDER.

Our Heavenly Father, help us when we fail to see and know the truth and its blessed influence for good. Help us to combat bravely the evil in the world and to look to Thee for encouragement and success. Help us, if we fail, to regain our footing and to reach the higher because of the effort which Thy love prompts. We gratefully accept the power which Thy wisdom gives and thank Thee for the opportunity to use its strength. Be Thou our guide and we shall fear no failure, nor overestimate the worth of success. So shall we "rejoice in the Lord always," — in failure because of Thy help and in success because of Thine approval. In the name of Jesus Christ our Lord and Redeemer. Amen.

WILLIAM E. GIBBS.

A singer sang a song of tears,
  And the great world heard and wept
For the song of the sorrows of fleeting years,
  And the hopes which the dead past kept:
And souls in anguish their burdens bore,
  And the world was sadder than ever before.

A singer sang a song of cheer,
  And the great world listened and smiled,
For he sang of the love of a Father dear
  And the trust of a little child;
And souls that before had forgotten to pray,
  Looked up and went singing along the way.

EMMA C. DOWD.

Almighty God, our heavenly Father, our trust is evermore in Thee, and we would keep that trust as a song within our hearts, which may cheer and bless and strengthen us. When the night is dark and the day is dreary may that song be with us, and when cares oppress and sorrows meet us, may our prayers still rise to Thee, for Thou art the God of our lives. Let not the day's discouragements depress us, nor its failures find us weak or helpless, nor its trials leave a stain upon our souls. But because we have Thy song of love within our hearts may we march to heavenly music, and ever go upon our way rejoicing. Amen.

PAUL REVERE FROTHINGHAM.

It is only the sincerity of human feeling that abides. As for a thought, we know not, it may be deceptive; but the love, wherewith we have loved it, will surely return to our soul; nor can a single drop of its clearness or strength be abstracted by error. Of that perfect ideal that each of us strives to build up in himself, the sum total of all our thoughts will help only to model the outline; but the elements that go to construct it, and keep it alive, are the purified passion, unselfishness, loyalty, wherein these thoughts have had being.

MAETERLINCK.

O God, our Heavenly Father, help us to take up the cares of this day with an unselfish heart, and in loyalty to what is right and good. Keep us in right relation to those with whom our lot is cast, in sympathy with the unanxious joy of the world and with the deeper life which is its source. We desire to enter into the thought and the love of the most hopeful souls, that, in all the needful pauses of the day, we may find cheer, incentive, and the ampler rest: through Jesus Christ, our Lord. Amen.

CHARLES H. LEONARD.

" Does the road wind up-hill all the way? "
" Yes, to the very end! "
" Will the day's journey take the whole long day? "
" From morn to night, my friend! "

" But is there for the night a resting-place? "
" A roof for all when the dark hours begin."
" May not the darkness hide it from my face? "
" You cannot miss that inn."

" Shall I meet other wayfarers at night? "
" Those who have gone before."
" Then must I knock or call when just in sight? "
" They will not keep you standing at that door."

" Shall I find comfort, travel-sore and weak? "
" Of labor you shall find the sum."
" Will there be beds for me and all who seek? "
" Yea, — beds for all who come! "

CHRISTINA ROSSETTI.

Our Heavenly Father, we thank Thee for this new day. May it be an open door to faithful service. Open our eyes that we may see all vexations, distresses, and toil as angels in disguise sent to strengthen and fulfil us, to prepare us for larger blessings at our journey's end. As the blue sky of Thy loving kindness is broader and more enduring than the clouds that sometimes hide it, so teach us to trust Thine unfailing love that overarches and outlasts all weariness and pain. When life and strength fail us here, may we find them transformed and glorious in the city of God hereafter. Be Thou our shield and our reward now and forever. Amen.

JOHN M. WILSON.

*Those homelier wildflowers, which we call weeds;
yellow japanned buttercups and star-disked dande-
lions, lying in the grass, like sparks that have leaped
from the kindling sun of summer; the profuse daisy-
like flower which whitens the fields, to the great dis-
gust of liberal shepherds, yet seems fair to loving eyes,
with its button-like mound of gold set round with milk-
white rays; the tall-stemmed succory, setting its pale
blue flowers aflame one after another; the red and
white clovers; the broad, flat leaves of the plantain, —
"the white man's foot," as the Indians called it; —
those common growths which fling themselves to be
crushed under our feet and our wheels, making themselves so cheap in this perpetual martyrdom that we
forget, each of them is a ray of the divine beauty.*

OLIVER WENDELL HOLMES.

Our Heavenly Father, however poor and mean
and commonplace our lives may seem to be, in our
better moments we think of ourselves as Thy children. We may have failed sometimes but we shall
not utterly fail. In Thy sight, nothing is common
or worthless. No life shall be cast as rubbish to the
void. However commonplace our tasks may seem,
let us feel ourselves in partnership with God, and
go forth to the duties of the day with high hope and
sense of dignity. So shalt Thou make even our
little lives of some real service to the world. We
pray to Thee in the spirit of Him, who though the
humblest of all, was yet Master of all. Amen.

GEORGE L. PERIN.

There's a real grace of character in forgetting the things which disturb the harmony of life.
HAMILTON W. MABIE.

Touch your lips with gladness and go singing on your way,
Smiles will strangely lighten every duty;
Just a little word of cheer may span a sky of gray
With hope's own heaven-tinted bow of beauty.
Wear a pleasant face wherein shall shine a joyful heart,
As shines the sun, the happy fields adorning;
To every care-beclouded life some ray of light impart,
And touch your lips with gladness every morning.
NIXON WATERMAN.

O Thou who art from everlasting to everlasting, Our God and Father, we flee unto Thee as the One who is able to save us from all foes within and without. We confess our weakness and our many grievous faults, and beseech Thee to touch us by Thy Spirit, that with penitent and lowly hearts we may seek Thee as our everlasting Friend and Helper. Be patient yet a while with our shortcomings and frowardness. Suffer us yet a little that Thine infinite grace and compassion may arouse us from our spiritual slumber unto the glorious life of obedience and love. In this new day we would be made to feel Thy presence and the light and joy and peace, which Thou dost promise to all who diligently seek Thee through Jesus Christ Our Lord. Amen.

CLARENCE E. RICE.

Now is the high tide of the year,
  And whatever of life hath ebbed away
Comes flooding back with a ripply cheer,
  Into every bare inlet and creek and bay;
Now the heart is so full that a drop overfills it,
We are happy now because God wills it.

JAMES RUSSELL LOWELL.

Holy, holy, holy, Lord God Almighty! early in the morning we approach unto Thee. The whole round of creation is burdened with the exuberance of Thy life, and everywhere is hallowed ground. We come with unshod feet. The sun, mighty minister of Thy great goodness, flooding the world with light and piercing all things with his fiery arrows, calls back to life the sleeping earth, and assures us that we are partakers of Thy light and Thy love and Thy life. O most glorious God! may these Thy mercies, fresh every morning, be with us through the day to strengthen us to do Thy will, we ask in the name of Him who came that we may have life and have it abundantly. Amen.

FRANK W. COLLIER.

Man hath much need of courage; and need to brace
His spiritual nerve in solitude;
Self-trusting, self-sustained, and self-imbued;
Seeking God in his own heart's secret place.
To perfect self, and in that self embrace
  The triune essence of truth, beauty, and good;
This is fulfilment, this beatitude
Throned high above base fears and hopes more base.
What shall it profit us, if, gaining all
  The privilege of priest-made paradise,
We lose therewith our self which is the soul?
And wherefore should we shrink from even the fall,
If haply we should fail with steadfast eyes
Fixed only on so bright, so pure a goal?

JOHN ADDINGTON SYMONDS.

Heavenly Father, we thank Thee for the gift of
a new day, for the tasks which it brings, and for the
strength with which we rise to its requirements.
Help us, through all this day, to remember Thee.
Thou art our strength, our guide, our inspiration.
Fill us with the courage born of faith. Let us feel
that, seeking to do right, we shall be moved and
aided by an unseen Power. In all our experiences
this day, help us to speak the truth, to be loyal to
friendship, to be steadfast in principle, to fight the
good fight and to keep the faith. Bless our endeavors
to give heart and hope to other souls; and grant
them the presence of Thy loving spirit. Amen.

JOHN CLARENCE LEE.

Let a man start out at breakneck speed in the morning, pushing and driving and hurrying as if it were a matter of life and death to accomplish a given task before noon, and he will generally end by working himself into a fever of anxiety and harassing care before night, and the man who, under any pretext whatsoever, whether for the sake of wealth or learning or pleasure, has pursued this mad, rushing, whirling method of life for fifteen or twenty years, will find himself thoroughly disqualified for the normal enjoyment of life thenceforward to the end of his days.

GEORGE L. PERIN.

Most gracious God! Thou who hast sustained us through the night watches, and who now openest to us the day, with its promise of good and opportunity for service, we still depend upon that heavenly faithfulness which never fails. We look to Thee for the quickening of our best powers. We would be laborers together with Thee to-day, not as driven to irksome tasks, but as honored with a welcome privilege. Whether we plant or water may we do it faithfully, and then trust Thee for the desired increase. May it please Thee to quiet our anxieties, to lay to rest our unworthy fears, and to assure us of Thine over-ruling providence; and thus through all our toiling may we enjoy large measures of the peace that passeth understanding. Amen.

JAMES EDWARD WRIGHT.

I do not say you can make yourself merry and happy when you are in a physical condition which is contrary to such mental condition, but by practice and effort you can learn to withdraw from it, refusing to allow your judgments and actions to be ruled by it. "What does that matter?" you will learn to say. "It is enough for me to know that the sun does shine, and that this is only a weary fog that is round about me for a moment. I shall come out into the light beyond presently." This is faith,—faith in God, who is Light.

GEORGE MacDONALD.

Our Father, residing in the light incomprehensible and who art seeing and providing all good for Thine immortal household, when mid investing clouds we shall hail Thy presence, transforming weakness into perfect strength and sighs and groans into joy and swelling songs, above all the many rightful subjects of Christian petition, we pray that Thou wilt always press us near to Thee to feel Thy loving heart-beats and dwell in the light in which is no darkness at all. We pray not to be spared any of our full part of the burdens needful to this day, but to be given the measure of grace to maintain unfaltering steps. Behold with compassion the errors that befall us as we, too, compassionate others. Amen.

JACOB STRAUB.

We are all perhaps familiar with the story of the little housemaid, who, when she was asked why she thought she had become a Christian, replied, after a little hesitation, " Because I sweep under the mats." A very poor reason at first sight, and only significant from the fact of the master-motive underlying the fact itself. A child's reasoning — but did not quaint old Herbert employ the same fine logic when he sang

" *Who sweeps a room as for Thy laws,*
　　Makes that and the action fine! "
　　　　　　　　　WILLIAM MOODIE.

Dear Lord of Life and Light, at the dawn of another day we rise to thank Thee for Thy watchful care, imparting strength and vitality during the closed hours of the night. Thy gift of eternal life is ours by Thy creatorship and love, and we would pray that in no way during this coming day shall we dishonor our birthright by evil thought or action. Help us to aspire to hold fast and develop Thy holy characteristics, normal to us and made active by our wills. We thank Thee for the goal revealed to us as our destiny, the spirit displayed by our Master, Jesus Christ, and like Him may we lean on Thee daily for the strengthening of our faith and the maturing of our plans. Amen.

CHARLES E. LUND.

They are tired of what is old,
We will give it voices new;
For the half hath not been told
Of the beautiful and true.
GEORGE MACDONALD.

The common problem, yours, mine, everyone's,
Is not to fancy what were fair in life
Provided it could be — but finding first
What may be, than find how to make it fair
Up to our means, a very different thing.
ROBERT BROWNING.

Thou Infinite Heart! our hearts go out after Thee, not for past, not for future, not for what was, though dear, not for what may be, though in vision precious, — not these the burden of our prayer. Our hearts crave peace, comfort with what is. May we confide in Thee so utterly that the old pain is eased, the anxious foreboding is dispelled, self-will merged in divine will, self-direction yielding to divine leading. Lo! our prayer is answered in the making and we are helped. Amen.

STANFORD MITCHELL.

Today is your day and mine, the only day we have, the day in which we play our part. What our part may signify in the great whole, we may not understand, but we are here to play it, and now is our time. This we know, it is a part of action, not of whining. It is a part of love, not cynicism. It is for us to express love in terms of human helpfulness. This we know, for we have learned from sad experience that any other course of life leads toward weakness and misery.

DAVID STARR JORDAN.

Our Father, Author alike of the morning light and Guardian through the darkness and shadow of the night, grant us the right spirit as we go forth to the unknown experiences of this day. We would not look eagerly for our own comfort and happiness, but would find them as Thy free gift while we are employed in giving comfort and happiness to others. Illuminate our lives with happy thoughts, cheerful words and blessed hopes, that we may go forth with no purpose but to do Thy will, and seeking no reward more glorious than Thine approval whispered into loving and attentive hearts, in Thy name. Amen.

LEWIS G. WILSON.

A Persian fable says: "One day
A wanderer found a lump of clay,
So redolent of sweet perfume
Its odors scented all the room.
   "What art thou?" was his quick demand;
   "Art thou some gem from Samarcand,
Or spikenard in this rude disguise,
Or other costly merchandise?"
   "Nay, I am but a lump of clay."
   "Then whence this wondrous perfume — say?"
"Friend, if the secret I disclose,
I have been dwelling with the rose,"
Sweet parable! and will not those
Who love to dwell with Sharon's Rose,
Distil sweet odors all around,
Though low and mean themselves are found?
Dear Lord, abide with us, that we
May draw our perfume fresh from thee.

ANONYMOUS.

Our Father, which art in heaven, — we thank Thee
for the memory of those who lived in Thy spirit and
labored in Thy love. The fragrance of their lives
abides with us. We thank Thee for the prophets
of great hopes, — for those who have seen the invisible, and have searched patiently for the city of
their God. We bless those who by their pure hearts
and unselfish lives have revealed unto us our greater
selves. Help us to learn of them the way of life.
Help us to live in such thoughts and deeds as made
them truly great. Keep our hearts so pure to-day,
our vision of the Master life so clear, that our path,
before and after us, shall be as the light of day. Amen.

FREDERICK W. BETTS.

Tell you what I like the best;
  'Long about knee-deep in June,
'Bout the time the strawberries melts
  On the vine, — some afternoon
Like to jes' git out and rest,
  And not work at nothing else.

Orchard's where I'd ruther be —
Needn't fence it in for me!
  Jes' the whole sky overhead,
  And the whole airth underneath.

JAMES WHITCOMB RILEY.

Help us, O Thou who art the Lord of life, that we may this morning praise Thee for the beauty of the world and for the joyful privilege of wandering in the green fields and by the sparkling brooks, and of resting tired body and weary limb beneath the sweet orchard shade, gazing with gladdened eyes at the blue canopy above, all forgetful of the toil and din of the far off city. O may our hearts this day be in tune with nature and in harmony with Thyself; and as we contemplate Thy works this and every day may our hearts go out in loving and practical sympathy toward those whose lives are spent within the narrow confines of sunless courts. Hear us for the Saviour's sake. Amen.

FRANCIS W. BRETT.

Give us, O give us the man who sings at his work. Be his occupation what it may, he is equal to any of those who follow the same pursuit in silent sullenness. He will do more in the same time — he will do it better — he will persevere longer. One is scarcely sensible of fatigue while he marches to music. The very stars are said to make harmony as they revolve in their spheres. Wondrous is the strength of cheerfulness, although past calculation its power of endurance. Efforts to be permanently useful, must be uniformly joyous — a spirit all sunshine, graceful from very gladness, beautiful because bright.

THOMAS CARLYLE.

Almighty God, we turn to Thee in adoration and praise as we pause upon the threshold of this new day. Grant, we pray Thee, that a song be in our hearts as we go about the duties of the passing hours. Whatever our experiences, whether of joy or sorrow, may we truly value the truthful spirit. If Thou callest us to bear burdens or to stand upon the mountain top of exultant achievement may we not forget to sing of Thee. Yea, O God, we would be ever of the company of trusting souls, for such are near to Thee. And when earthly days are past and the life of the freed spirit is over, grant that our lives may blend in full accord with the music of love, in sunshine of joy, in the beauty of holiness. We praise Thee now and ever. Amen.

STEPHEN H. ROBLIN.

Full-leafed in pride of deepest green,
The earth in the sunshine basks serene,
Where linden blossoms crowded cling,
A thousand bees are murmuring.
As showers drift from the freshened land
With a seven-barred bow is the rain-cloud spanned.
The wild rose yields her subtlest scents
Where hay cocks pitch their fragrant tents.
      The longest day's too brief for June,
      The night too short for such a moon!
                         SARA ANDREW SHAFER.

We thank Thee, our Father, for the wonderful
world in which we live; for the glory of the heavens;
for the beauty of the earth; for the bright morning
following the star-crowned night; for the song of
birds, the hum of bees, the fragrance of flowers, and
the laughter of children, for the industry of men
and women, for all Thy gifts of love. As again the
lengthening shadows creep across our pathway,
may we redouble our energies that no labor of love
may be left undone. So fill us with Thy presence,
so lead us by Thy Spirit this day, that in our homes
we may be patient, in our occupations sweet, in our
social relations brotherly, in all things Christlike,
for Jesus' sake. Amen.

ARTHUR WRIGHT.

Let me go where'er i will
I hear a sky-born music still:
It sounds from all things old,
It sounds from all things young,
From all that's fair, from all that's foul,
Peals out a cheerful song.

It is not only in the rose,
It is not only in the bird,
Not only where the rainbow glows,
Nor in the song of woman heard,
But in the darkest, meanest things
There alway, alway something sings.

'Tis not in the high stars alone,
Nor in the cups of budding flowers,
Nor in the redbreast's mellow tone,
Nor in the bow that smiles in showers,
But in the mud and scum of things
There alway, alway something sings.

RALPH WALDO EMERSON.

Dear Father in heaven, we thank Thee for all the sweet voices of the world, not only for the harmonies of the great masters of song but for the sweet voice of the mother as she sings her song of love, for the bird in the spring time. We thank Thee for the music in the prattle of children, and the kindly word spoken everywhere. The world is full of music if only we have music in our own hearts. We pray, as we set forth again this morning, for spirits in tune with all that is sweet and good. Wherever we go this day, let the world sing to us and make us glad. Amen.

GEORGE L. PERIN.

A little bird with plumage brown,
Beside my window flutters down,
A moment chirps its little strain,
Then taps upon my window-pane.
And chirps again, and hops along,
To call my notice to its song;
But I work on, nor heed its lay,
Till, in neglect, it flies away.

So birds of peace and hope and love
Come fluttering earthward from above,
To settle on life's window-sills,
And ease our load of earthly ills;
But we, in traffic's rush and din
Too deep engaged to let them in,
With deadened heart and sense plod on,
Nor know our loss till they are gone.

PAUL LAURENCE DUNBAR.

My voice shalt Thou hear in the morning, O Lord, in the morning will I direct my prayer unto Thee, and will look up; and looking up, may we not fail to realize that, amid the turmoil of this outward life, Thou art ever present to give peace and rest in the inner life. Should we fail to recognize that presence we shall lose the comfort which Thou art ever ready to bestow, and must ourselves bear burdens which Thou wouldst gladly bear for us or take from us. Thou knowest our frame and rememberest that we are dust. Open our spiritual vision to behold that Divine resources are subject to our daily prayer. In the name of Jesus, the Christ. Amen.

O. W. SCOTT.

Blessed are the poor in spirit, for theirs is the kingdom of Heaven.

Blessed are the pure in heart, for they shall see God. Blessed are the peacemakers, for they shall be called the children of God.

Blessed are ye when men shall revile you and persecute you, and shall say all manner of evil against you falsely for my sake.

MATTHEW v. 3, 8, 11.

O God, our Heavenly Father, we thank Thee that Thou dost overrule our weakness, failure and sins to the accomplishment of Thy divine plan for us. We recall with pleasure our successes in the past year, and if we have failed, wilt Thou show us where and when and teach us the way of amendment. We thank Thee for our Hope and Faith which have come to us from the Bible. Here, on every page and in every biography, have we learned of Christ Jesus, the Way, the Truth and the Life. We thank Thee that through Him our sins are forgiven, and we have learned to know Thee, O blessed Father, which knowledge is eternal life. May we walk with Him, moment by moment in a life of loving service to all mankind, during all the remaining days of our life. Amen.

E. M. WARNER.

One flag, one land, one heart, one hand,
One nation, evermore!
OLIVER WENDELL HOLMES

And for your country, boy, and for that flag, never dream a dream but of serving her, though the service carry you through a thousand hells! No matter what happens to you — no matter who flatters or abuses you — never look at another flag, never let a night pass but you pray God to bless that flag.
EDWARD EVERETT HALE.

Thine, O God, is the kingdom. And blessed is the nation whose God is the Lord. We believe that Thy hand has been in the founding and the fortunes of this land. We do homage to it for its ideals, its principles, its glorious company of apostles of truth, its noble army of martyrs for liberty and humanity; we love and cherish it as our home and our shrine; but we hallow it, we stand in awe of it, as the scene of Thy special activity, the instrument of Thy holy purposes. May its vision not pass; may the clouds that hang over it be dispersed by the clear shining of the sun of righteousness and peace; may the dream of freedom with fraternity be realized here, even here, upon these shores, that Thy saving health may be known among all nations. Amen.

C. ELLWOOD NASH.

Far up the crag, 'twixt sea and sky,
Where winds tempestuous, blowing by,
   Leave giant boulders swept and bare;
   Where forked lightnings fitful flare,
And petrels sound their stormy cry.

A dainty bluebell, sweet and shy,
Lifted its head complacently,
   As guarded by the tenderest care,
    Far up the crag.

And now, whenever fear draws nigh,
In thought I stand 'twixt sea and sky,
   And, as of old in my despair,
   I bless the Power that set it there—
That tiny thing with courage high,
    Far up the crag!

                FLORENCE E. COATES.

Eternal Presence, may we now speak to Thee? or, consciously within Thy presence, should our lips be still? Art Thou the Infinite Mercy, and shall we say, be merciful? Shall we persuade the love that can not once withhold itself? We would not ask, were prayer to change established law. But, we will open here our hearts, and so receive the blessedness that seeks us and has sought us, — sought us as the sunlight sought us early, — seeks us as the raindrops seek us in the storm. Not more canst Thou withhold the goodness from us. We wait receptively, unbarring all our rust-hinged doors to welcome the true favors that now find us. In sweet trust, asking or unasking, we abide ever in Thee. Amen.

PERRY MARSHALL.

God is a kind Father. He sets us all in the places where he wishes us to be employed, and that employment is truly " our Father's business." He chooses work for every creature which will be delightful to them, if they do it simply and humbly. He gives us always strength enough and sense enough for what He wants us to do; if we either tire ourselves or puzzle ourselves, it is our own fault. And we may always be sure, whatever we are doing, that we cannot be pleasing Him if we are not happy ourselves.

JOHN RUSKIN.

Father Divine, Thou art indeed kind. Thine are the ways of kindness, of wisdom, and of love, — the ways of pleasantness and the paths of peace. In simple and humble spirit as becometh Thy children, may we walk with Thee accomplishing the work to which Thou dost call us. Our work is Thy work, our business the Father's business; the business of justice, mercy and truth. When loyal and true, we are what we are, and do what we do by Thy grace. So help us to honor Thee in all the duties of life, — " Not slothful in business, — fervent in spirit," — pleasing Thee and therefore happy ourselves. Amen.

ISAAC P. CODDINGTON.

Threefold is the form of Space:
Length, with ever restless motion,
Seeks eternity's wide ocean;
Breadth with boundless sway extends;
Depth to unknown realms descends.

All as types to thee are given;
Thou must onward strive for heaven,
Never still or weary be,
Wouldst thou perfect glory see;
Far must thy researches go
Wouldst thou learn the world to know;
Thou must tempt the dark abyss
Wouldst thou prove what Being is.

Naught but firmness gains the prize, —
Naught but fulness makes us wise, —
Buried deep, truth ever lies!

            PROVERBS OF CONFUCIUS.

Our Heavenly Father, help us this day to make good our privilege to feel and think of Thee as we do. Help us this day to make ourselves part of our brotherhood, and our brotherhood part of Thee. We know not what the day hath in store for us, but we pray Thee to help us have in store for it our better heart, our better hands. Send Thy holy spirit into our life to calm and to strengthen; that we may be steadfast and true; that we may give and be forgiven. Bless all Thy children this day, and may our labor end as it began, in Thee, with Thee, for Thee. Amen.

LOUIS H. BUCKSHORN.

O Impatient Ones! Do the leaves say nothing to you as they murmur to-day? They are not fashioned this spring, but months ago; and the summer just begun will fashion others for another year. At the bottom of every leaf-stem is a cradle, and in it is an infant germ; and the winds will rock it, and the birds will sing to it all summer long, and next season it will unfold. So God is working for you and carrying forward to the perfect development all the processes of our lives.

HENRY WARD BEECHER.

O Eternal Father, giver of all spiritual grace, we thank Thee for Thy presence in our hearts. May we realize that Thou hast the best possible plan for every human life. Help us to be patient and joyful in the consciousness that Thou art carrying forward Thy blessed work in us. Thy love, O Lord, is equal to Thy wisdom, and Thou wilt always do what is best for us. May Thy holy will be our delight, so that we may each trust in Thee at all times and cheerfully say, Thy will, O Lord, not mine, be done. Thou who dost care for the birds and the lilies art ever mindful of us, Thy children. Deliver us from worry and may Thy peace guard our hearts and minds in Christ Jesus. Amen.

GEORGE H. CHENEY.

*Let us hope that one day all mankind will be happy
and wise; and though this day never should dawn
to have hoped for it cannot be wrong. And in any
event, it is helpful to speak of happiness to those who
are sad, that thus at least they may learn what it is
that happiness means. They are ever inclined to
regard it as something beyond them, extraordinary,
out of their reach. But if all who may count themselves
happy were to tell, very simply, what it was that
brought happiness to them, the others would see that
between sorrow and joy the difference is but as between
a gladsome, enlightened acceptance of life and a hostile
gloomy submission; between a large and harmonious
conception of life, and one that is stubborn and narrow.*

MAETERLINCK.

O Lord, we thank Thee for the special providence
which is over everything which Thou hast created,
and wherein Thou residest with all Thine infinite
perfections. We thank Thee that Thou carest for
us all, that in our day of joy we know it is Thou who
fillest our cup, by giving us the faculties which make
it run over at the brim. We thank Thee that Thou
art with us in our days of hardship and of calamity,
that when our own heart cries out against us, Thou
art greater than our heart, and, understanding all
things, blessest us in secret ways; and when we are
cast down and go stooping and feeble, with hungering
eyes and a failing heart, that Thou still art with us,
and leadest us from strength to strength and blessest
us continually. Amen.

THEODORE PARKER.

Were any of us really disappointed or melancholy in a hayfield? Did we ever lie fairly back on a haycock and look up into the blue sky, and listen to the merry sounds, the whetting of scythes and the laughing prattle of women and children, and think evil thoughts of the world or our brethren? Not we! Or, if we have so done we ought to be ashamed of ourselves, and deserve never again to be out of town during hay-harvest.

THOMAS HUGHES.

Dear Heavenly Father, we devoutly thank Thee for the beautiful open face of Nature shining upon us; for the splendor of the fields where the birds wing their merry flight; for the breath of the flowers and the grass beneath the scythe, like the odor of incense; and most of all, for the merry shouts of women and children and men in the meadow, in the heyday of happiness, as they fill their souls with the freedom of the children of God, and live in the open where no evil breath can come. Grant that we may live spiritually forever in the fragrant hay-fields of life, where the birds sing and the children shout, and where no covering or roof can ever shut out the sunshine of life's eternal bliss. Amen.

ROBERT S. KELLERMAN.

A story is told of a king who went into his garden one morning and found everything withering and dying. He asked an oak that stood near the gate what the trouble was. He found that it was sick of life and determined to die, because it was not tall and beautiful like the pine. The pine was out of heart because it could not bear grapes like the vine; the vine was going to throw its life away, because it could not stand erect and have as fine fruit as the pomegranate; and so on throughout the garden. Coming to the heart's-ease, the king found its bright face uplifted, as full of cheerfulness as ever. Said the king, "Well, heart's-ease, I am glad to find one brave little flower in this general discouragement and dying. You don't seem one bit disheartened." "No, your majesty. I know I am of small account; but I concluded you wanted a heart's-ease when you planted me. If you had wanted an oak, or a pine, or a vine, or a pomegranate, you would have set one out. So I am bound to be the best heart's-ease that ever I can."

WILLIAM MOODIE.

Like the wise King of old, I pray Thee, gracious Lord, give unto me wisdom. May Thy Pillar of Light guide my footsteps so that I go not astray in the wilderness of sin and selfish ambition. Help me to acquire a pure heart and a contented spirit. Amidst all the vicissitudes of fortune, let faith induce me to say, "Whatever God doeth is well." Amen.

M. M. EICHLER.

What shall I do to be just?
  What shall I do for the gain
    Of the world — for its sadness?
Teach me, O seers that I trust!
  Chart me the difficult main
    Leading out of my sorrow and madness.
  Preach me the purging of pain.

Shall I wrench from my finger the ring
  To cast to the tramp at my door?
Shall I tear off each luminous thing
  To drop in the palm of the poor?
    What shall I do to be just?
  Teach me, O Ye in the light,
    Whom the poor and the rich alike trust;
  My heart is aflame to be right.

HAMLIN A. GARLAND.

Infinite Spirit, Thou seest us just as we are. In Thy sight there can be no make-believe; we need not seek to offer Thee as a penance for our sins some cheap alms to the poor, for Thy favor cannot be bought. We pray simply that we may be just, — that we may be true. If we have wronged anyone, help us to right the wrong. If we have been false to ourselves or false to our neighbors, O Lord, make us true, — we seek no easy admission to a far-off heaven, we seek Thy presence here and now, today, by the only pathway open, the pathway of righteousness and truth. That we may enter this pathway, grant us we pray Thee the illumination of Thy Holy Spirit. Amen.

GEORGE L. PERIN.

The law of worthy life is fundamentally the law of strife. It is only through labor, painful effort, by grim energy and resolute courage, that we move on to better things.

THEODORE ROOSEVELT.

If we would please God we must watch every stroke and touch upon the canvas of our lives; we may not think we can lay it on with a trowel and yet succeed. We ought to live as miniature painters work, for they watch every line and tint.

SPURGEON.

As we begin this new day, O our Father, may such energy and vigor, such strength and courage, such faith and hope be ours that the problems and tasks awaiting us may be boldly and gladly met as challenges to our powers. May that abundant life be in us which shall make our difficulties a tonic, and the struggle to achieve high aims a joy. May we be resourceful, equal to life, adequate to every situation, able to stand this universe, — men who can. May we count it a privilege to live, to have a vision of life's possibilities, and to have the fellowship of so many good men and women by the way. Amen.

GEORGE R. DODSON.

With place, with gold, with power — oh, ask me not
With these my little hour of life to blot.
A little hour indeed! and I would fain
Its moments spend in what is worth its pain.
What traveler would faint through troublous lands
To gather only what must leave his hands
The moment that he takes his homeward ship?
Earth's goods and gauds give every man the slip;
But wealth of thought and richer wealth of love,
Must pass for coin in any world above.
The good to others done while here I strive
Is all at last that shall my dying shrive;
And, setting sail, my slight self-conquest's store
Is all my freight if I shall come to shore.

ANONYMOUS.

O Father, God! The span of our influence is both near and far; may it also be direct and strong. Thou hast planted mighty virtue and unquenchable love in our hearts. Love knows the secret of imparting virtue's value to all the wretchedness in life. So, we beseech Thee, direct our hearts to altitudes of holiness and set our feet in the highways of helpfulness. May the charm of gentleness be in every service to-day, and may the tone of tenderness carry love's message over all barriers to the hearts that need. Thus would we keep our confidence with Thee and bind ourselves more profitably to our fellows. So shall Thy great name be honored among men. Amen.

J. O. RANDALL.

What seems to grow fairer to me as life goes by, is the love and peace and tenderness of it. Not its wit and cleverness and grandeur of knowledge, but just the laughter of little children, and the friendship of friends, and the cosy talk of the fireside, and the sight of flowers and the sound of music.

J. R. GREEN.

Now that Thou givest us the light of a new day, grant that it carry with it the brightness of hope and courage for whatsoever the day may offer. Always behind the clouds is the shining that never fails; always beyond the labor which irks us is the joy of attainment. Open our eyes that we may see the best which shall be in the day; its love of friends, its sights of beauty, its music, its wisdom such as no day before could possess, its voices of the Spirit awaiting the listening ear, its tears of compassion and sympathy. Give us our daily bread such as shall feed the heart and enrich the mind and grant us forgiveness when we are blind to the common treasures of this Thy world. Amen.

GEORGE A. THAYER.

Methought that in a solemn church I stood.
Its marble acres, worn with knees and feet,
Lay spread from door to door, from street to street.
Midway the form hung high upon the rood
Of Him who gave His life to be our good;
Beyond, priests flitted, bowed, and murmured meet
Among the candles shining still and sweet.
Men came and went, and worshipped as they could;
And still their dust a woman with her broom,
Bowed to her work, kept sweeping to the door.
Then saw I slow through all the pillared gloom
Across the church a silent figure come.
"Daughter," it said, "Thou sweepest well my floor!"
"It is the Lord!" I cried, and saw no more.

GEORGE MACDONALD.

Our Father, who art ever with us, help us this day so to reveal Thee through our common tasks, our relations with one another, in our homes and at our work, that men may know and love Thee better. This is Thy most beautiful world. May we not mar its glory by our selfishness, but by the gentleness and sweetness of our lives make it more beautiful. May we this day not add to another's burden of care or pain. But may we by our words and deeds sweeten and brighten and strengthen the lives of those whom we meet. For Thy goodness and mercy to us, for the opportunity of service, for love and sympathy, we thank Thee and pray that our devotion to Thy truth may reveal the thankfulness of our hearts. **Amen.**

ARTHUR L. WEATHERLY.

For I, a man, with men am linked,
And not a brute with brutes; no gain
That I experience must remain
Unshared; but should my best endeavor
To share it, fail — subsisteth ever
God's care above, and I exult
That God, by God's own ways occult,
May — doth, I will believe — bring back
All wanderers to a single track.

ROBERT BROWNING.

Father of all souls in all worlds, our best friend forever, in Thy good keeping we cannot wander beyond Thy loving care. We thank Thee for life, for the fair world we live in, enriched by Thy countless benefits, for the glad tidings of Thy fatherly love that never fails, for the brotherhood that binds together all Thy children, and for the immortal hope that beckons us up and on. By faithful living may we make life divine, and by brotherly service show Thee our gratitude and love. May the gospel of Jesus prevail in all hearts, speedily bring all wanderers home, draw our souls heavenward, and prepare us for higher and larger realms of service, where we shall forever live to Thy glory. Amen.

RUSH R. SHIPPEN.

That man has a liberal education who has been so trained in youth that his body is the ready servant of his will, and does with ease and pleasure the work that it is capable of; whose intellect is a clear logic engine, ready to spin the gossamer as well as forge the anchors of the mind — one full of life and fire but whose passions are trained to come to heel by a rigorous will; the servant of a tender conscience; who has learned to love beauty, to hate vileness and to respect others as himself; such a one is in harmony with nature; they will get on together.

THOMAS HENRY HUXLEY.

Our Father, we would face this day in conscious companionship with Thee. Give us to know Thy will, to do Thy work. Help us to interpret aright Thy constant revelation of love in nature and in the experiences of life. Give us strength so to will and so to act that we may make this day rich in the joy that comes from helpful living. May divine impulse find quick expression in righteous deed. In Thine unresting effort to make this world Thine own may we join with glad hearts. Rejoicing in Thy love, strong in the consciousness of Thy presence, may we go to our day's work with unwavering purpose to do Thy will. Amen.

LATHAN A. CRANDALL.

A lily grows mysteriously, pushing up its solid weight of stem and leaf in the teeth of gravity. Shaped into beauty by secret and invisible fingers, the flower develops we know not how. But we do not wonder at it. Every day the thing is done; it is Nature, it is God. We are spiritual enough at least to understand that. But when the soul rises slowly above the world, pushing up its delicate virtues in the teeth of sin, shaping itself mysteriously into the image of Christ, we deny that the power is not of man. A strong will, we say, a high ideal, the reward of virtue, Christian influence — these will account for it. Spiritual character is merely the product of anxious work, self-command, and self-denial. We allow, that is to say, a miracle to the lily, but none to the man. The lily may grow; the man must fret and toil and spin.

HENRY DRUMMOND.

This morning, our God, we need Thee! Give us Thyself afresh in the holy inspiration of heart warmth and burning love, that today we may have power from above while we walk and toil with things and folks of earth. May we be the vase to hold the blossoming beauty of Thy unfolding. So may that beauty which Thou givest unfold in acts which we are led to perform, and the holiness of this day set fast character drawn from Thee. Thus may we all who are Thy children gladden the earth with unfolding beauty and kindness and shut out the things that are earthy. Amen.

E. E. SMALL.

The more simply you live, the more secure is your future; you are less at the mercy of surprises and reverses. An illness or a period of idleness does not suffice to dispossess you; a change of position, even considerable, does not put you to confusion. Having simple needs, you find it less painful to accustom yourself to the hazards of fortune. You remain a man, though you lose your office or your income, because the foundation on which your life rests is not your table, your cellar, your horses, your goods and chattels, or your money. In adversity you will not act like a nursling deprived of its bottle and rattle. Stronger, better armed for the struggle, presenting like those with shaven heads, less advantage to the hands of your enemy, you will also be of more profit to your neighbor.

CHARLES WAGNER.

O Thou who art ever the same, with the growing light of a new day, we would again take Thy name upon our lips; and again invite the dear consciousness of Thy presence. We do not know what this day may yield us. It may bring disaster; perhaps cherished hopes must be surrendered; plans may miscarry, clouds may gather, and storms may rage, but we will not be unmanned. We will not surrender our hold upon Thee. May we thus be enabled to meet disaster with courage, and unlooked for joy with the poise of humility. Guard our goings-out and our comings-in, and lead us into the beauteous paths of ripe content. Amen.

JAMES HARRY HOLDEN.

Love wore a suit of hodden gray
And toiled within the fields all day.

Love wielded pick and carried pack
And bent to heavy loads the back.

Though meagre fed and sorely lashed,
The only wage Love ever asked,

A child's wan face to kiss at night,
A woman's smile by candle light.

MARGARET SANGSTER.

Our Father in Heaven, we thank Thee for love. How rich a gift it has been to us, and how exhaustless. It has been the source of all other gifts. We thank Thee for the brightness and gladness with which love invests the sunny day, and more for the patience and hope which it inspires when the sky is overcast and the way grows weary. In joy or sorrow we can ask nothing better than that it be our constant guest. We thank Thee for home life which offers us every hour its opportunity to give and to receive love. May it be to us the symbol of Thy great household which Thy love pervades. And as we thus think of it may our home life grow to us more holy and divine and Thy love for all Thy children more personal and tender until Thy kingdom come and Thy will be done on earth as it is in heaven. Amen.

VINCENT E. TOMLINSON.

The entire object of true education is to make people not merely do the right things, but enjoy the right things — not merely industrious, but to love industry — not merely learned, but to love knowledge — not merely pure, but to love purity — not merely just, but to hunger and thirst after justice.

JOHN RUSKIN.

O Father, fill us with Thy love today, with love for Thee, and love for the morning light and all Thy glory. Fill us with love for the work that Thou dost give us to do, with love for the truth that Thou dost reveal to us and with love for the ideals of purity and righteousness that Thou dost set before us. May we have love for all Thy children. Make us realize that they are all our brothers and sisters. Make us strive to have Thy will done in their lives. Make us eager to have them know Thee. Amen

CHARLES B. BLISS.

If you were toiling up a weary hill,
Bearing a load beyond your strength to bear,
Straining each nerve untiringly and still
Stumbling and losing foothold here and there
And each one passing by would do so much
As give one upward lift and go his way,
Would not the slight reiterated touch
Of help and kindness lighten all the day?

If you were breasting a keen wind which tossed
And buffeted and chilled you as you strove,
Till baffled and bewildered quite, you lost
The power to see the way, and aim and move,
And one, if only for a moment's space,
Gave you a shelter from the bitter blast,
Would you not find it easier to face
The storm again when the brief rest was past?

SUSAN COOLIDGE.

Our Father, as we thank Thee for the friendly service and sympathy that bless and strengthen our daily lives, we pray that our gratitude may move us to give a like service and sympathy as freely as we receive. In the day to whose beginning Thou hast brought us, let our hearts and hands be ready to meet the needs of those with whom we come in touch. So influence our wayward wills that we shall not walk in selfish ways, nor forget the ties that bind us to one another, and to Thee. Keep us conscious of our birthright as Thy children, that our acts and aims may be filial and fraternal and loyal to Jesus Christ Our Lord. Amen.

COSTELLO WESTON.

It matters little where I was born,
Whether my parents were rich or poor,
Whether they shrank from the cold world's scorn
Or walked in the pride of wealth secure;
But whether I live an honest man,
And hold my integrity firm in my clutch,
I tell you brother, plain as I am,
It matters much.

FROM THE SWEDISH.

Dear Father in Heaven, good Giver of all,
  For birth in a land fair and free,
For parents with pluck, if not the best luck,
  Who toiled and who suffered for me.
Who never knew fear, though the scorners were near,
  Whom circumstance filled not with pride,
I thank Thee! These gifts, more than all on the lists,
  Have mattered with me, and abide.

While striving and struggling my manhood to build,
  To live like Thine own perfect Son,
I find on Earth's face not just one single place
  Where such work so well can be done
As in the fair land which from Thy gracious hand
  Comes to me a home to enjoy,
Where man, who should grow, may all liberty know
  In seeking the soul's high employ.
                                        Amen.

FREDERICK C. PRIEST.

*Don't object that your duties are so insignificant;
they are to be reckoned of infinite significance, and
alone important to you. Were it but the more perfect
regulation of your apartments, the sorting away of
your clothes and trinkets, the arranging of your
papers,* — "*Whatsoever thy hand findeth to do, do
it with all thy might,*" *and all thy worth and constancy.
Much more, if your duties are of evidently higher,
wider scope; if you have brothers, sisters, a father,
a mother, weigh earnestly what claim does lie upon
you on behalf of each, and consider it as the one thing
needful, to pay them more and more honestly and
nobly what you owe. What matter how miserable
one is if one can do that? That is the sure and steady
disconnection and extinction of whatsoever miseries
one has in this world.*

THOMAS CARLYLE.

Creator of things, Father of Spirits, standing at
the dawn of a new day we seek Thy blessing. We
know not what awaits us, Thou knowest, grant us
guidance! Help us to see all our duties in the light
of Thy countenance. Thou hast made the little
and the large, help us to see our duties in their relation to Thy plans Whatsoever we do, help us
to do all to Thy glory. Help us to sweep our floors
as to Thy laws, right our rooms as a part of Thy
universe, care for our clothes as gifts from Thee.
Help us to see Thee in the souls Thou hast sent into
the world, to treat them as thinking-thoughts of
Thine, expressions of Thy life. May we owe no man
anything but to love, may the sun never set on an
unpaid bill. For Thy name's sake. **Amen**.

O. P. GIFFORD.

Write it on your heart that every day is the best day in the year. No man has learned anything rightly until he knows that every day is doomsday. Today is a king in disguise. Today always looks mean to the thoughtless, in the face of an uniform experience that all good and great and happy actions are made up precisely of these blank todays. Let us not be so deceived, let us unmask the king as he passes.

RALPH WALDO EMERSON.

Our Father, we thank Thee for this morning that ushers in the only day of which we have promise. Whether it proves to be a day of sunshine or of clouds, — of joy or of sorrow, — may we live it with thankfulness, with perfect confidence that Thou wilt always give us that which is for our own good. Help us to spend this day in doing well what our hands find to do; may our souls breathe the spirit of love and helpfulness to all, and may we have abundantly the influence of Thy divine spirit to keep us pure. Amen.

LUTHER F. McKINNEY.

I like the man who faces what he must
With heart triumphant and a step of cheer;
Who fights the daily battle without fear;
Sees his hopes fail, yet keeps unfaltering trust
That God is God; that somehow, true and just,
His plans work out for mortals; not a tear
Is shed when fortune, which the world holds dear,
Falls from his grasp; better, with love, a crust
Than living in dishonor; envies not,
Nor loses faith in man; but does his best,
Nor even murmurs at his humbler lot;
But with a smile and words of hope, gives zest
To every toiler; he alone is great
Who by a life heroic conquers fate.

SARAH KNOWLES BOLTON.

Gracious Father, last night we laid ourselves down in peace to sleep, but it was Thou who madest us to dwell in safety, and when we awoke this morning we found ourselves still with Thee. Thy loving favor was keeping faithful watch and ward while we slumbered. We thank Thee for Thy kindly care of our lives during the darkness and danger of the night. Confident of Thy continued presence and armed with Thy unfailing strength, we would go forth to meet the duties and delights of the new day. God with us, we will overcome every temptation, endure every trial, bear every burden, and improve every opportunity of character-building and service-rendering, in the trustful and courageous spirit of Jesus Christ our Lord. Amen.

RALPH E. CONNER.

How large a part of our Godward life is travelled, not by clear landmarks seen far off in the promised land, but as travellers climb a mountain peak, by putting footstep after footstep, slowly and patiently, into the prints which someone going before us, with keener sight, with stronger nerves, tied to us by the cord of saintly sympathy, has planted deep into the pathless snow of the bleak distance that stretches up between humanity and God. . . . So we ascend by one another. We live by one another's blessings.

                            PHILLIPS BROOKS.

Our Father, we thank Thee for the light of a new day. May a new spirit and new courage come to our hearts. We thank Thee for all those who by patient toil and self-forgetting effort have made life as sweet and precious to us as it is. If we can no longer hear the voices nor see the faces of those we love or have reason to revere, may we be able to see their foot-prints and to take the way they trod, though that way seem steep and hard. May we be assured that the upward way leads to the expanding view and brings us to the splendor of the setting sun or of the still more glorious dawn. Amen.

HILARY BYGRAVE.

*A prince went into the vineyard to examine it.
He came to a peach tree, and said, "What are you
doing for me?" The tree said, "In the spring I
give my blossoms and fill the air with fragrance, and
on my boughs hangs the fruit which men will gather
and carry into the palace for you." "Well done!"
said the prince. To the chestnut he said, "What
are you doing?" "I am making nests for the birds,
and shelter cattle with my leaves and spreading
branches." And the prince said, "Well done!"
Then he went down to the meadow and asked the grass
what it was doing. "We are giving our lives for others,
for your sheep and cattle that they may be nourished."
And the prince said, "Well done!" Last of all he
asked the tiny daisy what it was doing, and the daisy
said, "Nothing, nothing. I cannot make a nesting-
place for the birds, and I cannot give shelter for the
cattle, and I cannot send fruit into the palace, and I
cannot even give food for the sheep and cows, —
they do not want me in the meadow. All I can do
is to be the best little daisy I can be." And the prince
bent down and kissed the daisy, and said, "There
is none better than thou."*

ANONYMOUS.

Help us, O Father, not to wait for the great
opportunities which may never come. Help us to
do with faithfulness the duties which lie close at
hand. In our homes this day and wherever we
may be — at school or on the street or at our
work — fill our hearts with the spirit of Christ and
let that spirit speak in every word which passes
our lips and shine from our faces and work with
our hands. Amen.

WALTER A. TUTTLE.

I will be glad all day for this cool draught
  And the clear drops I dash upon my brow;
For the fresh glint of sunlight on the tree
  And the bird singing on the bough.

I will be glad for that stored strength of life
  Which lasts the day because the spirit wills;
For the live air that wings from far and breathes
  The vigor of the everlasting hills.

What scope of toil, what loss or what reward,
  I do not know.   It is enough that now
I pledge the day's good cheer with this cool draught
  And the drops dashed upon my brow.

                              CHARLES P. CLEAVES.

Our Father, we are nursed in Thine arms, we
are rested in the heart of Jesus, so that we know no
more the emptiness of earth and the poverty of time,
for our citizenship is in heaven, already do we walk
the streets of gold.   Out of the highest rapture may
we come to do earth's plainest work, earth's hardest
toil, with patient hearts and willing hands, knowing
that death can be but for a moment, that all things
are meant, in the sovereignty of God to give themselves up to the rule of life.   Thus may Thy children
be loyal citizens, patient workers, honest merchant-
men, wise parents.   Be with all men who trust
Thee; melt the mountains before their coming, and
open the gates of difficulty ere they reach them,
and give them to feel that the greatness of Thy
mercy is the proof of its divinity.   Amen.

JOSEPH PARKER.

For I am persuaded, that neither death, nor life, nor angels, nor principalities, nor powers, nor things present, nor things to come.

Nor height, nor depth, nor any other creature, shall be able to separate us from the love of God which is in Christ Jesus our Lord.

ROMANS viii. 38–39.

These verses seem to me to express completely the remedial power of God's love. In this rough and tumble world of ours, of hard conditions, of disasters many, of untold misery, there are temptations enough for men to lose faith in God's love. It is well now and then to have an outburst of faith like this with the assurance that nothing can ever separate any child of God from the divine compassion and the divine care.

GEORGE L. PERIN.

Our Heavenly Father, it is good for us to believe that through all storms and all darkness and all sickness and all infirmity, even through death itself, Thy love abides. As we enter upon this day, we know not whither we shall go, but we thank Thee for the assurance that we may not go away from Thee. Thou followest us with Thy care and wrappest us around with Thy love, as with a garment. In all that we do today may we know that Thou seest us, and if our way be steep, may we be sure that Thou lovest us. Amen.

GEORGE L. PERIN.

Begin the morning by saying to thyself, I shall meet this day with the busybody, the ungrateful, the arrogant, deceitful, envious, unsocial: All these things happen to them by reason of their ignorance of what is good and evil. But I who have seen the nature of the good that it is beautiful, and of the bad that it is ugly, can neither be injured by any of them — for no one can fix on me what is ugly — nor can I be angry with my neighbor, nor hate him. We are made for coöperation; to act against one another, that is contrary to nature; and it is acting against one another to be vexed and turn away.

MARCUS AURELIUS.

Eternal Spirit of Love, teach us the power of love. Help us to learn that love is supreme, and hence envieth not, nor vaunteth itself, nor seeketh its own, but suffereth long and is kind. We, who in Jesus of Nazareth have seen the glory of Thy likeness and experienced the sweetness of Thy love, desire like Him to reveal Thee in our lives, to be loving and gentle, sincere and generous, to coöperate with friend and stranger in all that is good, to live so that they can work with us for the advancement of everything righteous. Fill us, therefore, with Thy spirit, and send us forth today in Thy service. Amen.

WILLIAM W. GUTH.

" God! " let the torrents, like a shout of nations.
Answer! and let the ice-plain echo, " God! "
" God! " sing, ye meadow streams, with gladsome
    voice
Ye pine groves, with your soft and soul-like sounds!
And they, too have a voice, yon piles of snow,
And in their perilous fall shall thunder, " God! "

Ye living flowers that skirt the eternal frost!
Ye wild goats sporting round the eagle's nest!
Ye eagles, playmates of the mountain storm!
Ye lightnings, the dread arrows of the clouds!
Ye signs and wonders of the elements!
Utter forth " God! " and fill the hills with praise!
               SAMUEL TAYLOR COLERIDGE.

Heavenly Father, how long have Thy servants thirsted after Thee — Thou spring of everlasting life! In this land of our home the meditations of ages surround us, and through the treasured thoughts of the wise in many generations we are lifted into a light beyond the solitary soul. Countless are Thy witnesses, Eternal God! the stars without number are but a little part of them; and the prayers and aspirings of every heart of man can never cease to speak Thee. Humbled and blind amid Thy manifold glories, may we find rest in the simplicity of Christ, and be among the pure in heart who alone can see Thee. Amen.

JAMES MARTINEAU.

O God, my master God, look down and see
If I am making what Thou wouldst of me.
Fain might I lift my hands up in the air
From the defiant passion of my prayer;
Yet here they grope on this cold altar stone,
Graving the words I think I should make known.
Mine eyes are Thine. Yea, let me not forget,
Lest with unstaunchèd tears I leave them wet,
Dimming their faithful power, till they not see
Some small, plain task that might be done for Thee.
My feet, that ache for paths of flowery bloom,
Halt steadfast in the straitness of this room.
Though they may never be on errands sent,
Here shall they stay, and wait Thy full content.
And my poor heart, that doth so crave for peace,
Shall beat until Thou bid its beating cease.
So, Thou dear master God, look down and see
Whether I do Thy bidding heedfully.

ALICE BROWN.

O God, our Heavenly Father, from whom cometh
to us again this gift of life, may we be able to use
as Thou wouldst have us the fresh revelation and
energy of each morning hour. May we be helped
to see more clearly that task with all its blessings,
which Thou placest within our reach today. Freshen
our souls anew with the coming sunlight and
quicken our will that we may perceive and fulfil
our present duty gladly, eagerly, successfully, however humble in the spirit of those who remember
that if done for Thy sake and beneath Thy laws
even servile labors shine. Amen.

HOBART CLARK.

We thank Thee for all that Thou hast made, and that Thou hast called it Good! We thank Thee! We enter into Thy work, and go about Thy business.
EDWARD EVERETT HALE.

O, it is great, and there is no other greatness. To make some work of God's creation a little fruitfuller, better, more worthy of God; to make some human hearts a little wiser, manfuller, happier, — more blessed, less accursed, — it is a work for God.
THOMAS CARLYLE.

Heavenly Father, we would begin the day with noble purpose; may we scorn all meanness, and lift up our heads unto the Lord as men who have a great expectation. Our hope is in a living God; Thou wilt not allow our life to wander into darkness; if for a small moment we are forsaken, we shall be gathered with ineffable and everlasting mercies. In the confidence of Thy presence, in the assurance of Thy sustaining grace, we look steadfastly to heaven, and then we look hopefully to earth, and we know that, having begun the day with prayer and praise and pious expectancy, its hours shall all be gladdened and its even-tide shall be a benediction. Guide us with Thine eyes; sustain us by Thy mighty power; keep us this day without sin. Amen.

JOSEPH PARKER.

The scenery around your house may be monotonous, without a mountain or sea or lake or hill; but an upward look at the clear sky will put you in instant communication with infinite beauty and majesty. No spot on earth is common or barren over which the skies bend in solemn silence. No human life need be barren or common which is connected by the great network of moral law with any other being.

J. H. CARLISLE.

Our God and Father, the author of beauty, the rewarder of all them that seek Thee, we, Thy children, come to Thee at the opening of this new day. May we have hearts so pure that we shall see Thee; minds so open that we shall talk with Thee; and lives so true that we shall reveal Thee. Let toil become to us as a sacrament. Reveal to us the beauty of life as well as of holiness and help us to live with upturned faces, so that we may catch the glory of Thy presence, and reflect it to all around us. May we walk with Thee, thinking Thy thoughts, having Thy visions of beauty and of life. When life's evening shall come gather us in Thine arms of love to be with Thee in the home which Thou hast prepared for us and hast beautified with earth's fairest treasures through Jesus Christ, Our Lord. Amen.

JOHN GALBRAITH.

How good is man's life, the mere living! How fit to
    employ
    All the heart and the soul and the senses forever in
    joy!

                                    ROBERT BROWNING.

        I am glad to think
I am not bound to make the world go right;
But only to discover and to do,
With cheerful heart, the work that God appoints.
        I will trust in Him,
That He can hold His own; and I will take
His will, above the work He sendeth me,
To be my chiefest good.

                                    JEAN INGELOW.

Our Heavenly Father, all Thy works prove Thy
goodness; the world Thou givest us is good; the
powers with which Thou dost endow us are adapted
to deeds of goodness. We know full well that we do
evil as well as good. Some of our days close in sadness. . . . At the beginning of this day we pledge ourselves to try harder than ever to do something good,
to make somebody happy, to keep our minds filled
with pure thoughts, to set our ambitions on worthy
objects; and we pray that Thou who art "the Power
not ourselves that makes for righteousness" shalt
work with us that through our effort and Thy help
the day shall end in joy and peace. Amen.

LEE S. McCOLLESTER.

Our lives are songs; God writes the words,
And we set them to music at pleasure;
And the song grows glad, or sweet, or sad,
As we choose to fashion the measure.
We must write the music, whatever the song,
Whatever its rhyme or metre;
And if it is sad, we can make it glad,
Or, if sweet, we can make it sweeter.

ELLA WHEELER WILCOX.

We thank Thee, O God, that Thou hast made us responsive to all the beauty and gladness about us, and that we may make our lives one grand, sweet song. We know there is much that may spoil the song. But we thank Thee, that if we follow the great Leader, we can change all discordant notes into harmony. Help us through Him to tune our lives into accord with Thine. Especially may we live in peace with each other. Make us strong to return good for evil, to meet irritability with patience, unkindness with gentleness and harsh words with quiet speech. So may our lives " be filled with music, and the cares that infest the day, shall fold their tents like the Arabs, and as silently steal away." Amen.

JAMES M. PAYSON.

Back of the canvas that throbs the painter is hinted
  and hidden,
  Into the statue that breathes the soul of the sculptor
    is bidden,
Under the joy that is felt lie the infinite issues of
  feeling;
  Crowning the glory revealed is the glory that crowns
    the revealing.
Great are the symbols of being, but that which is sym-
  bolled is greater;
  Vast the create and beheld, but vaster the inward
    creator.

RICHARD REALF.

Thou, Lord, who hast created us surely for good
and not evil, for Thou art good and doest good, wilt
go with us through all the day. Help us to keep in
mind Thy presence, that we may walk before Thee
and be perfect, that we may walk with Thee and be
pleasing to Thee, that we may walk after Thee,
humbly, reverently. May we prize the glories that
come with the hours, not suffering them to make us
conceited or self-centered, or unduly independent,
but utilize them as means to make us more fully a
part of Thee. Give us this day complete victory over
each temptation as it arrives, and may we feel when
night falls that we have acquitted ourselves well in
the campaign, and done what we could to make, not
only ourselves, but the world around us, better. Amen

JAMES MUDGE.

Each night is followed by its day,
Each storm by fairer weather,
While all the works of nature sing
Their songs of joy together.
Then learn, O heart, their songs of hope!
Cease, soul, thy thankless sorrow;
For though the clouds be dark today,
The sun will shine tomorrow.

T. EDGAR JONES.

Father of light! Who causeth light to shine out of darkness and maketh day to follow the night; we thank Thee for Thy loving care that has brought us from the slumber and rest of night to behold the light of a new day. May we rejoice in it, and cheerfully enter upon its duties and experiences. May the grace of Thy presence make our sunshine, that we may walk in the light of heaven, breathe its atmosphere and engage in its service; doing Thy will in the service of one another and in the service of love, truth and goodness. May the light of faith, hope, and love shining within us, dispel all darkness and sorrow from our lives, that light which shines so lustrously from the life of Jesus Christ our Lord. Amen.

ROBERT T. POLK.

Never say, " It is nobody's business but my own what I do with my life." It is not true. Your life is put into your hands as a trust, for many others besides yourself. If you use it well, it will make many others happy; if you abuse it, you will harm many others besides yourself.

JAMES M. PULLMAN.

Almighty Father, whom, though we have not seen, we love, we know not what this day may bring forth but we know that it shall be for good as our trust is in Thee. We look up and adore Thee, and we believe and love and obey. Throughout all the hours of this day may we be " diligent in business, fervent in spirit, serving the Lord." We believe in the victory of good over evil, of light over darkness; help us to bear our part courageously in the battle. Be merciful to us and make us merciful to one another. May we be numbered with those who are pure in heart, and see God in the humblest service to the humblest people. We beseech Thee to answer according to Thy love not only these prayers which we utter with our lips but also the silent prayers of our heart. Amen.

HAROLD PATTISON.

Prince Florimel and Prince Carimel were twin brothers, the sons of a king, and no one could tell which of the two ought to succeed to the throne, for they were both exactly the same age. So one day they went to a wise magician, and asked him which of them ought to be king after their father's death. "He who is most worthy," said the magician. "But how shall we find out who is most worthy?" "He who possesses the magic flower that grows in the enchanted forest shall be found most worthy," he answered. So the two brothers travelled through the enchanted forest until they found the magic flower; but it grew in such a dangerous place that Carimel would not attempt to reach it. Florimel, however, clambered down the rocks and plucked the flower; and when he had got it, what do you think he did with it? Why, he gave it to his brother, for the name of that magic flower was Unselfishness.

WILLIAM MOODIE.

Our Father, with thankful hearts for all Thy goodness to us in the past, — we seek Thy Holy Spirit's guidance for the day before us. Help us to live not for self alone, but for the good of all with whom we mingle. May the needy, suffering, and struggling ones all about us gather strength because of our devotion to Thee. So inspire us to forget ourselves, that we may the better remember our Master, and the privileges and duties of a life's service to Thy children. Wilt Thou not, Infinite One, thus help us, this day, and in all the days to come, to live to Thy glory! Amen.

LEWIS P. BATES.

*To do something for someone else; to love the un-
lovely; to give a hand to the unattractive; to speak
to the uncongenial; to make friends with the poor and
folks of lowly degree; to find a niche in the church of
the Lord, and to do something out of sheer love for Him;
to determine in His house to have His mind; to plan
to win at least one for the Master; to aim to redeem
past time that is lost; to will to let one's light shine;
to cut off practices that are sinful and costly; to add the
beauty of holiness — this is to make one's life a thing
of beauty and this is to grow in grace, for growing in
grace is simply copying the beautiful life of the alto-
gether lovely One.*

EDWARD F. REIMER.

Infinite Father, we rejoice that it is possible for us
to be workers together with Thee by giving our sympathy, love and help to Thy needy children. As Thou
hast honored us by appointing us to such a gracious
ministry, may we seek to honor Thee in return by trying to do Thy blessed will. In all lowly and gentle
ways, may we do what we can to bind up the broken-
hearted, to relieve the distressed, to strengthen the
weak. Let none who suffer look to us in vain for some
manifestation of the Christ-like Spirit. May we so
meet and treat the sad, the lonely, the tempted, that
they shall take knowledge of us that we have been
with Jesus. So may His heavenly teaching bear sweet
fruit in our conduct and characters, and so may the
Kingdom which He came to establish grow apace in
the world. In His name. Amen.

WILLARD C. SELLECK.

Let me feel that I am to be a lover. I am to see to it that the world is better for me, and to find my reward in the act. Love would put a new face on this weary old world in which we dwell as pagans and enemies too long; and it would warm the heart to see how fast the vain diplomacy of statesmen, the impotence of armies and navies and lines of defence, would be superseded by this unarmed child. This great, overgrown, dead Christendom of ours still keeps alive at least the name of a lover of mankind. But one day all men will be lovers: and every calamity will be dissolved in the universal sunshine.

RALPH WALDO EMERSON.

What manner of love hast Thou bestowed upon us, dear Lord, that we should be called Thy children! As Thou hast loved us, so teach us each to love the world. This day someone will go forth to business on land or sea burdened with heavy cares: some father disheartened and discouraged will take up the trials of yesterday wondering what the end will be — some mother dismayed with her lot will cry "How long?" Help us, O Lord to minister to them in word or look, in prayer or gift. As the sun shall this day bring light and life to this old earth causing it to yield its highest purpose, so grant that Thy love may give through us a new inspiration to all mankind. Hasten the time when all shall love Thee as Thou hast loved the world. Then will each love the other. Then will the sword and the spear be molten into the plowshare and the pruning hook, and the desert shall bud and blossom as the rose. Amen.

EDWIN ALONZO BLAKE.

Thou art, O God, the life and light
Of all this wondrous world we see:
Its glow by day, its smile by night,
Are but reflections caught from thee.
Where'er we turn, thy glories shine,
And all things fair and bright are thine.

THOMAS MOORE

Almighty God, our Heavenly Father, who hast safely brought us to the beginning of this day, defend us in the same with Thy mighty power. Grant that this day we fall into no sin. Create in us a clean heart and renew a right spirit within us. Open our eyes that this day may be a fresh disclosure of Thyself, the Unseen Presence; endow us with Thy strength that, in joy and pain, it may lead us into Thy house not made with hands, eternal in the heavens. Enable us so to use the things of the world that while they abide we may not lose Thy presence, and when they pass we may not stand alone. So shall the spirit of Christ inflame us. Amen.

FREDERICK W. PERKINS.

It ain't no use to grumble and complain,
It's just as cheap and easy to rejoice;
When God sorts out the weather and sends rain,
Why, rain's my choice.

JAMES WHITCOMB RILEY.

When you get into a tight place, and everything goes against you, till it seems as if you could not hold on a minute longer, never give up then, for that's just the place and time that the tide will turn

HARRIET BEECHER STOWE.

Father, we pray Thee that in every emergency of our lives we may be faithful to the duty which the day demands, and with reverent spirits acquit us like men, doing what should be done, bearing what must be borne, and so growing greater from our toil and our sufferings, till we transfigure ourselves into noble images of humanity, which are blameless within and beautiful without, and acceptable to Thy spirit. So may Thy kingdom come and Thy will be done on earth as it is in heaven; for Thine is the kingdom and the power and the glory, the dominion and honor forever and ever. Amen.

THEODORE PARKER.

It was only a glad "Good Morning"
  As she passed along the way;
But it spread the morning's glory
  Over the livelong day.
CARLOTTA PERRY.

Smile upon the troubled pilgrims
  Whom you pass and meet;
Frowns are thorns, and smiles are blossoms,
  Oft to weary feet.
Do not make the way seem harder
  By a sullen face;
Smile a little, smile a little,
  Brighten up the place.
ELLA WHEELER WILCOX.

Father, in this morning hour, we would look into Thy face and feel the sweetness of that transforming influence which is forever baptizing Thy world with light and gladness, adding beauty to beauty and glory to glory. Baptize us anew, with this all-pervading spirit and send us out into this day's work to meet its varied experiences with trusting hearts and smiling faces. May we each send forth a brightening, gladdening influence to cheer and strengthen and uplift every weary, troubled pilgrim whom we meet on this day's journey. So may it be ours to enter into closer and diviner fellowship with Thee, our Father, whose greatest joy is to impart joy and blessing to Thy waiting children. Amen.

ANNETTE J. SHAW.

There are nettles everywhere,
But smooth green grasses are more common still;
The blue of heaven is larger than the cloud.
ELIZABETH BARRETT BROWNING.

Flower in the crannied wall,
I pluck you out of the crannies; —
Hold you here, root and all, in my hand,
Little flower — but if I could understand
What you are, root and all, and all in all,
I should know what God and man is.
ALFRED TENNYSON.

O Thou, Who hast gemmed the heavens with round, revolving worlds, the earth with beauty and the coronet of our minds with royal faculties, we do not know what " the little flower is, root and all, and all in all " and yet, dear Lord, through the clear and the convincing revelation of Thy dear Son; through the divine image which Thou hast implanted within us; through the mighty and the persuasive witness from experience, we do feel and believe that Thou art the great creator, preserver and benefactor; That Thou hast called us to do a noble, a specific work; that we ought not to neglect the gift that is in us; to this end wilt Thou help us to be pure, brave, faithful and strong, that we may fight the good fight, and win the crown of righteousness. Amen.

ALBERT HAMMATT.

O ye, so far above me on the Height,
I cannot hear your voices as ye stand
Facing the vast, invisible to me.
But I can see your gestures of delight,
And something guess of that wide, glorious sea,
The glimmering isles of that enchanted land,
The winds which from that ocean freshly blow.
And so your Vision lifts me toward the Height,
Although ye have forgot me far below.

But you, my brother, you, my near of kin,
Who some few steps above me on the steep
Look smiling back to cheer me ever on,
Who lend a hand as I the chasm leap,
And stay your haste that I the crag may win,
Thinking it scorn for Strength to climb alone;
You with your morning song when sings the lark,
You, with unflagging purpose at high noon,
And quiet-hearted trust when comes the dark, —
To you I owe it that I climb at all.

MARY FRANCES WRIGHT.

Spirit of the Infinite Life! We praise Thee that our visions of the Divinest rise far beyond the borders of our known and familiar fields, that the resources of our unwearied life are in those mysterious regions that we have not explored. And yet we rejoice that the shadows of these holy visions fall across our common ways, reporting thus from the Infinite and the unknown the possibilities of greater fortunes yet to be. In this life of Thee may we dwell, seeing Thee in the life about us and evermore seeking to lead the life toward those high places that are always waiting the coming of those who aspire toward Thee. Amen.

E. L. REXFORD.

The flowers got into a debate one morning as to which of them was the flower of God: and the rose said: " I am the flower of God, for I am the fairest and the most perfect in beauty and variety of form and delicacy of fragrance of all the flowers." And the crocus said: " No, you are not the flower of God. Why, I was blooming long before you bloomed. I am the primitive flower; I am the first one." And the lily of the valley said modestly: " I am small, but I am white; perhaps I am the flower of God." And the trailing arbutus said: " Before any of you came forth I was blooming under the leaves and under the snow. Am I not the flower of God?" And all the flowers cried out: " No, you are no flower at all; you are a come-outer." And then God's wind, blowing on the garden, brought this message to them: " Little flowers, do you not know that every flower that answers God's spring call, and comes out of the cold, dark earth, and lifts its head above the sod and blooms forth, catching the sunlight from God and flinging it back to men, taking the sweet south wind from God and giving it back to others in sweet and blessed fragrance — do you not know they are all God's flowers?"

LYMAN ABBOTT.

Our Heavenly Father, in Thy sight, there are no nations, there is no north and no south, no east and no west; there is no black and no white; Jew and Gentile, bond and free, — all are Thine. O, Lord, give us so much breadth of sympathy that we shall be able to understand at least dimly the universality of Thy love. Amen.

GEORGE L. PERIN.

Sound, sound the clarion, fill the fife!
To all the sensual world proclaim
One crowded hour of glorious life
Is worth an age without a name.

WALTER SCOTT.

Do not pray for easy lives. Pray to be stronger men. Do not pray for tasks equal to your powers. Pray for powers equal to your tasks. Then the doing of your work shall be no miracle. But you shall be a miracle. Every day you shall wonder at yourself, at the richness of life which has come to you by the grace of God.

PHILLIPS BROOKS.

Our Heavenly Father, we thank Thee for the rest of the night and the joy and beauty of the morning. This day we accept as a loving tribute of Thy Love to Thy children. May we not mar it by unhallowed thoughts, unkind, hasty and regretful speech and shameful and evil deeds. May ours be the illumination which comes from moral and spiritual conquest. May we feel the ties that bind us tenderly to Thee and to one another; and work for that large human brotherhood, which holds in its strong embrace even the most distant and isolated member of the human family. May we go forth to our work with a deep and abiding faith in the power of good over evil and willing to do our share in the building up of Thy kingdom of love and righteousness, peace and good will here upon earth. Amen.

HENDRIK VOSSEMA.

We learn wisdom from failure much more than from success, often discover what will do by finding out what will not do, and probably he who never made a mistake never made a discovery. Horne Tooke used to say of his studies in intellectual philosophy that he had become all the better acquainted with the country through having had the good luck sometimes to lose his way.

SAMUEL SMILES.

Our Father, in the strength of our nightly rest and daily bread we go forth to whatever needs us or awaits us. Nothing from Thee is too difficult for us to attempt; nothing too grievous for us to bear. Teach us how priceless is Thy gift of life, how close we are to the fountain of strength, how sure of success is every effort to bring good to pass. Reverently and believingly would we hearken to Thee in our inmost souls. Let not our failures dishearten us, or the delay of results cause chill of doubt or fear. May our presence have strength and peace for others, and our lives proclaim that Thou livest and art good to all. In the name of Christ we lift our prayer. Amen.

SAMUEL C. BEANE.

At Bannockburn Lord Randolph Murray was being sorely pressed by a large body of cavalry. Sir James Douglas got leave from Bruce to go to his aid, but just as he came up he found the English in disorder, and many horses galloping away with empty saddles. "Halt!" he cried to his men; "These brave men have already repulsed the enemy; let us not diminish their glory by seeking to share it."

WILLIAM MOODIE.

O God of Hosts! On many a field of battle wilt Thy soldiers fight this day. Help them to be brave and true. Give them a glorious victory. Help us who watch to give them full credit for their valor. May we not diminish by seeking to share their glory. May we not render their deeds commonplace by insisting that "It is so easy, so natural, for them to be good," implying that their struggle has not been hard or that their victories had not been what ours have proven to be. Help us, O Lord, with valor to fight our own battles and run our own race and with gratitude to be glad in others' victories. Amen.

J. FRANK CHASE.

The bee that sips her sweets from flowers fair,
Flying on careless wing now here, now there,
With azure skies above, green sward below,
And soft south wind to bear her to and fro,
Might seem the soul of self-devoted ease,
Her life a draught of nectar without lees.
Not so! Her prime is full of strenuous deed
That shames our own in generous meed
Of work for other's good. Long summer days
She builds her golden house, with guerdons stays
Her Queen, uprears her young, and stores her food —
Then sudden shuns her wealth, her home, her brood,
And seeks new haven on an unknown sea,
Leaving her life-work to posterity.

HENRY HOYT MOORE.

Gracious Father in heaven, and all about me, Thy gentleness doth ever tend to make life greater and richer. Thy providence is so wholesomely good, I would fain be completely at home in it. Thou art very gracious. Help me to be as gracious in my way as Thou art in Thy wonderful way. When I acknowledge that Thou art good and wise, there comes a joyous freedom to my spirit that makes life a sweet pleasure. I desire ever to work in the fulness of this faith without grudging, without suspecting, an open, glad and fruitful service. Oh, help me then to love my fellows more, and Thee sincerely! Amen.

ELIHU GRANT.

Drudgery is the gray angel of success. . . . Look at the leaders in the professions, the solid men in business, the master-workmen who begin as poor boys and end by building a town to house their factory-hands, they are drudges of the single aim. . . . "One thing I do." . . . Mr. Maydole, the hammer-maker of Central New York, was an artist: "Yes," he said, "I have made hammers for twenty-eight years." "Well, then you ought to be able to make a pretty good hammer by this time." "No, sir," was the answer, "I never made a pretty good hammer — I make the best hammer made in the United States."

WILLIAM C. GANNETT.

O Lord, we remember our daily duties before Thee, the hard toil which Thou givest us in our manifold and various avocations, and we pray Thee that there may be in us such a confidence in our nature, such earnest obedience to Thee, we reverencing all Thy qualities and keeping Thy commands, that we shall serve Thee every day, making our life one great act of holiness unto Thee. May our continuous industry be so squared by the golden rule that it shall nicely fit with the interests of all with whom we have to do, and so by our handicraft all mankind shall be blessed. Amen.

THEODORE PARKER.

His larger life ye cannot miss
In gladly, nobly using this.
                                    BAYARD TAYLOR.

There are saints enough if we only know how to find them — sainthoods of the fireside and of the market place. They wear no glory round their heads; they do their duties in the strength of God; they have their martyrdoms and win their palms, and though they get into no calendars, they leave a benediction and a force behind them on the earth when they go up to heaven.
                                    PHILLIPS BROOKS.

Our Father, in Whose life are our lives, help us to use all things nobly and so find joy in Thee. We thank Thee for faithful souls who in humblest station have reflected Thy life and have worked for blessing. In Thy strength they have sought to build Thy kingdom, and though they have had no glory of men they yet have wrought for Thee and have won place in Thy heart. Because they have aided the world and others have entered into their labors their good work shall remain and its quiet influence shall be a benediction. Though they have lived obscure lives and have filled obscure places they have been precious in Thy sight and are numbered with Thy saints. May we, like them, eternally serve Thee. Amen.

GEORGE H. YOUNG.

We can't choose happiness either for ourselves or for another; we can't tell where that will lie. We can only choose whether we will indulge ourselves in the present moment, or whether we will renounce that for the sake of obeying the divine voice within us, — for the sake of being true to all the motives that sanctify our lives. I know this belief is hard; it has slipped away from me again and again; but I have felt that if I let it go forever, I should have no light through the darkness of this life.

GEORGE ELIOT.

O God, Thou knowest the hours in which we desire Thee. Thou knowest that Thou hast made us to love truth and to walk in the light and when we are unjust, unkind, unloving, then we are not true to ourselves, — then we forget that we are living souls and that Thou art our Father. Let us not draw nigh to Thee with our lips while our hearts are far from Thee, but, knowing how dependent and frail we are, may we feel that it is a good and helpful thing to draw nigh unto Thee by faith and prayer, — and to take thought of that Infinite Love which holds us all in its arms of strength and mercy. Lift up our minds today, warm our affections, and deepen within us the feeling of reverence, of gratitude, and guide all the longings of our hearts aright. Amen.

JOSHUA YOUNG.

Life may be given in many ways,
And loyalty to truth be sealed
As bravely in the closet as the field,
So bountiful is fate;
But then to stand beside her,
When craven churls deride her,
To front a lie in arms and not to yield,
This shows, methinks, God's plan
And measure of a stalwart man,
Limbed like the old heroic breeds,
Who stands self-poised on manhood's solid earth,
Not forced to frame excuses for his birth,
Fed from within with all the strength he needs.

JAMES RUSSELL LOWELL.

Heavenly Father, in this new day may we recognize
a new opportunity for seeking Thy purpose in us; to
become stronger children of Thine, and worthier
followers of Thy Son. Whatever be our trial give us
courage to stand without compromise, for that which
we believe to be true; give us grace to rise superior
to praise or blame, timidity or self-interest; to be
loyal to the best in us, and be ever ready to protest
against wrong and injustice. Help us to know ourselves as temples of Thine; to know that the essential
principal in us is not dust, but God; to rise to that
dignity of sonship that compels one to choose the
right and say: " Here I stand, I cannot do otherwise."
In His name. Amen.

HERBERT H. GRAVES.

*All we have willed or hoped or dreamed of good, shall
  exist;*
  *Not its semblance, but itself; no beauty, nor good,
  nor power*
*Whose voice has gone forth, but each survives for the
  melodist,*
  When eternity affirms the conception of an hour.
*The high that proved too high, the heroic for earth too
  hard,*
  *The passion that left the ground to lose itself in the
  sky,*
Are music sent up to God by the lover and the bard;
  *Enough that he heard it once: we shall hear it
  by and by.*

ROBERT BROWNING.

O God, our heavenly Father! we come before Thee
at this morning hour, thanking Thee for Thy loving
care, that has protected us through the night, and for
the blessed sleep, that has brought refreshment to
our bodies and minds. We are grateful, O Father,
for this new day, rich in hope and promise and opportunity, and we pray that, as its hours pass, we may
be kept very near to Thee, that the "Words of our
mouth and the meditations of our heart, may be acceptable in Thy sight," that when the day is done, and
we come to Thee at its close, we need in no wise to be
ashamed. Amen.

NELLIE MANN OPDALE.

How often does the chopper of some stone,
While toiling at his task of heave and shock,
Find in the heart-space of a severed rock
The impress of some fern that once had grown,
Full of aspiring life and color-tone,
Deep in the forest where the shadows flock,
Till, caught within the adamantine block,
It lay for ages hidden and unknown!
So many a beauteous thought blooms in the mind
But unexpressed, droops down into the soul
And lies unuttered in the silence there
Until some opener of the soul shall find
The fern-like fossilled dream, complete and whole,
And marvel at its beauty past compare.

ALFRED L. DONALDSON.

O mighty Potter, to whose steadfast eyes
    A thousand years lie open as one day,
Thy patient hand set firm on life's great wheel
    This heavy, shapeless clay.

Rough and imperfect, yet it owns Thy touch;
    Spare not, nor stay, the pressure of Thine hand:
Make known Thy power; and soon, or late, let love
    Perfect what love hath planned!

              Amen.

L. H. HAMMOND.

The dark green summer, with its massive hues,
Fades into Autumn's tincture manifold;
A gorgeous garniture of fire and gold
The high slope of the ferny hill indues.
The mists of morn in slumbering layers diffuse
O'er glimmering rock, smooth lake, and spiked array
Of hedgerow thorns a unity of gray.
All things appear their tangible form to lose
In ghostly vastness. But anon the gloom
Melts, as the sun puts off his muddy veil.
And now the birds their twittering songs resume,
All summer silent in the leafy dale.
In spring they piped of love on every tree,
But now they sing the song of memory.

HARTLEY COLERIDGE.

Ever blessed Father, in Whose pleasant world we
are glad to awake again, looking forward to a happy
and useful day, we beseech Thy loving guidance
through these hours. May we look abroad with gratitude and love upon this beautiful earth, doubly
beautiful in the waning summer time, when a new
splendor comes across the hills, and Thou dost reveal
Thyself, as of old, in the burning bush. Grant that
we may look through nature up to nature's God.
Grant that the mists of doubt and uncertainty which
often hide Thee from us may be dispersed in the sunlight of a happy faith, and that the heart, so often sad
and silent, may once more lift its cheerful song to Thee.
Amen.

ALFRED GOODING.

*No rare creative inspirations throng
My quiet spirit, silent, sad and lone;
No Sapphic flame hath on its altar shone;
No music to my nature doth belong.
Thou art the sunlight, I am Memnon's stone,
Thou art the zephyr, I give back its song;
The harp Æolian can do no wrong
To the soft airs which wake an answering tone:
Upon my soul, Oh, then breathe tenderly;
Subdue the discord, still the jarring strain;
So may the harp-strings yield but melody.
If notes discordant give thy keen ear pain,
Set the fine chords again to harmony;
Let but sweet echoes of thyself remain.*

ADA FOSTER MURRAY.

O Thou Who art the source of all that is and the giver of all that makes life blessed, we thank Thee that Thy providence abides through every change and that Thou dost cheer the loneliest lot with the comfort of Thy presence. Thou hast been with us in times past and now on this last day of the summer months, we would thank Thee for the blessings of the closing season and ask for the continuance of Thy unfailing care and the enrichment of our souls with the gifts of Thy Spirit. Bring us into harmony with all that is pure and good, and enable us to walk in the light of Thy favor and in the paths of Thy commandments. Amen.

CHARLES H. VAIL.

'Neath harvest moon the stricken summer lies
Still smiling bravely in her brightest bloom,
Her heart yet holds no hint of gloom,
No trace of sadness in her sunlit eyes.
We love thee, Summer, child of Paradise —
A myriad host announce thy coming doom
Chanting the requiem of thy wintry tomb,
While lovingly look down the tender skies;
A holy hush is in the hazy air
As in thy radiant beauty thou dost sleep!
Nature, arrayed in rainbow colors fair,
Is strong of heart her vigil long to keep:
We know the secret thou dost seek to tell, —
Thou art immortal, Summer, fare thee well.

ANNA A. GORDON.

Heavenly Father, behind all changes dost Thou lurk in eternal constancy. Never lingering, each good of life gives place to the better Thou hast in store, and in glory and gladness resigns to that which comes after. From the good that is, may we learn to pass cheerfully to the better that is to be, — from the cool morning and sunny noon to the purple gloaming and the star-lit night, from the tender spring and glowing summer to the golden autumn and snow-pure winter, from the sweet life that now is to that fulness of realization whose sweeter splendors eye hath not seen nor the heart of man conceived. We place our hands in Thine and would walk with Thee in holiest trust and serenest peace. Amen.

THOMAS W. ILLMAN.

" I will be happy all the day
Let come what may."
'Twas early morning when the word was said,
And like a journey 'cross a weary plain
There stretched the hours, but I was comforted
As heart and voice sung o'er the sweet refrain,
" I will be happy all the day
Let come what may."

" I will make hope and only hope
My horoscope."
The sombre, brooding clouds of discontent
Oppress one's spirit like a throbbing pain;
One frets and moans in one's environment,
But with a look ahead I sing again,
" I will make hope and only hope
My horoscope."

FREDERICK A. BISBEE.

Yea, Lord, we thank Thee that we may hope and be happy all the day for Omnipotence is our Father and our changeless Friend, and we have naught to fear. We are glad of life and thank Thee for all that makes it heroic or beautiful or sweet. We rejoice in our home, in our dear ones, and in the precious human loves that reflect the love divine. Pardon our sins, we pray Thee, and work out Thy purposes in us. May we work and hope on and be glad in Thee filling this day so full of useful employ that when the night shall come, we shall lie down to sleep upon Thy loving bosom like tired but happy children, and so find rest and refreshment for another day with men and Thee. Amen.

CARL F. HENRY.

There's a dance of leaves in that aspen bower,
There's a titter of winds in that beechen tree,
There's a smile on the fruit, and a smile on the flower,
And a laugh from the brook that runs to the sea.
               WILLIAM CULLEN BRYANT.

O sweet September! thy first breezes bring
The dry leaf's rustle and the squirrel's laughter,
The cool, fresh air, whence health and vigor spring
And promise of exceeding joy hereafter.
               GEORGE ARNOLD.

O Lord, we thank Thee for the spring, which brought her handsome promise, for the gorgeous preparation which the summer made in his manly strength, and we bless Thee for the months of autumn, whose sober beauty now is cast on every hill and every tree. We thank Thee for the harvests which the toil and the thought of man have gathered already from the surface of the ground, or digged from its bosom. We bless Thee for the other harvests still growing beneath the earth, or hanging abundant beauties in the autumnal sun from many a tree, all over our blessed Northern land. Amen.

THEODORE PARKER.

Do right, and God's recompense to you will be the power to do more right. Give, and God's reward to you will be the spirit of giving more: blessed spirit, for it is the Spirit of God Himself, whose Life is the blessedness of giving. Love, and God will pay you with the capacity of more love; for love is Heaven, love is God within you.

FREDERICK W. ROBERTSON.

O Lord, we thank Thee for Thy manifold gifts unto the children of men. Thou givest life and all the sustenance of life. Thou givest our fair and beautiful world. Thou givest us the power of hope and faith and thought. From Thine own giving may we learn that it is more blessed to give than to receive. Teach us, O Lord, to give more freely and more gladly, and may we learn how our own life, and joy and growth are involved in the spirit in which we give and serve. In all our giving and all our serving may we keep before us the vision of the Master who gave Himself that we might live. Amen.

GEORGE L. PERIN.

Our birth is but a sleep and a forgetting:
  The soul that rises with us, our life's star,
Hath had elsewhere its setting,
  And cometh from afar.
Not in entire forgetfulness,
And not in utter nakedness,
  But trailing clouds of glory, do we come
From God who is our home:
  Heaven lies about us in our infancy,
  At length the man perceives it die away
And fade into the light of common day.
                 WILLIAM WORDSWORTH.

O Eternal God, Who art without beginning of days or end of years, from Whom cometh all our life; pardon, we beseech Thee, the sins of Thy children, wherein we have darkened Thine own image within us. Let not our light die away amid the common toil and daily care, but so glorify our life with Thy spirit, that we may gladly present both souls and bodies to Thy service an acceptable sacrifice, and, learning to love Thee above all things, may be approved in Thy sight as true disciples of Thy Son Jesus Christ. Amen.

WILLIAM E. GASKIN.

A haze on the far horizon,
The infinite tender sky,
The ripe, rich tint of the corn-fields,
And the wild geese sailing high,
And all over upland and lowland
The charm of the goldenrod —
Some of us call it Autumn,
And others call it God.

WILLIAM H. CARRUTH.

Once more, O God, Thou partest the curtains of night to bless us with a new day. In its dawning Thou revealest Thyself to us anew. Fresh beauties break upon our vision; new evidences of Thy goodness appear; new joys rise in our hearts. We thank Thee for the harvest of corn that feeds our bodies and the harvest of beauty that feeds our souls; for the blue of the distant hills and the wide stretch of meadow and prairie; for golden flower and flying bird; for the nearness of Thy presence in the brooding haze; for the thoughts unutterable that rise within us. In thankfulness may we go forth to our daily tasks and live in consciousness of Thy eternal presence and love. Amen.

RODNEY F. JOHONNOT.

I come under your windows, some fine morning, and play you one of my adagio movements, and some of you say, — This is good, play us so always. But, dear friends, if I did not change the stop sometimes, the machine would wear out in one part and rust in another. How easily this or that tune flows! you say, there must be no end of such melodies in him. I will open the poor machine for you one moment, and you shall look. Every note marks where a spur of steel has been driven in. It is easy to grind out the song, but to plant these bristling points which make it was the painful task of time.

OLIVER WENDELL HOLMES.

We thank Thee, Father, for Thy love which, like the morning light, fails not to greet us at each opening day. While its radiant beams light up the pathway from our hearts to Thine, we come, with eager steps, for morning worship and for praise. Take Thou, we pray, the hand outstretched out to Thee and lead us safely through another day. Grant us the strength to do our very best and leave results with Thee. We do not ask for ease, but victory; not for the praise of men, but for the blessing of our God upon our heaven-appointed task. Grant us the joy supreme of knowing, when the sun has set, that we have left undone no duty to our God or fellowman. Amen.

J. W. ANNAS.

Admit into thy silent breast
  The notes of but one bird
And instantly thy soul will join
  In jubilant accord.

The perfume of a single flow'r
  Inhale like breath of God,
And in the garden of thy heart
  A thousand buds will nod.

Toward one star in heaven's expanse
  Direct thy spirit's flight,
And thou wilt have in the wide world,
  My child, enough delight.
                JOHANNA AMBROSIUS.

Our Father in Heaven, as Thou turnest the earth once more toward the light to give us another day may we not forget that all things come of Thee. Thou givest us this beautiful earth, adorned with a thousand varied beauties, crowded with opportunities and possibilities, for our home. Day and night, sunshine and the rain, labor and trial, joy and victory, all are from Thy hand. Whatever the circumstances of our life, whatever our labor and place, help us to remember that life is a school in which to learn, an arena where we may fight and win. May we gain wisdom and strength to win the victory which is life eternal, and in finding that may we find peace and content in Thee. Amen.

FREDERICK A. TAYLOR.

Give me the gospel of the fields and woods —
The sermons written in the book of books;
The sweet communion of the things of earth
Fresh with the warm baptism of the sun.
Give me the offertory of bud and bloom,
The perfect caroling of happy birds.
Give me the creed of one of God's fair days
Wrought in the beauty of its loveliness;
And then, the benediction of the stars,
His eloquent ministers of the night.

JAMES RAVENSCROFT.

Heavenly Father, we praise Thee for the breaking day, the singing birds, the dew in the meadows, the fragrance of the flowers, ascending like old-time incense from Jewish altar, the sun gilding the hill-tops, the veiled stars, the gliding river, mirroring in its depths, sedge and tree and overhanging sky. Thou hast ordained that we nestle in the bosom of nature and feel the touch of God. Pour strength into our beings from bird and flower, and Thy spirit which moves in them, that our youth may be renewed like the eagle's. So shall the memories of earth enrich our heaven. We praise and supplicate in the name of Jesus. Amen.

L. A. FREEMAN.

Just whistle a bit if the day be dark
  And the sky be overcast:
If mute be the voice of the piping lark,
  Why, pipe your own small blast.

And it's wonderful how o'er the gray sky-track,
  The truant warbler comes stealing back.
But why need he come? for your soul's at rest,
  And the song in the heart, — ah, that is best.
  PAUL LAURENCE DUNBAR.

Our Heavenly Father, we thank Thee for the as
surance that all things work together for good to then
that love Thee. Help us to live this day in joyous
faith in that promise. May we realize that behind all
clouds the sun still shines, and that the Father's
wisdom never errs, and his love never fails. Give us
courage for this day's conflicts, grace for its trials, and
strength for its duties. Guide our feet in the way of
Thy commandments and fill our souls with the joy
of Thy presence. May our lives no less than our lips
praise Thee. Amen.
  CHARLES F. RICE.

For each true deed is worship; it is prayer,
And carries its own answer unaware.
Yes, they whose feet upon good errands run
Are friends of God, with Michael of the sun;
Yes, each accomplished service of the day
Paves for the feet of God a lordlier way.
The souls that love and labor through all wrong,
They clasp His hand and make the Circle strong;
They lay the deep foundation stone by stone,
And build into Eternity God's throne!

EDWIN MARKHAM.

Our Heavenly Father, we, Thy children, turn to Thee in gratitude and hope for this new day of opportunity. May our high calling in Christ Jesus loom large before our eyes. Deliver us, we humbly beseech Thee, from making ourselves and our concerns chief in thought and effort. May we find our lives in saving those whose sky is dark, whose burdens are heavy, and whose faith is perishing. With zest, as do the angels, when we hear Thy Spirit's voice, may we turn and obey. To let these hours of service prove to us, not only that Thou art, but that Thou art the rewarder of them that diligently seek Thee. Through Jesus Christ, our Lord. Amen.

DeWitt S. Clark.

Good name, in man or woman, dear my lord,
Is the immediate jewel of their souls.
Who steals my purse, steals trash; 'tis something,
*   nothing;*
'Twas mine, 'tis his, and has been slave to thousands;
But he that filches from me my good name,
Robs me of that which not enriches him,
And makes me poor indeed.

SHAKESPEARE.

God of all righteousness and charity, breathe upon me the spirit of thine own charity and righteousness, that I may deal worthily with the good name of every human being with whom I have to do. Help me, that I may bring no injury to the fair fame of any. May the law of kindness be in my lips, and the spirit of helpful justice in my heart. Inspire me to come, whenever I ought, to the rescue of the slandered, that I may deliver them into the liberty of human fellowship. And not to me alone, O God, but to all men, teach this divine lesson of fair judgment and sweet help, that they may live together as children in thy gracious family. Amen.

WILLIAM N. CLARKE.

I searched for love in heart of city's hum;
I searched for love upon the shining sand
Of ocean beach; and then on towering cliffs I sung
A pleading song that love unto my heart might come;
         But love came not.

I searched for love no more, but labored sore
To ease those hearts whom sorrow'd touched before,
Faint hope that in sweet work I'd surely find
Some compensation for a fate unkind —
         When, lo! love came.
                              BESSIE L. RUSSELL.

For love and life and light and breath and ease,
For work, success and hope, for power to please,
For conscience clear, for faith without alloy,
For common share in common human joy,
I thank Thee, gracious God!

For loneliness and shadow, sickness, care,
For failure, doubt, remorse, death, and despair,
For sleepless nights, for aching heart and brain,
For common share in common human pain,
I thank Thee, gracious God! Amen.
   MARGARET WENTWORTH.

In fallow fields the goldenrod
And purple asters beck and nod.
The milkweed launches fairy boats;
In tangled silver the cobweb floats.
Pervasive odors of ripening vine,
Fill the air like a luscious wine.
The gentian blooms on the browning waste;
With coral chains is the alder laced.
　　The blackbirds gather, and wheel and fly,
　　The swallows twitter a low " Goodbye! "
　　　　　　SARA ANDREW SHAFER.

Father in Heaven, we love Thee, we cannot help
it. Thy blessings around us on every side tell us of
Thy love. Our love leaps involuntarily from our hearts
responsive to these numberless delights. We thank
Thee for the rich harvests that burden the fields, for
the acres of beauty that reach over hill and through
meadow, for the stars that make cheerful the night.
Help us to bless Thee when the storms come to disappoint and destroy. May we realize that the tempest
comes from the Good Father, that He has sent it, a
great blessing in disguise. Great Father, help us to
know and feel that everything coming from Thee is
good. So may Thy Kingdom come to Thy children
of earth. Amen.

CHARLES EDWARD DAVIS.

Once, out of all the anguish and the sorrow of my heart,
I wrote a song, and put my pent-up passion in its art.
And the great world never heeded this soulful human
   groan,
For it bore a burden infinitely heavy of its own.

Once, out of all the happiness and joy within my breast,
I made a little song and blithely sent it on its quest.
And the great world, with its infinitely many joys,
   divine,
Still had room and instant welcome for this little song
   of mine.

WILLIAM F. DIX.

O God, I thank Thee that Thou hast numbered me with the children of the day. O Immanuel, make Thy Presence to be a sun within me this day. May I dispel clouds or reveal the rainbows ever half-hidden in robes of mists. May I melt snows and bring spring-time freshets of joy. May I shed light that shall turn groans into songs. May I shine on till I shall stand before the Great White Throne that is encompassed with an unbroken rainbow, and take up the angelic music among that starry host of souls who have found the true "music of the spheres," and are:

   "Forever singing as they shine,
   'The hand that made us is divine.'"
Amen.

ELLIOTT F. STUDLEY.

All is best, though we oft doubt
  What the unsearchable dispose
Of highest wisdom brings about,
  And ever best found in the close.
Oft He seems to hide His face,
  But unexpectedly returns,
And to his faithful champion hath in place
  Bore witness gloriously.

JOHN MILTON.

Our Father, we have ever dwelt in Thee, though sometimes we have forgotten it. While our eyes slept, it may be that to our spirit's sight a ladder was set up on the earth and the top of it reached to heaven, and on it Thy angels were ascending and descending to help us. Now again, O Father, comes to us from Thy hand of love the food and the tasks of a new day. Help us then to put away the error from which we fled or should have fled yesterday. This morning let us set up the stone of our Bethel that through the day we may be reminded in all we do, that Thou art in this place with us. Whether we see Thee or not, let us take courage and make this a day nearer Thee. Fill us with Jesus' own large sympathies for others, with Jesus' purpose to seek and to serve the right, and especially grant us Jesus' complete trust in Thy perfect goodness. In His name, we ask it. Amen.

MERRILL C. WARD.

As far as earth is from the sky,
  So Love is high.
Where Alpine lakes their vigils keep
  Is Love more deep.

In Nature there no boundaries are
  That tell how far Love goes;
Love's measure, as each countless star,
  God knows.

    .   .   .   .   .   .

One only thing we know: Love comes to stay;
Though God's to give, it is not even His
  To take away.

                     MARIAN ALDEN.

O God, our Heavenly Father, we recognize our dependence upon Thee for the bounties of Thy never-failing Providence, and as we enter upon this new day to which Thou has safely brought us, we ask Thy help that we may receive it as a gift from Thee and may consecrate ourselves more perfectly in the least things as well as in the greatest, to Thy service. Help us to be faithful to all the duties and responsibilities of our lot. Deliver us from all useless discontent, all idle doubts and foolish fears. In all our dealings may we be simple and sincere. Strengthen us to do at every moment that which we feel to be right and good in Thy sight, and through loyal obedience to Thy will may we rise into a clearer vision of the things that belong to Thy heavenly kingdom. Amen.

WILLIAM H. FISH.

Some people are always grumbling because roses have thorns. I am thankful that thorns have roses.
ALPHONSE KARR.

There are those who want to get away from all their past; who if they could, would fain begin all over again. Their life seems one long failure. But you must learn, you must let God teach you, that the only way to get rid of your past is to get a future out of it.
PHILLIPS BROOKS.

Our Heavenly Father, the remembrance of Thee fills life with all that is most beautiful and bright. Our deepest sorrows, our most bitter experiences come when we forget Thee. No life can be a failure which strives to do Thy will. Sorrow may come to us, but just as an artist may darken a flower, in painting, before retouching it to make its color all the brighter, so we know that Thou, who givest color to the flowers, may for a season permit sorrow to darken our lives; but Thou art only in the midst of Thy work. At Thy retouch, life becomes the more beautiful. Help us to pray, not simply, "Lord, remember me," for it is not possible for Thee to forget Thy children; we pray "assist us to be always mindful of Thee." Amen.

E. McP. AMEE.

The sooner we read, mark, learn, and inwardly digest a little Eastern apothegm of Howard Hinton's the better: Two balls were together in a box, a gold and a gilt ball. The gilt ball was carefully done up in tissue paper, and securely wedged into one corner; but the gold ball was loose, and went rolling about with every movement of the box. "Oh, please, do take care of yourself!" said the gilt ball, peeping out apprehensively from the folds of the tissue paper. "Why, where's the harm?" answered the gold ball, as it took a fresh lurch to an opposite corner. "Oh, how can you?" cried the other; "you'll rub it off." "Rub what off?" asked the gold ball. . . The gold won't rub off . . . Only the gingerbread gilt.

ELLICE HOPKINS.

Heavenly Father, we hear the loving call of this new day and on the wings of the morning we would speed to the work and worship of the beautiful hours Thou hast given us. We thank Thee that Thou hast made us for the hurry of the market place as well as for the quiet of the home. May our own lives be brightened by contact with our fellowmen. May the pure gold of the Spirit of Christ be ours in purity of personal thought, in the benediction of words of strength and sweetness and in the varied service we may render our neighbors in the name of Jesus our Lord and Saviour. Amen.

JAMES F. ALLEN.

O heart of mine, we shouldn't worry so!
What we've missed of calm we couldn't have, you know!
What we've met of stormy pain,
And of sorrow's driving rain,
We can better meet again,
      If it blow!

For we know, not every morrow can be sad;
So, forgetting all the sorrow
      We have had,
Let us fold away our fears,
And put by our childish tears,
And through all the coming years,
      Just be glad.

JAMES WHITCOMB RILEY

Heavenly Father, Thy very name fills our hearts with confidence and peace. For we know that out of Thy Fatherly goodness all earthly providences are bestowed and administered for our good. So, for our unwilling submission, when Thou hast led us into hard and thorny pathways, we ask Thy generous forgiveness; and for our ingratitude when pleasure and prosperity have attended us, we entreat Thy tender patience. As Thou hast commanded us to rejoice in Thy salvation, may our hearts be filled with gladness to-day; and, as Thou hast counselled us that when we lack wisdom, we may ask of Thee, we beseech Thee to bestow upon us now and evermore the wisdom of cheerfulness and joy. In the name of Jesus, Amen.

EDMUND L. SMILEY.

We all shrink, like cowards, from new duties, new responsibilities. We do not venture to go out of the beaten track of our daily life. Close to us, on each side of the road, are those whom we might help or save with one good action, one kind word. But we are afraid. We say: "I am not prepared; I am not ready; I have not time; I am not qualified; find some better person; send some one else." Perhaps we have only one talent, and, therefore, instead of using it, we hide it, and when the Master comes we shall meet him with the old answer: "I was afraid, and went and hid thy talent in the earth. Lo! there thou hast that is thine."

JAMES FREEMAN CLARKE.

From the base sin of selfishness, O Lord, deliver us. Teach us by Thy life of ministry and sacrifice for others that the more fully and willingly we lose ourselves in service for our fellowmen, the more surely we shall find ourselves in Thee. As we go forth this day in paths that Thou hast prepared for us, help us to so forget ourselves in acts of kindness and words of comfort that each one whom our lives may touch, may become thereby a happier, purer, stronger soul. Take Thou the care of these lives of ours, while, with Thee, in busy streets and crowded shops where greed is grasping and sin is lurking, we shall try to care for souls of others, who need the help that we might give. Then, at the eventide today or on the morrow, it will be our joy like Thine to find ourselves again in hearts made happy, in lives inspired, in souls redeemed. Amen.

GEORGE B. DEAN.

Before God's footstool to confess
A poor soul knelt and bowed his head,
"I failed!" he wailed. The Master said,
"Thou didst thy best — that is success!"
ANONYMOUS.

Straight from the Mighty Bow, this truth is driven:
"They fail, and they alone, who have not striven."
Fly far, O shaft of light, all doubt redeeming,
Rouse men from dull despair and idle dreaming.
High Heaven's Evangel be, gospel God-given;
They fail, and they alone, who have not striven.
CLARENCE URMY.

We thank Thee, O God, for the light that reveals to us the divine estimate of life, that lifts the veil of mystery from struggle and sacrifice and enables us to interpret their meaning as elements of successful living. We praise Thee for the truth that assures us that we are in this world to win, to overcome, to be more than conquerors. We pray that we may be too busy to dream and too brave to doubt. Strengthen us for life's conflict, help us to carry our burdens cheerfully, fight courageously, strive lawfully, that we may be worthy to be counted among those who shall receive the crown of righteousness and hear at last the "Well done" of the Master. Amen.

GEORGE S. SCRIVENER.

Be diligent and faithful, patient and hopeful, one and all of you; and may we all know, at all times, that verily the Eternal rules above us, and that nothing finally wrong has happened or can happen.

THOMAS CARLYLE.

If you entered the workshop of a blacksmith, you would not dare to find fault with his bellows, anvils and hammers. If you had not the skill of a workman, but the consideration of a man, what would you say? "It is not without cause the bellows are placed there; the artificer knew, though I do not know, the reason." You would not dare to find fault with the blacksmith in his shop, and do you dare to find fault with God in His world?

ST. BERNARD.

We thank Thee, O loving Father, that we are not alone in the universe with longing for the higher life. There are a thousand revelations of Thee in our fellowmen. And when we cannot find Thee, for blindness, in nature or in ourselves, we can see Thee revealed in the lives heroic that surround us. In the abstract Thou art hard to find; in the lives of men Thou art always visible. We thank Thee that there is a contagion of rightness and that love is a vital seed that fills the world with its kind. We are fearful of love sometimes, fearing to waste it on a loveless world. Help us to see that every atom we give becomes an ocean to ourselves. Amen.

ALBERT C. GRIER.

To be at all — what is better than that?
I think if there were nothing more developed, the clam
in its callous shell in the sand were august enough
I am not in any callous shell;
I am cased with supple conductors, all over
They take every object by the hand, and lead it within
me;
They are thousands, each one with his entry to himself;
They are always watching with their little eyes, from
my head to my feet;
One no more than a point lets in and out of me such
bliss and magnitude,
I think I could lift the girder of the house away if it
lay between me and whatever I wanted.

WALT WHITMAN.

Our Heavenly Father, we thank Thee for all the
delicate beauty as well as for the rugged strength of
these bodies in which Thou hast set us to live. But
more wonderful than the habitation of the soul is the
soul itself. Thou hast made us a little lower than
the angels, Thou hast crowned us with glory and
honor, and we join reverently in the words of the great
poet-prophet who said of man — " In action how like
an angel, in apprehension how like a God!" O
Lord, we thank Thee for this great thought of our own
life. Yet let us not be vain nor proud. We pray
rather that we may be inspired to live so earnestly
and so nobly that we shall prove our title now to all
that we have dreamed as our natural birthright. So
shall we feel ourselves to-day sons and daughters of
God. Amen.

GEORGE L. PERIN.

*I do believe the common man's task is the hardest
The hero has the hero's aspiration that lifts him to his
labor. All great duties are easier than the little ones,
though they cost far more blood and agony.*

PHILLIPS BROOKS.

*Thus man is made equal to every event. He can
face danger for the right. A poor, tender, painful body,
he can run into flame or bullets or pestilence, with duty
for his guide. . . . I am not afraid of accident as long
as I am in my place. . . . Every man's task is his
life-preserver. The conviction that his work is dear to
God and cannot be spared, defends him.*

RALPH WALDO EMERSON.

O Thou Who art the giver of every good and perfect gift, help us better to understand the measure of
Thy giving; that we count not those blessings only
which make life smooth and easy and of tame comfort
but the things that make life resolute and hearty, and
that put to test the vigor of our souls, that give us
chance to prove our high nobility and unfaltering courage; the things that build for the soul's fine substance
of eternal worth — these are Thy blessings, too, for
which we thank Thee. Give us entrance into Thine
eternal living through strong activity and zest of life;
that manhood have its eager challenge and womanhood its glowing opportunity to assert themselves as
winning joy through bafflement and Thy strong peace
that passeth not away, through steadfast consecration to high service. Amen.

GEORGE H. BADGER.

If I can put one touch of a rosy sunset into the life of any man, or woman I shall feel that I have worked with God. He is in no haste; and if I do what I may in earnest I need not worry if I do no great work. Let God make His sunsets; I will mottle my little cloud. To help the growth of a thought that struggles toward the light, to brush with gentle hand the earth stain from the white of one snowdrop — such be my ambition.

GEORGE MACDONALD

Help us, our Father, to know that we have here at hand all that we need to make this day what it ought to be; that we need not look afar, but in the duty of this present moment, in the opportunity to learn, to serve and thus to grow, which the morning offers, is all that is necessary to make this day sound and serviceable; in such a day we shall find enduring joy and from it Thou, the Giver of all days, wilt derive satisfaction, since it will do its full share in fulfilling Thy purpose. And may we see that if we make our todays what they should be Thou wilt take care of the tomorrows. Amen.

HERBERT E. BENTON.

My neighbor hath a little field,
Small store of wine its presses yield,
And truly but a slender hoard
Its harvest brings for barn or board.
Yet tho' a hundred fields are mine,
Fertile with olive, corn and wine;
Tho' Autumn piles my garners high,
Still for that little field I sigh.
For ah! methinks no otherwhere
Is any field so good and fair.
Small tho' it be, 'tis better far
Than all my fruitful vineyards are,
Amid whose plenty sad I pine —
"Ah, would the little field were mine!"
Large knowledge void of peace and rest,
And wealth with pining care possest —
These by my fertile lands are meant.
That little field is called Content.

ROBERTSON TROWBRIDGE.

Heavenly Father, as prayed Thy servant of old, so we this morning repeat "Give us neither poverty nor riches." Help us this day, in whatsoever state we are, therewith to be content. May no complaining word proceed out of our mouths. Above all may no murmuring thought lodge within us. So shall we rest in peace with Thee, and God, even our God, shall bless us. Yet, O Lord, forbid that we should remain satisfied with any portion, which our best effort, with Thine assistance, can improve. Then shall we grow in grace and more and more approach the stature of true men and women, in Christ Jesus. Amen.

M. EMORY WRIGHT.

Forenoon and afternoon and night — Forenoon
And afternoon and night, — Forenoon, and — what?
The empty song repeats itself. No more?
Yea, that is life. Make this forenoon sublime,
This afternoon a psalm, this night a prayer,
And time is conquered, and thy crown is won.

      EDWARD ROWLAND SILL.

Help me, O Lord, if I shall see
 Times when I walk from hope apart,
Till all my days but seem to be
 The troubled week-days of the heart.

Help me to find, in seasons past,
 The hours that have been good or fair,
And bid remembrance hold them fast,
 To keep me wholly from despair.

Help me to look behind, before,
 To make my past and future form
A bow of promise, meeting o'er
 The darkness of my day of storm.

        Amen.

PHŒBE CARY.

The iris-pillar suggested the burning bush on Horeb. In Moses' time, nature, in the regard of science, was a mere bush, a single shrub. Now it has grown, through the researches of the intellect, to a tree. The universe is a mighty tree; and the great truth for us to connect with the majestic science of these days, and to keep vivid by a religious imagination, is, that from the roots of its mystery to the silver-leaved boughs of the firmament, it is continually filled with God, and yet unconsumed.

T. STARR KING.

Almighty God, our Heavenly Father, who in all ages has been revealing Thyself to men as a God of righteousness and love, we approach Thy throne of grace this morning confessing our unworthiness and pleading Thy forgiving love. While humbling ourselves before Thee because of the consciousness of our unworthiness, we yet approach Thee, our Father, with filial trust and confidence, yea, with gladness of heart and holy boldness in the all-prevailing name of Jesus Christ our Lord. We bless Thee for Thy watchful care over us amid all the dangers, temptations and difficulties of the past. Truly Thou hast been with us, and although Thy people have often been surrounded by fire, the bush has not been consumed. In the future as in the past, be Thou our God and Guide and finally bring us into Thine everlasting Kingdom, through Jesus Christ our Lord. **Amen.**

A. K. MacLennan.

Would you like to hear what sort of questions the school-boys had to answer eighteen centuries ago? Very well; you shall. A rabbi, who lived nearly twenty years before Christ was born, set his pupils thinking by asking them, "What is the best thing for a man to possess?" One of them replied, "A kind nature;" another, "A good companion;" another, "A good neighbor." But one of them, named Eleazer, said, "A good heart." "I like your answer best, Eleazer," said the master, "for it includes all the rest."

FRANCIS AUGUSTUS COX.

Our Father in heaven, we are happy to believe that Thou dost wish us to have the best. Thou dost teach us that the best possession we can have is a good heart, for out of the heart are the issues of life. Thou art the searcher of hearts, — if our hearts are hard Thou canst give us hearts of flesh, if they are sinful Thou canst create clean hearts within us. Even if they are desperately wicked Thou canst make them new. Grant us, therefore, Thy Holy Spirit we humbly beseech Thee, that our hearts may be pure and good. Thus may we ever possess the best possible treasure, and thus may we perfectly love Thee and worthily magnify Thy holy name. Through Jesus Christ our Lord. Amen.

WILLARD T. PERRIN.

Month of fruits and falling leaves,
Under thy opalescent skies
The vagrant summer idly lies,
While coming Autumn deftly weaves
Rare tints for tall ungarnered sheaves
Of goldenrod, kissing the eyes
Of purple asters as she dyes
The vine that swings beneath the eaves.

And all the bending hedgerows seem
A Joseph's coat of colors. Hues
That shame the rainbow's royal arch
Set all the harvest fields a-gleam
With beauty, fresh with fragrant dews
To crown the season's onward march.

GEORGE W. SHIPMAN.

Author and Giver of every good and perfect gift whose infinite presence and power underlie all growth and life and activity, Who revealest Thyself in the varied forms of beauty which come so rapidly in the revolving year, in the green grass and blossoming roses and lilies and refreshing, fast-succeeding fruits, we thank Thee that Thou art now crowning the year with Thy goodness and inviting us to gather in from tree, garden, field, forest, mine, what will feed, clothe, protect us during the wintry season given us, free from arduous labors, to find enjoyment in books, music and social intercourse. These blessings remind us to present to Thee the fruits of the spirit, love, joy, peace, long suffering, kindness, goodness, faithfulness, meekness, temperance. Amen.

CALVIN S. LOCKE.

One answered, on the day when Christ went by,
"Lord, I am rich; pause not for such as I.
My work, my home, my strength, my frugal store,
The sun and rain — what need have I of more?
Go to the sinful who have need of Thee,
Go to the poor, but tarry not for me.
What is there Thou should'st do for such as I?"
And He went by.

Long years thereafter, by a palace door,
The footstep of the Master paused once more
From whence the old voice answered piteously, —
"Lord, I am poor, my house unfit for Thee;
Nor peace nor pleasures bless my princely board,
Nor love nor health; what could I give Thee, Lord?
Lord, I am poor, unworthy, stained with sin, —"
Yet He went in.

MABEL EARLE.

We who are poor in spirit, turn to Thee who art the giver of every good and perfect gift, to hold out our empty hands and pray that Thou wilt make us rich. During the past days and years we have been out in Thy world striving for more things and then more things and yet more things, forgetful of the fact that a man's life consisteth not in the abundance of the things which he possesseth. Now, realizing the poverty of our real lives, we ask Thee to bestow upon us those eternal riches which pertain to the human soul and possessing which we shall have treasure in that heaven within where moth and rust do not corrupt nor thieves break through and steal. So shall we be rich indeed. Amen.

FRANK OLIVER HALL.

Be strong!
We are not here to play, to dream, to drift.
We have hard work to do, and loads to lift.
Shun not the struggle; face it. 'Tis God's gift.

Be strong!
Say not the days are evil, — who's to blame?
And fold the hands and acquiesce — O shame!
Stand up, speak out, and bravely, in God's name.

Be strong!
It matters not how deep intrenched the wrong,
How hard the battle goes, the day how long,
Faint not, fight on! Tomorrow comes the song.
MALTBIE DAVENPORT BABCOCK.

O our Father, we thank Thee for this new morning. Truly the light is sweet and a pleasant thing it is for the eyes to behold the same. Lift Thou upon us the light of Thy countenance and bid us go in peace. So shall we begin the day aright. With gentle skill Thou dost deal with us. Thou art not careless with us or hasty or impatient. Help us to be strong in Thee. May we be able to cast out of our lives everything that would grieve Thee and harm us. With a loving spirit may we serve Thee this day. May we be rooted and grounded in love. However hard the battle may go give us courage and confidence to believe that through Christ, strengthening us, we can do all things required of us. Lord, increase our faith. Amen.

J. E. HAWKINS.

Nobody proves God's being. But, suddenly, one sees God is here. One speaks and God answers. Thereafter all is sure.

EDWARD EVERETT HALE.

There is nothing that so persuades us of the great realities of moral and spiritual being as the man in whom God is manifest, the type of our human nature at its best, and the indorsement of the sublime faith that God in humanity is the supreme revelation of Himself!

HORATIO STEBBINS.

Blessed Father, as the morning light has triumphed in its struggle to overcome darkness, so Thou dost gently but irresistibly call us from slumber to the glories and duties of the new day. May we be strong in the sweet assurance that the unfolding hours are full of blessing because Thou art caring for us. Help us to do Thy will by enabling us to minister to those around us. May the words of our mouth and the industry of our hands reveal Thy guiding love. Enable us to order our ways by the habit of trust that we have learned through Thy constancy. Wilt Thou disappoint our fears, steady our hearts, and show us the way of obedience, peace and service that we may realize the good through the day and rejoice in it, as disciples of Christ. Amen.

JAMES D. CORBY.

Thou knowest not what argument
Thy life to thy neighbor's creed hath lent;
All are needed by each one;
Nothing is good or fair alone.

RALPH WALDO EMERSON.

Men will not be content to live every man for himself,
nor to die every man for himself. In work, in art, in
study, in trade — in all life, indeed, the children of God,
called by a Saviour's voice, will wish to live in the com-
mon cause. They will live for the common wealth, —
this is the modern phrase. They will bear each other's
burdens, — this is the phrase of Paul. They will live
in the life of love. And it will prove true as it was
promised, that all things are added to the community
which thus seeks the Kingdom of God and His Right-
eousness.

EDWARD EVERETT HALE.

Eternal God, who dost still create the light, and
make the morning and the evening of our days, by
Thy light we look to Thee. In Thy light we worship
Thee. Gird us with strength to work with Thee to
bring Thy Kingdom in. May we lose and find ourselves again in the larger whole of life by ministering
to others' needs; by bearing others' burdens; by
sharing their joys and tears and the common fruits of
toil, thus making our life and faith in Thee become
their own. Let Thy work appear unto Thy servants,
and establish Thou the work of our hands upon us;
yea, the work of our hands establish Thou it; and let
Thy beauty and Thy glory be upon us forever and
ever. Amen.

C. E. HOLMES.

Master, to do great work for Thee, my hand
  Is far too weak! Thou givest what may suit,
  Some little chips to cut with care minute,
Or tint, or grave, or polish. Others stand
Before their quarried marble, fair and grand,
  And make a life-work of the grand design
  Which Thou hast traced; or, many-skilled, combine
To build vast temples, gloriously planned.
Yet take the tiny stones which I have wrought
  Just one by one, as they were given by Thee,
Not knowing what came next in Thy wise thought.
Let each stone by Thy master-hand of grace
  Form the mosaic as Thou wilt for me
And in Thy temple-pavement give it place.

FRANCES RIDLEY HAVERGAL.

Father, we are shortsighted and weak, and hence cannot do our best work without Thine aid. We rejoice in the privileges and opportunities of this day. Thou hast counted us worthy to work for Thee. Thou canst use our loaves and fishes, but dost require us to bring thus our little all for Thy blessing. We are inspired with hope to make our consecration to Thee. Make this a day of glorious service. Guide us in our thoughts and work. Glorify Thyself in our life. And wherever the close of this day may find us may it be with the feeling that we have done our best by Thy blessing and help. Amen.

J. W. FULTON.

" Whatever the weather may be," says he —
*   " Whatever the weather may be,*
It's the songs ye sing, an' the smiles ye wear,
That's a-making the sun shine everywhere;
An' the world of gloom is a world of glee,
Wid the bird in the bush, an' the bud in the tree
An' the fruit on the stim o' the bough," says he,
" Whatever the weather may be," says he —
*   " Whatever the weather may be!"*

JAMES WHITCOMB RILEY.

O Father of Lights, with whom can be no variation, neither shadow that is cast by turning, help us today so to trust Thee that our joy may be unclouded. Thy love is unchanging in its radiance and warmth. Therefore let it glow in me and through me light someone who may be in darkness. O strong Son of God, who art the same, yesterday, today, yea, and forever, enable us, we beseech Thee, to be brave and cheery as though Thyself wast in the darkest hours as in the brightest. Teach us that the storm and trial is just our opportunity to shine. Cleanse us of all disobedience and darkness. Be our constant Comforter. Let others see that it is Christ within us. Amen.

THOMAS W. SMITH.

Look up to God, and say, " Make use of me for the future as Thou wilt. I am of the same mind; I am equal with Thee. I refuse nothing which seems good to Thee. Lead me whither Thou wilt. Clothe me in whatever dress Thou wilt. Is it Thy will that I should be in a public or private condition; dwell here, or be banished; be poor or rich? Under all these circumstances I will make Thy defence to men. I will show what the nature of everything is."

EPICTETUS.

Merciful Father, we begin this day, knowing not what the end may be, with thoughts of Thee and Thy loving kindness. May this be to us a day of joy, a day upon which we can look back and say we have been blessed by Thee. We pray for that spirit that enabled others to labor in the cause of love and righteousness, and while we may not be able to accomplish all the good we have set our hearts upon, may the thought that our lives and our labors have not been in vain, inspire us and others with courage to continue the work of helping and blessing our fellowmen. Amen.

DONALD FRASER.

Men deny the Divine Existence with as little feeling as the most assert it. Even in our true systems we go on collecting mere words, playmarks and medals, as the misers do coins; and not till late do we transmute the words into feelings, the coins into enjoyments. A man may for twenty years believe the immortality of the soul; in the one-and-twentieth, in some great moment, he for the first time discovers with amazement the rich meaning of this belief, and the warmth of this naphtha-well.

RICHTER.

O Thou Who slumberest not, nor sleepest, in the dawn of this new day we look trustingly to Thee. While the night has been enfolding us, Thy loving care has held us in the everlasting arms. May this day be for us a fresh consecration. May we be ennobled in Thee. May we share Thy life in things small or great. However humble our lives — however emptied our experience of that which wins the plaudits of men, may we manifest Thee. By us may Thy Kingdom come and Thy will be done. Amen.

GEORGE H. YOUNG.

Thou wilt not hold in scorn the child who dares
Look up to Thee, the Father, — dares to ask
More than Thy wisdom answers. From Thy hand
The worlds were cast; yet every leaflet claims
From that same hand its little shining sphere
Of star-lit dew; thine image, the great sun,
Girt with his mantle of tempestuous flame,
Glares in mid-heaven; but to his noontide blaze
The slender violet lifts its lidless eye,
And from his splendor steals its fairest hue,
Its sweetest perfume from the scorching fire.

OLIVER WENDELL HOLMES.

Thou great Spirit of life and power, we do not shrink in terror before Thee, but come to Thee in trust and love. Though we cannot fathom the mystery of Thy life nor measure the might of Thy power, yet we have learned to call Thee Father; and even as the violet lifts its face to the noonday sun to find the secret of its life, so we lift our faces to Thee, to find the secret of our lives. Thou answerest us with tenderness. Thou speakest to us in love. Fresh from sleep, we put our hands in Thine to be led forth to the duties of the day. May we go forth with that confidence and hope, which are born of trust in Thee, our Father. Amen.

GEORGE L. PERIN.

Now believe me, God hides some ideal in every human soul. Some time in our life we feel a trembling, fearful longing to do some good thing. Life finds its noblest spring of excellence in this hidden impulse to do our best. There is a time when we are not content to be such merchants or doctors or lawyers as we see on the dead level or below it. The woman longs to glorify her womanhood as sister, wife or mother. Here is God, — God standing silently at the door all day long, — God whispering to the soul that to be pure and true is to succeed in life and that whatever we get short of that will burn up like stubble, though the whole world try to save it.

ROBERT COLLYER.

God of all power and might, come into our lives with Thy might and Thy power. Awaken us from that slumber of death-in-life which easily and sweetly steals through the door, and, like some new Delilah, binds the strong will within. Come, come as the fresh morning sun, to drive away the mist of our sloth and indecision. Come, enter; and bring with Thee the upstirring power and the wide radiance of the life divine. Come, enter, and abide! When Thou art absent, though life be easy, it doth not satisfy us; but when Thou art present, though life be hard, it doth also content us. O God of all power and might, come Thou into our lives with Thy might and Thy power. Amen.

MELVIN BRANDOW.

If you really want to help your fellowmen, you must not merely have in you what would do them good if they should take it from you, but you must be such a man that they can take it from you. The snow must melt upon the mountain and come down in a spring torrent, before its richness can make the valley rich. And yet in every age there are cold, hard, unsympathetic wise men standing up aloof, like snow banks on the hill tops, conscious of the locked up fertility in them and wondering that their wisdom does not save the world.

PHILLIPS BROOKS.

O Thou, who hast kept us safely during the uncon·sciousness of our slumbering hours and brought us refreshed to this morning light, prepare us for the duties of this day by filling us with the assurance that we are Thine, and that Thou lovest us. Help us to be more like Thee, to love Thee more and serve Thee better. May we manifest our love to Thee by our willingness to be of service to our fellowmen. Make us warm-hearted and true, helpful and kind, reflecting Thy love and doing Thy will. We are glad to live in this beautiful world. And we pray that we may be faithful co-laborers with Jesus Christ, in bringing light, love and joy to all lives. Amen.

EUGENE M. GRANT.

A few more smiles of silent sympathy, a few more tender words, a little more restraint in temper, may make all the difference between happiness and half-happiness to those I live with.

STOPFORD A. BROOKE.

> *Others shall sing the song,*
> *Others shall right the wrong,*
> *Finish what I begin,*
> *And all I fail to win,*
> *What matter, I or they,*
> *Mine or another's day,*
> *So the right word be said,*
> *And life the sweeter made?*

JOHN GREENLEAF WHITTIER.

Father, so little of the world in which we live is Thy world, so much our world, the petty, dwarfed world of our own small vision, that we lose heart and fail to do our share. Help us to see that, as in the densest swamps the sweetest flowers grow, so, even in our darkest hours, we still may be sweet at heart, saying the word, doing the deed, giving the sympathy, that will make the world sing and blossom. If there are times when pain and darkness obscure our vision of Thee, help us to look on to the sunset of our day, when the black pall is transfigured at the touch of Thy glory, — when sorrow and failure transcended by gentleness are our beauty and salvation. Amen.

JOHN M. DAVIDSON.

There is not a man in the world who is not saved by hope every day of his life. Rob one of hope and you have robbed him of his power. Nothing may so quickly unnerve a man and render him helpless as to take hope out of his heart. What is poverty? What is sickness? What is disaster? What are daily burdens? What signifies the desertion of friends, what of death itself so long as a man can hope? The man who hopes will brush every difficulty out of the way. He will put aside every suggestion of failure. Take hope out of a man's heart and you have taken all. Put hope into a man's heart and you have given all.

GEORGE L. PERIN.

We thank Thee, O God, for the light of another morning, for the privilege of entering upon another day. We shall meet with those who do not understand life nor the world in which we live. It is to them only a place to bear burdens, to toil, to endure. Give us, O Father, understanding minds and hearts. Teach us to know that life is a great opportunity, that Thy plans for each one are very broad, that the world is full of open doors; and inspired by this knowledge may no despondent soul cross our path without being helped and made to feel that every life through the love of God and the guidance of God may be made sublime. Amen.

ALEXANDER DIGHT.

Ho! for the bending sheaves,
Ho! for the crimson leaves
   Flaming in splendor!
Season of ripened gold,
Plenty in crib and fold,
Skies with a depth untold
   Liquid and tender.
              JAMES RUSSELL LOWELL.

Source Infinite and Eternal of Light and Life; Creator of being flowing on forever; Minister far and wide of unspeakable bounty; Through whose power rise the riches of Nature; From whose abundance descend all gifts to man; Soul of our souls and safeguard of the world; To whom all Intelligence looks through every dawn; And by whose support the heart of man is stayed; Let there be to our steps paths of brightness; to our lives laws of justice, kindness, and trust, that we may abound in doing good and by grace, mercy, and truth duly shown, may obtain grateful remembrance evermore. **Amen.**

EDWARD C. TOWNE.

There is something in the autumn that is native to
    my blood
Touch of manner, hint of mood;
  And my heart is like a rhyme,
    With the yellow and the purple and the crimson
    keeping time.

The scarlet of the maples can shake me like a cry
Of bugles going by.
  And my lonely spirit thrills
  To see the frosty asters like a smoke upon the hills.
                    RICHARD HOVEY.

O Father, my heart is lonely till I feel Thy spirit near, and then the glory of the season brings a message to my soul. Help me now to see Thy master hand in the great beauty of the world. May my soul that feels the glad riot of color know that he who gives such beauty and bounty has for me far richer blessings in the great fields of the future. May this day, begun with Nature's rhythm be set with the music of holy purpose and noble service. And may the music sound not alone for me, but for others that we together may march forward in the spirit of Him who loved the lilies of the field and the fowls of the air. Amen.

CHARLES E. VARNEY.

Thousands of years ago a leaf fell on the soft clay, and seemed to be lost. But last summer a geologist in his ramblings broke off a piece of rock with his hammer, and there lay the image of the leaf, with every line and every vein and all the delicate tracery preserved in the stone through those centuries. So the words we speak and the things we do today may seem to be lost, but in the great final revealing the smallest of them will appear.

JAMES RUSSELL MILLER.

Our Father we thank Thee for the light of this new day. Tenderly Thou hast withdrawn the curtain of the night and shown us the beauties and glories of Nature, reminding us of Thine own blessed verdict in the dawn of creation, " Behold they are very good." Good indeed, is it to live in such a world, and we thank Thee for our being. We ask this morning, dear Lord, not for the perishing things of earth, but for continued power and disposition to enjoy Thee and Thy works, for a faith that never wavers and a hope that never grows dim, for such a portion of this world's goods as the wise may enjoy without harm and the righteous hold without wrong. Amen.

JAMES SALLAWAY.

Nay, I wrong you, little flower,
Reading mournful mood of mine
In your looks, that give no sign
Of a spirit dark and cheerless:
You possess the heavenly power
That rejoices in the hour,
Glad, contented, free and fearless, —
Lifts a sunny face to heaven
When a sunny day is given;
Makes a summer of its own,
Blooming late and all alone.

HENRY VAN DYKE.

We thank Thee, O Father, that, to those who obey the command of Jesus to consider them, the flowers become prophets of God and preachers of righteousness. We thank Thee for the worship which They render Thee, so pure, so brave, so glad, and so acceptable. They may not hinder Thee and Thou dost work Thy perfect will in them; O give us the wisdom and the grace to make Thee welcome to our hearts until in us also Thou shalt work Thy perfect will. So may we find our true use and felicity, and render unto Thee the praise that is Thy due. And this we ask through Jesus Christ, our Lord. **Amen.**

CHARLES R. TENNEY.

Season of mists and mellow fruitfulness!
* Close bosom friend of the maturing sun;*
Conspiring with Him how to load and bless
* With fruit the vines that round the thatch-eaves run;*
To bend with apples the moss'd cottage trees,
* And fill all fruit with ripeness to the core;*
To swell the gourd, and plump the hazel-shells
* With a sweet kernel; to set to budding more*
And still more later flowers for the bees,
* Until they think warm days will never cease,*
For summer has o'er brimmed their clammy cells.

                              JOHN KEATS.

Our dear Heavenly Father, Thou hast ever been wooing us by a thousand influences and voices to Thyself and our souls are ever restless till they rest in Thy love. The voices of nature everywhere speak to us of Thy goodness and Thy power and all verdure and blossom and fruitage is but the answer of the inanimate world to Thy call of life. Shall we do less than these, O God, when upon us Thou hast stamped Thine own image and made our being the house beautiful for Thine indwelling! We are Thy disciples indeed if we bear much fruit and have love one for the other. Mould us, fashion us, mature us, dear Lord, till the angels, watching at the gates and on the towers, say we look like Thee. And this we ask in Jesus' name. Amen.

GEORGE M. SMILEY.

I pluck an acorn from the greensward, and hold it to my ear and this is what it says to me: " By and by the birds will come and nest in me. By and by I will furnish shade for the cattle. By and by I will provide warmth for the home in the pleasant fire. By and by I will be shelter from the storm to those who have gone under the roof. By and by I will be the strong ribs of the great vessel, and the tempest will beat against me in vain, while I carry men across the Atlantic." " O foolish little acorn, wilt thou be all this?" I ask. And the acorn answers, " Yes, God and I."

LYMAN ABBOTT.

Almighty God, we believe that Thou art present and controlling in all the operations of Nature. Not a sparrow falls to the ground without Thy notice. All life is of Thy giving. Plants, animals, and worlds alike are governed by Thy laws. We realize in some measure Thy Omnipotence. We should fear to draw near to Thee if Thou hadst not revealed Thyself to us in Jesus Christ as a God of love. Thou, O God, art love. We believe that Thou wilt give to all Thy children eternal life. As from the acorn comes the oak, clothed in royal beauty, seemingly life from death, so from what seems death shall our immortal spirits rise to dwell forever with Thee. We adore Thee, O God. We love Thee for Thy goodness and Thy love shown to us. Be gracious unto us and bless us for our Saviour's sake. Amen.

CYRUS NORTHROP.

I suppose every day of earth, with its hundred thousand deaths and something more of births, — with its loves and hates, its triumphs and defeats, its pangs and blisses, has more of humanity in it than all the books that were ever written, put together. I believe the flowers growing at this moment send up more fragrance to heaven than was ever exhaled from all the essences ever distilled.

OLIVER WENDELL HOLMES.

Our Heavenly Father, Thou art in all nature and in all human history. If we really know our world and our fellowmen and ourselves, we shall know Thee. As we enter upon the work of this new day, we pray that we may feel Thy presence with us. Thou art never far away from us; we cannot get away from our world, and we cannot fly from ourselves. Thou art with Thy world and Thou art with Thy children. We ask not so much for Thy presence, as for the consciousness of Thy presence. May we learn to know Thee in the world about us and in the secret places of our own hearts. Then shall all life be fragrant and beautiful and this day somewhat divine. **Amen.**

GEORGE L. PERIN.

The best thing to take people out of their own worries, is to go to work and find out how other folk's worries are getting on.

MRS. A. D. T. WHITNEY.

Socrates thought that if all our misfortunes were laid in one common heap, whence every one must take an equal portion, most persons would be content to take their own and depart.

PLUTARCH.

Our Father in Heaven, the light of this new day is the light of Thy countenance, therefore we rejoice. In Thy sunshine our souls find strength for the burdens Thou dost give, and even through Thy shadows we reach the peace which passeth understanding. Yet Thou art comfort to us that we may comfort the troubled and the distressed with the comfort wherewith we ourselves are comforted. Set Thou our feet in the paths of service. Make us, we pray Thee, glad ministers of Thy mercy, and in binding up the wounds of others may we have balm for our own. By this day, may we grow in patience and power, and in the knowledge of Thy love. Amen.

LEON O. WILLIAMS.

Life has a thousand pages — love and scorn,
*   Hope and adventure, poverty and sin,*
Despair and glory, loneliness forlorn,
*   Age, sorrow, exile, all are writ therein — ;*
And on each page, however stern or sad,
*   Are words which gleam upon the crabbed scroll,*
Revealing words, that make our spirits glad,
*   And well are worth the study of the soul.*
We may not lightly shrink from any leaf,
*   For on it may be writ the word we need.*
God turns the page — whatever joy or grief
*   He opens for us, let us wisely read.*

PRISCILLA LEONARD.

Fill our souls with Thy light, O God, that we may ever hope. Give us the poise of endless progress. Make our souls free and joyous as the bird's wing. Give us the courage of our convictions in all places, under all conditions. Make us brave. Take away all forms of fear, whether of man, of nature, or of Thee, and make us feel that each is our mighty friend, but Thou supreme over all, faithful each moment to our being, in ten thousand sweet, true, tender, life-giving, life-sustaining ministries. Teach us to look for Thee everywhere, and to see Thy order, and Thy beauty, facing all things Heavenward. May our ideals be perfect holiness, perfect strength, perfect love, perfect service. Make our faith great in the higher estate, where our faculties, only dawning here, shall rise in a glorious morning of the soul. Amen.

A. N. ALCOTT.

Suppose a kindly word of mine
Could lift the clouds and bring sunshine;
*   Am I my brother's keeper?*

Suppose the weary worker toils,
For scanty pittance delves and moils;
*   Am I my brother's keeper?*

Suppose in penury and fear
My neighbor see the wolf draw near;
*   Am I my brother's keeper?*

.   .   .   .

Perhaps — who knows? — perhaps I'm not!
Self-centred soul! hast thou forgot
The marvel of our common lot,
*   The mystic tie that binds us all*
*   Who dwell on this terrestrial ball,*
*   Stupendous hope of time and song,*
*   The bourne for which the ages long?*
How hard our hearts must seem to Thee,
Exhaustless Fount of Charity!
                    HENRY NEHEMIAH DODGE.

We thank Thee, our Father, for the light of a new
day and for its opportunities of service for Thee and
Thy great Cause. We rejoice that Thou dost not
only set duty clearly before us, but also dost grant
power to perform it. May we realize not only that
we are " our brother's keeper," and that our lives are
helpful or harmful every day, but may we be in-
creasingly grateful that we may every day by Thy
grace be fellow-helpers and workers together with
God. Amen.

WILLIAM FULL.

It is of no use to dispute about the Indian Summer. I never found two people who could agree as to the time when it ought to be here, or upon a month and day when it should be decidedly too late to look for it. It keeps coming. For my part, I think we get it now and then, little by little, as " the Kingdom " comes. That every soft, warm, mellow, hazy, golden day, like each fair, fragrant life, is a part and out-crop of it; though weeks of gale and frost, or ages of cruel worldliness and miserable sin may lie between.

Mrs. A. D. T. Whitney.

Vouchsafe Thy blessing, O Heavenly Father, upon this morning service of thanksgiving and prayer. We thank Thee that each year Thou sendest seed-time and harvest, to us Thy children. For the beauty and bounty of the Autumn, for all Thy material gifts, for friends and home, and for our precious Christian faith, we are deeply grateful to Thee. Give us the attentive mind, the receptive heart, that we may see Thy providence and love in every event of life. Banish fear and doubt from our minds. Guard us from all temptations. May the Spirit of Christ abide in our hearts, and enable us to glorify Thee in all our works and lives. In its power and glory may Thy Kingdom come, and remain upon the earth forever. Amen.

Elbert W. Whitney.

Pleasant smiles, gentle tones, cheery greetings, tempers sweet under a headache or a business care or the children's noise; the ready bubbling over of thoughtfulness for one another, and the habits of smiling, greeting, forbearing, thinking in these ways; it is these above all else which makes one's home " a building of God; a house not made with hands," these that we hear in the song of " Home, Sweet Home."

WILLIAM C. GANNETT.

Almighty Father, the light of another day breaks in upon our lives, to reveal to us unfinished tasks and unsought duties. The sorrows and joys of the coming day are hidden from our sight, enswathed in the folded hours of toil. But Thou knowest all our heedless ways and tempers that chafe from impatience; Thou seest the measure of our needs and dost consider our desires. Give unto us the consciousness of Thine everlasting arms about us. And then when the shadows lengthen and the twilight hushes the hum of toil, our spirits shall know no weariness and bear no stain. Give ear unto this our morning prayer, O Thou Light of Light. Amen.

FRANCIS TREADWAY CLAYTON.

How can people help loving things, when they are full of life magnetism, that even a finger touch gets the thrill of ?

It is not the sunshine, or any other tangible why, that accounts for the pleasantness of old house corners. It is the pureness and the pleasantness that have clustered there; the very walls have drunk these in.

MRS. A. D. T. WHITNEY.

Our Heavenly Father, wilt Thou keep our home life bright and sweet? Guard our lips from harsh words, our lives from shame. If quarrels arise, help us to be the first to forgive and forget. In the hour of temptation may we say no, because of a father's splendid honor, and a mother's pure face! In the time of trial or seeming defeat may we be brave and of good cheer! Teach us that home is made dear, not by its furnishings, but by the memories and inspirations of the hours we spent under its roof with those who loved us and were always tender and true! Bind us together in the bonds of love and peace, and keep us always united and a happy family. Amen.

HENRY R. ROSE.

There are loyal hearts, there are spirits brave,
  There are souls that are pure and true;
Then give to the world the best you have,
  And the best shall come back to you.

Give love, and love to your heart will flow,
  A strength in your utmost need;
Have faith, and a score of hearts will show
  Their faith in your word and deed.

For life is the mirror of king and slave,
  'Tis just what you are and do;
Then give to the world the best you have,
  And the best will come back to you.

MADELINE S. BRIDGES.

Almighty Father, we come to Thee for a Father's blessing, that this day we may go about Thy work and enter into Thy business, alive in Thy spirit and strong in Thy strength. We ask this for ourselves, each of us, that we may be knit to each other as brothers with brothers, to bear each other's burdens. We ask it most of all for home, that in home-life there always may be joy and peace and love, each seeking another's good, brothers and sisters with sisters and brothers, fathers and mothers with their children, that home may be the place of Thy holy spirit and the home of joy. Today we would come and go as Thy messengers, in our own lives welcoming the Father, who is with us seeking Thy strength and asking for Thy good will. Bless us today with Thy blessing. Amen.

EDWARD EVERETT HALE.

We are never more discontented with others than when we are discontented with ourselves. The consciousness of wrongdoing makes us irritable, and our heart in its cunning quarrels with what is outside it, in order that it may deafen the clamor within.

In the conduct of life, habits count for more than maxims, because habit is a living maxim, become flesh and instinct. To reform one's maxims is nothing; it is but to change the title of the book. To learn new habits is everything, for it is to reach the substance of life. Life is but a tissue of habits.

HENRI-FRÉDÉRIC AMIEL.

Our Heavenly Father, we pray that our daily life may take on that dignity and calmness and tranquillity which are the possession of those who truly and inwardly trust and confide in the eternal Goodness, who believe that our days are ordered by a Higher Power, and that through all there runs a thread, — a chain of Infinite Love, binding us all to Thee and to one common universal good and blessedness. In this faith, keep us, O Holy Father, and, filled with love to Thee and to our neighbor, may we pursue our way and do our work, anxious only to have Thee in all our thoughts. In Thy name, Amen.

JOSHUA YOUNG.

*Thus pass away the generations of men! — thus
perish the records of the glory of nations! Yet, when
every emanation of the human mind has faded, when
in the storms of time the monuments of man's creative
art are scattered to the dust, an ever new life springs
from the bosom of the earth. Unceasingly prolific
Nature unfolds her germs, regardless though sinful
man, ever at war with himself, tramples beneath his
foot the ripening fruit!*

ALEXANDER VON HUMBOLDT.

Infinite Spirit, Thou buildest the monuments of
Thy power in the rocks of the mountains, but Thou
buildest the monuments of Thy love in the hearts of
men. When the bodies and the works of men have
perished the rocks will abide and the trees will bear
their fruit. But when the rocks have crumbled the
souls of men will abide. If that which is seen is
temporal, we thank Thee O Lord, that the unseen is
eternal. We are awed by the majesty of the seas and
the mountains. But we are inspired by the immortality of the soul. Heavenly Father, may we live
today as if made for eternity. So may our lives be
dignified and glorified. Amen.

GEORGE L. PERIN.

God doth not need
Either man's work, or His own gifts, who best
Bear His mild yoke, they serve Him best; His state
Is kingly; thousands at His bidding speed
And post o'er land and ocean without rest:—
They also serve who only stand and wait.

JOHN MILTON.

O God, who didst give to Thy servant light in his blindness and music in the heart, grant that I may this day be swift to run on all errands of mercy and truth, or patient to wait Thy will, if so Thou commandest. Make me as unswerving as are the stars above me, as trustful as the birds who sing at dawn, and fear not what the day may bring. May I be strong to resist all evil, and cleave to that which is good. May I be conscious that in the loneliest hour Thou art near, and in the most solitary place there is the communion of saints. May Thy power flow through human weakness, and may all the trials and testings of life lead me constantly to the Rock that is higher than I. So may Thy will be done in my life as it is in heaven. Amen.

W. H. P. FAUNCE.

I saw the long line of the vacant shore
The sea-weed and the shells upon the sand,
And the brown rocks left bare on every hand,
As if the ebbing tide would flow no more,
Then heard I, more distinctly than before,
The ocean breathe and its great breast expand,
And hurrying came on the defenceless land
The insurgent waters with tumultuous roar.
All thought and feeling and desire, I said,
Love, laughter, and the exultant joy of song
Have ebbed from me forever! Suddenly o'er me
They swept again from their deep ocean bed
And in a tumult of delight, and strong
As youth, and beautiful as youth, upbore me.

HENRY W. LONGFELLOW.

We give Thee hearty thanks, most Holy Father
that Thou hast not delivered up our souls to the
emptiness and longing of despair. In Thy mercy and
wisdom hast Thou ordained that we may taste ever
afresh the deepest joys of life and ever anew feel the
thrill of its loftiest inspirations. Like the sea is our
life for its largeness; like the sea in its ebbs and flows.
O Father of Life, flood our souls this day with a tide
from the ocean of Thine own love lifting our lives to
highest service and bliss. And Thine shall be all the
honor and praise. Amen.

E. W. LUTTERMAN.

The bird, let loose in Eastern skies,
  When hastening fondly home,
Ne'er stoops to earth her wing, nor flies
  Where idle warblers roam.
But high she shoots through air and light
  Above all low delay,
Where nothing earthly bounds her flight,
  Nor shadow dims her way.

So grant me, God, from every care,
  And stain of passion free,
Aloft, through Virtue's purer air,
  To hold my course to Thee!
No sin to cloud — no lure to stay
  My soul, as home she springs; —
Thy sunshine on her joyful way,
  Thy freedom in her wings!

THOMAS MOORE.

O God, who art both life and truth, the Author of
our being and the light which lighteneth all, the source
of our soul's life, and the goal towards which we strive,
as cleaves the lark at dawn the heavenly blue, so may
our souls be freed from sense, whose music siren-like
would seek to draw us from our flight to Thee. As
that same bird rejoices in the morning light, and
sounds its note of praise, so may our souls be tuned to
heavenly symphonies, and may the sunshine of Thy
love, resplendent in secure omnipotence, give glad
assurance to our hearts, nor cease to guide our way,
until we reach that central orb, our soul's true home,
and find eternal rest in Thee. Amen.

ALBERT B. SHIELDS.

There is ever a song somewhere, my dear;
  There is ever a something sings alway:
There's the song of the lark when the skies are clear
  And the song of the thrush when the skies are gray,
The sunshine showers across the grain,
  And the bluebird trills in the orchard tree;
And in and out, when the eaves drip rain,
  The swallows are twittering ceaselessly.

There is ever a song somewhere, my dear,
  Be the skies above or dark or fair,
There is ever a song that our hearts may hear —
There is ever a song somewhere, my dear —
  There is ever a song somewhere!

JAMES WHITCOMB RILEY.

O God, the Giver of all harmony and joy, before whom the morning stars sang together, by Whom the voice of the sparrow is heard, we thank Thee that we may serve Thee with gladness and come before Thy presence with singing. Put Thy new song into our mouths and help us to render the acceptable praises of the upright and pure in heart. Help us to love all Thy creatures and to delight in the songs Thou hast taught them. Especially enable us to bless our brother men, to hush their sighing and swell their singing, to strengthen the chorus of joy and praise with which Thou hast ordained the world shall be filled. We ask with confidence because we know Thy love. Amen.

J. FRANCIS COOPER.

The snow has capped 'yon distant hill,
*   At morn the running brook was still,*
From driven herds the clouds that rise
*   Are like the smoke of sacrifice;*
Ere long the frozen sod shall mark
*   The ploughshare, changed to stubborn rock.*
The brawling stream shall soon be done —
*   Sing, little bird! the frosts have come.*

                    Oliver Wendell Holmes.

Almighty God, our Heavenly Father, Thou art the giver of all good gifts, and all that comes from Thy hand is good. May we accept Thy providences. In the dreary days of winter as in the pleasant summer season, Thy mercies are new every morning and fresh every evening. Even when our hearts are chilled with grief and disappointment and failure, we would still put our trust in the eternal goodness. Help us, O God, to be truly grateful for everything that comes to us. In the winter of the soul may we learn the lessons of patience and resignation. Thus, with faith triumphant and with hearts full of gladness may we sing our songs of praise to Thy holy name forever and forever. Amen.

   Arthur W. Grose.

It is will alone that matters!
Will alone that mars or makes,
Will, that no distraction scatters,
And that no resistance breaks.

HENRIK IBSEN.

No man can choose what coming hours may bring
To him of need, of joy, of suffering;
But what his soul shall bring unto each hour
To meet its challenge — this is in his power.

PRISCILLA LEONARD.

Infinite God, Who perceivest the destinies of worlds and of men; Who bringest to pass all that we enjoy, and Who permittest all that we suffer; may I this day be enabled to recognize Thy Fatherly goodness, in the morning mists, even as in the noonday brightness! Should sorrow becloud my pathway, should disappointment make its keen thrusts, should temptation lay its attractive coils, may my soul be made aware of Thy consoling presence, enjoy the compensations of Thy grace, assert the potency of the wisdom from above! And mayest Thou reveal Thyself! So may be fanned to a flame the divine spark in my heart, whereby all are made partakers of the victory with and through our Lord, Jesus Christ. **Amen.**

ERNEST W. BURCH.

"*Yes,*" *she answered, lifting her eyes to his face;* "*I, too, have felt it, Hermas, this burden, this need, this unsatisfied longing. I think I know what it means. It is gratitude; — the language of the heart, the music of happiness. There is no perfect joy without gratitude. But we have never learned it, and the want of it troubles us. It is like being dumb with a heart full of love. We must find the word for it, and say it together. Then we shall be perfectly joined in perfect joy.*"

HENRY VAN DYKE.

Almighty God, forbid that we shall ever be satisfied with the rich gifts of Thy land, or until the gifts have brought us, appreciative, humble, grateful, to Thee, the giver of them all. Help us to see that this is their high office, disregarding which the noblest of them becomes a stumbling block, accepting which the humblest of them becomes a means of grace and of surpassing gladness. Move us, then, to such acceptance of Thy favors as shall bring us to Thee rejoicing, that we may need less the experiences which shall bring us to Thee weeping. And hallow all our human loves by lifting us to a common sense and acknowledgment of Thy transcendent love, as shown especially in Jesus Christ. Amen.

CHARLES R. TENNEY.

" What is the real good? "
I asked, in musing mood.
" Order," said the court;
" Knowledge," said the school,
" Truth," said the wise man,
" Pleasure," said the fool,
" Love," said the maiden,
" Beauty," said the page,
" Freedom," said the dreamer,
" Home," said the sage;
" Fame," said the soldier,
" Equity," said the seer.
Spake my heart full sadly —
" The answer is not here."
Then within my bosom
Softly this I heard:
" Each heart holds the secret;
Kindness is the word."

JOHN BOYLE O'REILLY.

Oh, Father, we are in a world of wonder and of bountiful promise. We scarcely know which to choose. Of all life's quests we would seek the highest and best. Thou art a Lord gracious and kind. Grace is but another name for kindness. It is this which is pronounced as a benediction Sabbath after Sabbath, and for which we lift up our faces morning after morning, to receive. Crown us with Thy loving kindness and tender mercies. But not for ourselves alone! As we meet the weary and heavy burdened in life, inspire us to show them the kindness of our God. As freely as we have received, so freely may we impart. Amen.

W. G. RICHARDSON.

What a blessed thing it is that we can forget! Today's troubles look large, but a week hence they will be forgotten and buried out of sight. Says one writer, " If you should keep a book and daily put down the things that worry you, and see what becomes of them, it would be a benefit to you." The art of forgetting is a blessed art, but the art of overlooking is quite as important.

AUGHEY.

Lord, we know not the path our feet must walk today; yet we are not anxious. " Thy word will be a lamp to our feet," and what we need to know Thou wilt reveal just when we need to know it. Help us not to forget that we are under our Father's care; that He knoweth our frame, that He will not unduly burden us; that He will not " suffer us to be tempted beyond that which we are able to bear;" that He will make " all things work together for good to them that love Him." So may this day be one of peace to us, and through us may some troubled heart find rest. Amen.

GEORGE SKENE.

Learn to laugh. A good laugh is better than medicine. Learn to tell a story. A well told story is as welcome as a sunbeam in a sick room. Learn to keep your own troubles to yourself. The world is too busy to care for your ills and sorrows. Learn to do something for others. Even if you are a bedridden invalid there is always something that you can do to make others happier, and that is the surest way to attain happiness for yourself.

                                        THE BEACON.

Father of all mankind, may the spirit of cheer mark this new day. May the smile of Thy benediction rest upon us, and give courage to meet the duty and bear the burden. Help us each moment to know something of the highest joy of serving Thee. May that joy never be absent from our pain. May it consecrate every pleasure. May it lift us nearer the stature of the Christ, that the light of our life may shed its beams on the pathway of other lives, — a light in their darkness, an assurance of sympathy in affliction, an inspiration to do and endure. So may all gladly go to their appointed duty, one with Thee, even as Christ, whose followers we aim to be. Amen.

CHARLES T. BILLINGS.

Take whatever is good in man, and argue that God is not only that, but infinitely better than that. In fashioning your conception of God, make it as resplendent in justice, as august in truth, as noble and pure in love, as radiant and wondrous in pity, as enduring as you please. Never be afraid that you will overdraw the divine character. God is never better in your thought or imagination than He is in Himself.

HENRY WARD BEECHER.

Almighty God, we thank Thee for the great thoughts and high hopes which lie deep in human hearts. We thank Thee for the visions of the perfect life which lead us ever toward the light. We long to follow those who lead the way to Thee. By faith and love may we be bound to them. As voices of Thy spirit may they be to us. Bless us this day with hunger for righteousness. Feed us with the bread of life. Endow us with high hopes and determined wills, that we may be faithful. Amen.

FREDERICK W. BETTS.

There was a man who smiled
Because the day was bright;
Because he slept at night;
Because God gave him sight
To gaze upon his child!
Because his little one
Could leap and laugh and run;
Because the distant sun
Smiled on the earth, he smiled.

He toiled and still was glad
Because the air was free;
Because he loved, and she
That claimed his love and he
Shared all the joys they had!
Because the grasses grew;
Because the sweet wind blew;
Because that he could hew
And hammer he was glad.

S. E. KISER.

O Lord, who dost bountifully provide for us the necessities and comforts of life, and makest us glad in the enjoyment of the same; grant, we beseech Thee, that we may so use these, Thy gifts, that in all our blessings we find Thee to be the source and author of all our happiness — of our health and prosperity, of our joys and hopes, and of the holy relations of friends and family; lest, resting content in that which is less, we fail to attain to that which is greatest — truly to know Thee and to love Thee, which is the very end of our being and the consummation of all bliss; through Jesus Christ our Lord. Amen.

WILLIAM H. P. HATCH.

I have seen
A curious child, who dwelt upon a tract
Of inland ground, applying to his ear
The convolutions of a smooth-lipped shell;
To which, in silence hushed, his very soul
Listened intensely; and his countenance soon
Brightened with joy; for from within were heard
Murmurings, whereby the monitor expressed
Mysterious union with its native sea:
Even such a shell the universe itself
Is to the ear of Faith; and there are times,
I doubt not, when to you it doth impart
Authentic tidings of invisible things;
Of ebb and flow, and ever-during power;
And central peace, subsisting at the heart
Of endless agitation.

WILLIAM WORDSWORTH.

Father of Lights, with whom can be no variation or shadow that is cast by turning, give to me the joy of the love that endures as seeing Him who is invisible; that where Thy speaking voice is, there may be my listening ear; that above the waste and clamor of the tasks that exhaust me in bodily strength, there may be supplied a power of will to do the right and a fellowship with all righteous men everywhere. Help me to remember that Life consists not in the abundance of the things I possess. Let my faith see through doubt, endure through temptation and privation, and cleave steadfastly to God, remembering that Love believing is Love triumphing. Through Jesus Christ our Lord. Amen.

ADOLPH A. BERLE.

When Jeremy Taylor had lost all — when his house had been plundered and his family driven out of doors, and all his worldly estate had been sequestered — he could still write thus: "I am fallen into the hands of publicans and sequesterers, and they have taken all from me. What now? Let me look about me. They have left me the sun and moon, a loving wife and many friends to pity me, and some to relieve me; and I can still discourse, and, unless I list, they have not taken away my merry countenance and my cheerful spirit and a good conscience; they have still left me the providence of God, and all the promises of the Gospel, and my religion, and my hopes of heaven, and my charity to them, too; and still I sleep and digest, I eat and drink, I read and meditate — and he that hath so many causes of joy and so great, is very much in love with sorrow and peevishness, who leaves all these pleasures, and chooses to sit down upon his little handful of thorns."

SAMUEL SMILES.

Father of all mercies, Who Thyself art more to us than the utmost of Thy gifts; we thank Thee for those blessings of our life which come like the manna fresh every morning and pass with the passing day. Still more we thank Thee for the blessings which abide, like a pillar of cloud by day and fire by night, witness of Thine own presence ever continuing with us. Give us grace and wisdom so to receive the ministries of this new day, that by means of them we may enter more fully into the Divine friendship and the everlasting habitations. Whatever may fail us, grant us such hold upon Thyself as shall be the having of all things, through Jesus Christ our Lord. Amen.

JAMES FAIRBAIRN BRODIE.

Native goodness is unconscious, asks not to be recog-
    nized;
But its baser affectation is a thing to be despised.
Only when the man is loyal to himself shall he be
    prized.

. . . .

If I live the life He gave me, God will turn it to His
    use.

                       BAYARD TAYLOR.

Live not without a friend! the Alpine rock must own
Its mossy grace or else be nothing but a stone.

Live not without a God! however low or high,
In every house should be a window to the sky.
                 WILLIAM WETMORE STORY.

    Eternal God, who hast neither dawn nor evening, yet sendest us alternate mercies of the darkness and the day; there is no light but Thine, without, within. As Thou liftest the curtain of night from our abodes, take also the veil from our hearts. Rise with Thy morning upon our souls: quicken all our labor and our prayer: and though all else declines, let the noontide of Thy grace and peace remain. May we walk, while it is yet day, in the steps of Him who, with fewest hours, finished Thy divinest work. Amen.

JAMES MARTINEAU.

I found it difficult the other night to cross a muddy street because of the deep shadow cast by my own body which stood between the electric light and the walk over which I was crossing. Not a little of the time, I fear, do we stand in our own spiritual light, making our own pathway black with ugly shadows cast by our own personality, while the light flashes all around us. If you would avoid the shadows walk toward the electric light in the heavens and let its beams fall in your face.

GEORGE L. PERIN.

Our pathway, Heavenly Father, is dark and lone. Sad and sinister suggestions born in our own hearts blind our souls and stay our steps. But with Thee there is no night. Light is Thy shadow. Unto Thee, therefore, we would turn in the sweet surrender of the spirit. In our darkness which leadeth unto death show us the way. Walking by Thy guidance, intent upon Thy will, may we rest with unforgetting memory upon Thy sevenfold promise of life. Give us the gift of the morning star. With Thee by our side may this new day bring us a new vision of duty, a larger girding for life, the nobler hope, the truth that makes men free. And unto Thee be thanks, praise and glory.

Amen.

FRANKLIN HAMILTON.

The first principle of Christianity is to forget one's self. When Wilberforce was straining every energy to get his bill for the emancipation of slaves passed, a lady once said to him, "Mr. Wilberforce, I'm afraid you are so busy about those slaves that you are neglecting your own soul." "True, madam," he said; "I had quite forgotten that I have one." That remark contains one of the deepest truths of Christianity.

HENRY DRUMMOND.

O Lord, give us the mind of the Master! We would look on our fellow creatures as he looked on them. We would be free from all taint of envy, jealousy, and sin. We would have his single eye and his hearing ear. We know that Thou art in man, for it is Thy spirit which quickens within him every pure thought and moves to every unselfish deed. Give us a due sense of humility and appreciation that we may enter into the secret thought and understand the sincere purpose of all the toilers of this present world! Thus would we abide forever with the saints, the seers, and the singers, of all climes and ages!

Amen

EBEN H. CHAPIN.

Do we not know that more than half our trouble is borrowed? Just suppose that we could get rid of all unnecessary and previous terror; just suppose that we could be sure of final victory in every conflict, and final emergence out of every shadow into brighter day; how our hearts would be lightened! How much more bravely we should work and fight and march forward! This is the courage to which we are entitled and which we may find in the thought that God is with us everywhere.

HENRY VAN DYKE.

O Gracious and Infinite Presence, Thou art the peace that dwells in the shade of night and the brightness and hope of this new day. We are gratefully conscious of the loving strength that stands ever ready to help. The call of the day's work is in our ears and the courage manfully to labor is in our hearts. Strengthen us, Father, when weariness of toil dissolves our noble resolutions; calm us when petty vexations distract from our holy purposes. May midday find us refreshed by Thy grace and eventide solaced by Thy benediction. And now as we go forth to duty let our hearts know no terror but the fear of wrong-doing and our minds no anxiety but the earnest desire to toil fruitfully. Grant that we may see beneath life's busy activities the great good Thou art working out among men and to this end learn to labor and to wait. Amen.

CHARLES R. EAST.

There is no thing we cannot overcome.
Say not thy evil instinct is inherited,
Or that some trait inborn makes thy whole life forlorn,
And calls down punishment that is not merited.
Back of thy parents and grandparents lies
The Great Eternal Will. That, too, is thine
Inheritance, strong, beautiful, divine,
Sure lever of success, for him who tries.
Pry up thy faults with this great lever, Will,
However deeply bedded in propensity,
However firmly set, I tell thee firmer yet
Is that strange power that comes from truth's im-
 mensity!

ELLA WHEELER WILCOX.

O Eternal Goodness, help us now, as another morning dawns, to readjust ourselves to Thy purpose of blessing. We believe that the most certain, significant and permanent fact of the universe is that Thou art our Father. Thus we are the heirs of Thy sufficient grace. There is no curse of ancestry for him who knows Thee as His parent. There is no weakness of the flesh for him who, through touch with Thee, becomes strong in the spirit. Help us all through this day to deny the chain of every earthly folly and sin, to stand erect and free as becometh children of the Infinite. So, finding and using the wisdom of our Master, who, most of all men, gained success, may we overcome the world. Amen.

GEORGE E. HUNTLEY.

All things seem rushing straight into the dark—
But the dark still is God.

GEORGE MACDONALD.

Love is and was my king and lord,
And will be, tho' as yet I keep
Within the court on earth, and sleep
Encompass'd by his faithful guard,

And here at times a sentinel
Who moves about from place to place,
And whispers to the worlds of space,
In the deep night, that all is well.

ALFRED TENNYSON.

O God, our Heavenly Father, we thank Thee
that Thou hast led us into this new day. We thank
Thee also, that, though its experiences are untried and
its issues involved in uncertainty, we are unafraid,
full indeed of glad expectation, because we know Thee
as our King and Lord. Help us in obedience and love
to keep close to Thee, so that, if ever quick darkness
shall come upon us, we may still be undisturbed because of Thy presence, to whom the darkness and the
light are both alike. This we ask in the name of Him
who loved us and gave Himself for us. Amen.

CHARLES R. TENNEY.

Let thy day be to thy night
A letter of good tidings. Let thy praise
Go up as birds go up, that when they wake
Shake off the dew and soar; so take joy home
And make a place in thy heart for her,
And give her time to grow and cherish her;
Then will she come and oft will sing to thee
When thou art working in the furrows; ay,
Or weeding in the sacred hour of dawn.
It is a comely fashion to be glad —
Joy is the grace we say to God.

JEAN INGELOW.

Our Father, we thank Thee for the blessings of night. In this new morning hour, we pray for stout hearts and strong to meet the day's work. May we go forth with a song on our lips and the joy of renewed youth in our souls. Amid the tumults of the day enable us to hear Thy becalming voice. Then, though in dreariest labor, we shall have glad hearts, though pressed by dullest cares, we shall keep uncrushed hopes, though distracted by earth's din, we shall hear heaven's music. Abide with us, Benign Spirit. Inspire us to do our duty, and to learn that therein, alone, may true joy be found. Amen.

GEORGE RUNYON LONGBRAKE.

The weather-prophet tells us of an approaching storm. It comes according to the programme. We admire the accuracy of the prediction, and congratulate ourselves that we have such a good meteorological service. But when, perchance, a bright crystalline piece of weather arrives instead of the foretold tempest, do we not feel a secret sense of pleasure which goes beyond our mere comfort in the sunshine? The whole affair is not as easy as a sum in simple addition, after all, — at least not with our present knowledge. It is a good joke on the Weather Bureau. "Aha, Old Probabilities!" we say, "You don't know it all yet; there are still some chances to be taken!"

HENRY VAN DYKE.

Our Heavenly Father, Thou hast covered us with the darkness and we have slept under the shadow of Thy care. Thou hast opened for us again the gates of the morning, and refreshed, we rise to praise Thee. The memory of mercies past inspires our hope for today. Reveal Thyself to us by Thy spirit and through Thy word; make nature to minister to us in the heavens above and the fields below; let every experience lead us toward Thyself. Help us to see Thy face in those about us, and honor Thee in loving, helpful ministry to them. Bring to us today a fresh and larger sense of Thy presence, forgiveness, and care, and so the assurance that all things are working together for our good. In the name of Jesus Christ our Saviour. Amen.

SAMUEL H. GREENE.

" I will lift up mine eyes unto the hills."
PSALM CXXI, I.

Peace is the message of the hills,
A peace that broods
Upon their mighty heads, and fills
Their forest solitudes;
The leaping mountain waterfalls,
As each unto the other calls,
Blend in a murmuring noise
Whose silver rushing music stills
The pretty play of human moods,
And bids the calmed soul rejoice
In the deep secrets of the woods,
The majesty of Nature's voice.
PRISCILLA LEONARD.

Dear God and Father of us all, Who maketh Thy sun to rise out of the sea and tintest the hills with the rosy promise of the day, we look up when we awake and seeing the light upon the mountains know that the day is coming to fill the world with beauty and glory. With thankful hearts we praise Thee, and pray that to us may be granted that loftiness of nature, that stability of character, that repose of mind and heart and life that is prefigured to us in the natural world. Grant that we may each become mediums of Thy love and hope to all who may chance to look up to us for guidance along the shores of life's tempestuous ocean. May the spirit of the Eternal find such expression in us and through us, this day, that all who come within the radiance of our joy may come into the consciousness of the joy of the Eternal. Amen.

THOMAS J. HORNER.

And he said unto me, O Daniel, a man greatly beloved, understand the words that I speak unto thee, and stand upright: for unto thee am I now sent, and when he had spoken this word unto me, I stood trembling. Then said he unto me, Fear not, Daniel, for from the first day that thou didst set thy heart to understand and to chasten thyself before thy God, thy words were heard, and I am come for thy words. . . . Then there came again and touched me one like the appearance of a man and he strengthened me and said, O man, greatly beloved, fear not: peace be unto thee, be strong, yea, be strong.

BOOK OF DANIEL.

Our Heavenly Father, we thank Thee that Thou art not far from us at any time. We have only to look up reverently and to our imagination Thou art standing near. We have only to wait in the darkness of the night to feel Thy presence with us. We have only to listen at any time to hear Thy voice. Thou deignest to stop and speak to us when we are in trouble, to guide our footsteps when we have lost our way, to renew our courage when we have become disheartened. O Lord, speak to us this day, saying to us, as unto him of old, " Peace be unto thee, be strong, yea, be strong." Amen.

GEORGE L. PERIN.

Let star-wheels and angel-wings, with their holy
   winnowings,
  Keep beside you all the way:
Lest in passion you should dash, with a blind and
   heavy crash,
  Up against the thick-bossed shield of God's judg-
   ment in the field.
                ELIZABETH BARRETT BROWNING.

*Be diligent and faithful, patient and hopeful, one
and all of you; and may we all know, at all times, that
verily the Eternal rules above us, and that nothing
finally wrong has happened or can happen.*
                THOMAS CARLYLE.

Almighty God, our Father in heaven, the giver of
every good and perfect gift, teach us, we pray Thee,
how to do Thy will on earth as it is done in heaven,
as the goal of our lives. Send down exceeding, abundantly above all that we can ask or think, the blessed
influences of Thy Holy Spirit, to transform each heart
and all the world into the kingdom of heaven. Give
us the Morning Star of Hope. Feed us from the Tree
of Life. Teach us Thy redeeming love. Grant that
we may have some part with Thee in the redemption
of the world, and be permitted to join with the whole
glad earth in the chorus, " Blessing and honor and
glory and power be unto Him that sitteth upon the
throne, and unto the Lamb forever and ever." Amen.
  F. N. PELOUBET.

What is the crown of the whole of life lived faithfully here? It is not a crown of gold or gems in another life; it is simply more life; a broader use of power, a healthier capacity, a larger usefulness. You are faithful unto death, through the misapprehensions and imperfections and absence of appreciation or gratitude in this preparatory world, and then there is offered to you inevitably and legitimately the crown of a larger, more serviceable, more effective life.

FRANCIS G. PEABODY.

To Thee, O Author of our lives, we speak thanksgiving and gratitude for Thy gifts of love and trust. Help us to bring them into full exercise this day. By them may we know the experience of burdens made light and yokes made easy. With them, let us realize that we are effective workers with Thee. Because of them, show us how all our tasks are transformed to divine endeavors. Through them, set free all other of our highest impulses. So, O God, shall we know the fulness of life, we and all our loved ones. So shall we see doubt change to faith and blindness to vision. So shall our influence through word and work be the ministry of hope and of joy to any disconsolate, and to any who are a weak guide to the source of strength. For newness of life, for all the fruits of the spirit, whereby the heart is ever young and in joyous companionship with the Christ, for all this we **pray now** and ever. Amen.

WILLIAM H. McGLAUGHLIN.

The child frightened in his play runs to seek his mother. She takes him upon her lap and presses his head to her bosom; and with tenderest words of love, she looks down upon him and smooths his hair and kisses his cheek, and wipes away his tears. Then, in a low and gentle voice, she sings some sweet descant, some lullaby of love; and the fear fades out from his face, and a smile of satisfaction plays over it, and at length his eyes close, and he sleeps in the deep depths and delights of peace. God Almighty is the mother and the soul is the tired child; and He folds it in His arms and dispels its fears, and lulls it to repose, saying "Sleep, my darling, sleep! It is I who watch thee."

HENRY WARD BEECHER.

Blessed Master! we thank Thee that every tired and weary child may find rest in the bosom of the Father. Each morning brings with it new cares, new duties, new privileges, new responsibilities; for all these, we need Thy protecting care, and pray for Thy divine guidance. When wearied and burdened with the cares of daily life, wilt Thou help us to flee to Thee as the frightened child flees to the loving mother; and wilt Thou encircle us with Thine arms of love, and whisper in our ears words of comfort and cheer and of forgiveness. Teach us to trust Thee in the morning, to walk with Thee through the day, and to commit our ways to Thee at all times. Amen.

SAMUEL M. DICK.

Certainly there never was a busier life than that of Jesus, — His whole great mission bounded by three hurried years. Yet in the morning He says to His friends: " Let us come apart and rest awhile;" and again when the evening is come He is in the mountain apart, alone. That is the place of worship in a world of work. It is not a refuge from duty, or a shirking of it; it is the renewal of power to meet one's duty and do it. The work of life is not to be well done with a hot, feverish, overwhelmed, and burdened mind; it is to be well done with a mind calmed and fortified by moments of withdrawal; and it is to be best done by one who from time to time pulls himself up in his eager life and permits God to speak to his soul.

FRANCIS G. PEABODY.

O Spirit of grace, who withholdest Thy blessing from none, take from us the tediousness and anxiety of a selfish mind, the unfruitfulness of cold affections, the weakness of an inconstant will. With the simplicity of a great purpose, the quiet of a meek temper, and the power of a well-ordered soul, may we pass through the toils and watches of our pilgrimage; grateful for all that may render the burden of duty light; and even in strong trouble rejoicing to be deemed worthy of the severer service of Thy will. Amen.

JAMES MARTINEAU.

God gives to every man
The virtue, temper, understanding, taste,
That lifts him into life, and lets him fall
Just in the niche he was ordain'd to fill.

WILLIAM COWPER.

Did you ever hear of a man who had striven all his life faithfully and singly toward an object, and in no measure obtained it? If a man constantly aspires, is he not elevated? Did ever a man try heroism, magnanimity, truth, sincerity, and find that there was no advantage in them — that it was a vain endeavor?

HENRY DAVID THOREAU.

Holy Father, help us to be thankful that no life is beneath Thy notice. If a sparrow cannot fall without Thee, how much more is Thine eye fixed upon Thy child. Teach us, O Lord, that there is a divine purpose in each life. But may we not try to choose this without Thee. Show us how to wait upon Thee in holy silence till Thou dost make it known to us. O Master, say to us: "As the Father hath sent me into the world even so have I sent you." When we have found at the Cross our little mission, O sustain us and help us to keep it steadily in view — let us share Thy holy enthusiasm when Thou didst say: "My meat is to do the will of Him that sent me and to finish His work." O Father, when we are depressed whisper to us: "Your labor is not in vain in the Lord." May our mission transform us into the likeness of Jesus, and may we say with Him at evening: "I have glorified Thee on the earth; I have finished the work Thou gavest me to do." Amen.

L. P. JOHNSON.

Though wrong may win, its victory is brief,
  The tides of good at first no passage find;
Each surge breaks, shattered, on the sullen reef, —
  Yet still the infinite ocean comes behind.

The road of Right has neither turn nor bend,
  It stretches straight unto the highest goal;
  Hard, long, and lonely? — yes, yet never soul
Can lose its way thereon, nor miss the end.

PRISCILLA LEONARD.

We thank Thee, Heavenly Father, that awaking, we are conscious that Thou art near. Walk with us, through the untried path of this day's duty and service. We rejoice that Thou art in Thy world. Within its striving is Thy calm. Around its restlessness is Thy rest. Thy purpose fashions its achievements; Thy love shapes its future. Help us to see it with clearer vision, to hold it fast with firmer faith. When wrong seems to triumph, may we know that it is already perishing, and hold hard by truth and love and faith. Give us grace to spend this day as becometh children of God in honor, in courtesy, in sympathy, in confident trust. When the way seems long and lonely, straight and steep, help us to sing as we march forward, since Thou art with us, Who hast said, " I will never leave thee nor forsake thee." Amen.

CHARLES C. P. HILLER.

She was a droll little figure of a girl with a quaint old face, that showed too early the lines of care and work, and her clothing betokened a poverty-stricken home. Evidently not much of brightness had touched her life, but her face always lightened up when she mentioned her school or her teacher. "Why is it that you love your teacher so well?" she was asked one day. Her eyes shone and her lips smiled happily as she replied, "Because she's glad to me!" What a tribute was that! What an evidence was that of a happy heart that radiated its gladness! If we cannot bring other offerings of much value to the children and the poor among us, how blessed are we if we can bring gladness!

ESTELLE M. HART.

Almighty God, teach us how to be glad. Put some gladness into our hearts. Show us where gladness is hidden in our little world about us, so that we may find it and use it. Give us the wisdom of Jesus, who, although a Man of Sorrows, yet spake ever of His joy and His peace. We feel that the secret of things must be gladness, that somehow there is a covered joy even in what we call our sufferings. Let us find that. Keep our hearts pure of the soiling of evil desire, for we know that no gladness can come from the muddy fountains of sin. Let our hands be busy at some good part of the world's work, for we know that idleness never went hand in hand with joy. Let our minds be open to acknowledge, love and obey the truth, for we feel that truth alone can satisfy our hearts. And let us feel to-day the duty of gladness we owe to our fellow-creatures. Let us give to them what we would receive from Thee. Amen.

FRANK CRANE.

But winter has yet brighter scenes — he boasts
Splendors beyond what gorgeous Summer knows;
Or Autumn with his many fruits, and woods
All flushed with many hues, come when the rains
Have glazed the snow and clothed the trees with ice,
The incrusted surface shall upbear thy steps,
And the broad arching portals of the grove
Welcome thy entering.

WILLIAM CULLEN BRYANT.

Our Father, we know that Thou wilt commune with us if only we truly seek Thee; Thou art the Infinite Consciousness and Thou dost include within Thyself our finite consciousness. We have our life in Thy life. This morning we would be mindful of Thy presence. The northern groves with snow-laden, bended branches bid us enter and worship. Thou dost send forth the rays of Thy sun and touch them aglow with the reflected beauty of the snow-flake. Thou hast also created us. The flake reflects the sun, and may we reflect Thee, through living righteously. Help us to do the right and to forego the wrong. Amen.

FRED ALBAN WEIL.

" *A commonplace life,*" *we say, and we sigh;*
But why should we sigh as we say?
The commonplace sun in the commonplace sky
Makes up the commonplace day.
The moon and the stars are commonplace things,
And the flower that blooms and the bird that sings,
But dark were the world and sad our lot
If the flowers failed and the sun shone not;
And God, who studies each separate soul
Out of commonplace lives makes His beautiful whole.
SUSAN COOLIDGE.

Our Infinite Father, we open our hearts to Thee, for where Thou art heaven is. As the morning sun gives light and life to Earth, so Thou givest light and life and joy to us. We say Good-morning to Thee, and as we listen Thy Good-morning comes to us. As it comes we glow and expand like the opening flower. May this glowing spirit of love be in all we say and do and think this day, and still continue through all days to come. When we are vexed and weary with trials and labor, make us to remember this morning glow of Thy Love that it may renew rest and peace within us. Help us, O our Father, to enter the beauty of this day and this life by claiming our heritage as " children of light " and going forth to fulfil the common duties of the day as " children of God." Amen.

WALTER DOLE.

No matter! so long as the world is the work of eternal goodness, and so long as conscience has not deceived us. To give happiness and to do good, there is our only law, our anchor of salvation, our beacon light, our reason for existing. All religions may crumble away; so long as this survives we have still an ideal, and life is worth living. Nothing can lessen the dignity and value of humanity so long as the religion of love, of unselfishness and devotion endures; and none can destroy the altars of this faith for us so long as we feel ourselves still capable of love.

HENRI - FRÉDÉRIC AMIEL.

Our Heavenly Father, we thank Thee for a night of peaceful rest, and we are glad to begin a new day with full assurance of Thy loving care. We hope for pleasant ways and large success, but Thy wisdom is better than our wishes and if it is appointed us to meet difficulties or temptations, we pray for strength to sustain a manly warfare. We have faith that whatever our condition Thou wilt still provide a way by which lofty purpose and resolute endeavor may use the circumstances of our life for a nearer approach to Thee and for service to our fellowmen. To this end be then the light of our way and the strength of our life, through Jesus Christ our Lord. Amen.

J. SMITH DODGE.

He was a friend to man, and lived in a house by the side of the road.

HOMER.

*There are hermit souls that live withdrawn
  In the peace of their self-content;
There are souls, like stars, that dwell apart,
  In a fellow-less firmament;
There are pioneer souls that blaze their paths
  Where highways never ran: —
But let me live by the side of the road
  And be a friend to man.*

*Let me live in a house by the side of the road,
  Where the race of men go by —
The men who are good and the men who are bad,
  As good and as bad as I.
I would not sit in the scorner's seat,
  Or hurl the cynic's ban: —
Let me live in a house by the side of the road
  And be a friend to man.*

SAM WALTER FOSS.

Our Father in Heaven, we come with thanksgiving for the light of another day and all the blessings which it brings from Thee. May the precious moments before us be filled with activity. Forgive us if we have been remiss in seizing our opportunities and so lead us this day that if we shall be called to Thee, the sweet voice of the Master may greet us with, " Inasmuch as ye have done it unto one of the least of these my brethren, ye have done it unto Me." In Jesus' name. Amen.

J. E. CHARLTON.

One old lady kept a sighing;
Said she wasn't young,
Didn't look as sweet's she used to,
Times were all unstrung;
Troubles doubled aches, and favors
Went a flying past,
Wrinkles stung like thorns, and eyesight
Kept a failing fast.

One old lady kept a saying
Life was like the spring,
Brighter blossoms always coming,
Birds around to sing;
Troubles came — and went; she let 'em,
Didn't count the throng.
Thanked the Lord 'most every morning
She'd been young so long!

JESSIE M. SHAW.

Our Heavenly Father, wilt Thou forgive us for the sighs and tears and frowns and doubts of yesterday? Especially wilt Thou forgive us for all that was little and petty and mean? May we begin again today with larger vision, higher hope and nobler ambition. May there be no sighs for lost beauty, no grief over faded youth and no lamentation over lost fortune. Thankful and glad for what we have, may we find our joy in using it for some high end. So may we conserve the youth of the heart and the light of the soul. Amen.

GEORGE L. PERIN.

There is never a sky of winter
  To the heart that sings alway;
Never a night but hath stars to light,
  And dreams of a rosy day.

The world is ever a garden
  Red with the bloom of May;
And never a stormy morning
  To the heart that sings alway!
                    FRANK L. STANTON.

O Thou who art the Love, the Light, and the Life in whom is no discord, no darkness, no disease nor death; but who art ever radiating sympathy, vision and health; we give Thee hearty thanks for the consciousness of Thy abiding presence when we possess a humble and contrite spirit. May we ever remember that nothing but our own selfishness, pride, and forgetfulness can break this constant communion with Thee. Open our hearts just now for the inflow of the divine Love in order that we may pass it on to others today. Open our eyes today that we may see Thee everywhere striving against selfishness in the lives of all men. Fill us with Thy Life today in order that there may go out to others a heavenly harmony, a song, a symphony, that will dispel discord, darkness and disease; that will overcome evil with good. Amen.

E. J. HELMS.

As the bird trims her to the gale,
  I trim myself to the storm of time,
I man the rudder, reef the sail,
  Obey the voice at eve obeyed at prime;
" Lowly faithful, banish fear,
  Right onward drive unharmed;
The port, well worth the cruise, is near,
  And every wave is charmed."
                         RALPH WALDO EMERSON.

Heavenly Father, keep our faces in the light and upward. Make us courageous in the storm. Help us to consecrate all our powers against the contrary winds and listen for the loving voice of Him who walks the rough waves and comes toward our frail barks. May we never be afraid; may we know peace and rest and trust. O Saviour, help us to know the reality of Thy love and friendship, and hear Thee say in the darkest hour, " All is well." May no storm be too severe, no burden too heavy, no task too hard. So let us believe and live. Amen.

CORTLAND MYERS.

Love thyself last: cherish those hearts that hate thee,
Corruption wins not more than honesty.
Still in thy right hand carry gentle peace,
To silence envious tongues. Be just, and fear not:
Let all the ends thou aim'st at be thy country's,
Thy God's, and truth's; then if thou fall'st, O Crom
*   well,*
Thou fall'st a blessed martyr!

SHAKESPEARE.

Father Almighty, we do trust in Thee, and we ask Thee for everything. Thou art pleased to give us everything. Thou dost give us the light by which we see. Thou dost give us this air which we breathe and with which we speak. Best of all, Thou hast shown us that we are one family of Thy children, alive in Thy life and strong in Thy strength. Thou dost give us the water that we drink and the food that we eat. Everything is Thine while it is ours. Now, Father, we are here to consecrate these gifts to Thy service, to come and go indeed as Thy children; when we speak, to speak the word that Thou shalt teach; when we act, to do the thing that Thou wouldst. Moreover, inspire us with Thine holy spirit, that we may so come and go in our Father's service, and for the coming of Thy kingdom in this world, that all men may be one, and may bear one another's burdens, and so fulfil the law of Christ. Amen.

EDWARD EVERETT HALE.

Each soul, alone unto herself, must bear
The heartache out of which man wins despair
Or hope according to his faculty.
Nathless one thing is certain; who hath known
Truth, beauty, goodness, shining in their sphere,
Shall not be lost through any lesser lure.
On black tempestuous waves he may be thrown;
Yet to the right port shall he surely steer,
And God Himself shall make his doing pure.

JOHN ADDINGTON SYMONDS.

O God, with the dawn we would lift our grateful hearts to Thee! We know not what Thou hast in store for us this new day, but we rejoice that we are in Thy thought, and that we cannot pass beyond the reach of Thy love. Helpless and weak, we pray for courage to be undaunted by the uncertainties of life, and that we may meet all its duties with a firm and tranquil mind. Grant that we may be helpful to all with whom we come in contact and forbid that we should judge others hastily or uncharitably. May our minds and hearts be open to the truth, that we may know and do Thy gracious will. Guided and guarded by Thee, may the day be full of peace, purity and power. Amen.

GEORGE M. HOWE.

There was never a song that was sung by thee,
But a sweeter one was meant to be.
There was never a deed that was grandly done,
But a greater was meant by some earnest one.
For the sweetest voice can never impart
The song that trembles within the heart.

And the brain and the hand can never quite do
The thing that the soul has fondly in view.
And hence are the tears and the burdens of pain,
For the shining goals are never to gain
But enough that a God can hear and see
The song and the deed that were meant to be.

BENJAMIN R. BULKELEY.

Almighty God, our Heavenly Father, who hast illumined the morning with the brightness of Thy life, we rejoice in the potency of the influence that brings us into communion with Thee. For the blessed revelation of Thyself, for life and all things that nourish it, for the earth and the fulness thereof, for daily comforts and mercies and for the Light that lighteth every man who cometh into the world, we give Thee thanks. We thank Thee too for the songs that we have sung and for the better songs that are in our hearts. We thank Thee for every noble deed and also for the dreams of nobler deeds that men have cherished. O Lord, bless our work and fill us with aspiration for nobler service. Bless the poor, the sick, and those that mourn. Hear this our prayer and answer our petition through Jesus Christ our Lord. Amen.

FRANK D. SARGENT.

Love the spot where you are, and the friends God has given you and be sure to expect everything good of them.

JOHN ALBEE.

When do we lift each other up? Must we gain a height first or can we reach up our feebleness together to the Hands that do offer us a mighty help from on high? Near doing, and near living, and near loving; these life-particles make the great heaven, as the little polarized atoms of light, all magnetized one way, make the great blue in which the stars burn forever.

MRS. A. D. T. WHITNEY.

No discontent could harass us if we had a deeper faith in Thee and a broader love for those about us. We praise Thee, therefore, that we may be rooted and grounded in Christ. And that our little lives may glorify Him by bringing forth abundant fruit. Thou dost give us the holy privilege of being co-laborers with Thee in the salvation of needy humanity. Around us are the countless opportunities for ennobling and gladdening the lives of those whose courage burns low, or who have never known the transforming companionship of Christ. We would not forget that we are debtors to Thee and to that great Host whose love and service has inspired us. May we be not selfish takers only, but generous givers. May there be less gloom, fewer shackles, less guilt in the world because we are mastered by the spirit of Christ. Amen.

PHILIP L. FRICK.

*Have you learned lessons only of those who admired
you, and were tender with you, and stood aside
for you?*
*Have you not learned great lessons from those who
reject you, and brace themselves against you?
or who treat you with contempt, or dispute the
passage with you?*

WALT WHITMAN.

Help us, O God, always to be hopeful; teach us
what it means to hope in Thee, and may we experience
the truth of the promise which says: "He will
strengthen your heart that hopes in Him;" but help
us not to indulge in too fond hopes nor to be too easily
elated by future dreams. May we see life clearly as
it is and be ready to accept courageously whatsoever
Thou sendest us. Help us to accept all our joys as
Thy blessings; all our duties as Thy commands, and
our sorrows as of Thine appointment, and help us to
believe that Thou wilt turn even that which seems
to harm us, into everlasting good and everlasting joy.
Amen.

JOHN F. MEYER.

Life should be a giving birth to the soul, the development of a higher mode of reality. The animal must be humanized: flesh must be made spirit; physiological activity must be transmuted into intellect and conscience, into reason, justice, and generosity, as the torch is transmuted into light and warmth. The blind, greedy, selfish nature of man must put on beauty and nobleness. This heavenly alchemy is what justifies our presence on the earth; it is our mission and our glory.

HENRI-FRÉDÉRIC AMIEL.

Our Father, this world is Thy world, and this day is Thy renewed gift of opportunity to learn life's lesson more perfectly. We need clearer insight into Thy designs, that we may loathe every form of selfishness, and love devotion. Give us to know the Christ more intimately, and in the strength of His apprehended presence help us to employ this day in practising the holy principles He taught. Assist us this morning to have, and throughout this day to keep, such an attitude of glad co-operation with Him, that work shall be shot through and through with joy in anticipation of its glorious result. So may this day be to us a time of real soul expansion; a wooing and a winning of that which is highest, even a purer, nobler character. Amen.

J. EDWIN LACOUNT.

'Tis the mind that makes the body rich,
And as the sun breaks through the darkest clouds,
So honor peereth in the meanest habit.
What, is the jay more precious than the lark,
Because his feathers are more beautiful?
Or is the adder better than the eel,
Because his painted skin contents the eye?

SHAKESPEARE.

In this world of mingled good and evil, amid the ceaseless struggle of the better with the worse, grant unto us our Father, the cheerful assurance that we are enlisted in the service of the good, bound for the better, and destined for the best. Reveal to us each day some task that we can do for Thee, some chance to bear with Christ the burden of another, some call to take the side of the right against the wrong. Help us to conquer hardship by patience, despair by hope, fear by courage, and hate by love; and may we find the peace, the power, the glory of Thy perfect will and Thy great kingdom reflected and reproduced in our hearts and lives. Amen.

WILLIAM DeWITT HYDE.

Call him not old, whose visionary brain
Holds o'er the past its undivided reign,
For him in vain the envious seasons roll
Who bears eternal summer in his soul.
If yet the minstrel's song, the poet's lay,
Spring with her birds, or children at their play,
Or maiden's smile, or heavenly dream of art,
Stir the few life-drops creeping round his heart,
Turn to the record where his years are told, —
Count his gray hairs, — they cannot make him old!

OLIVER WENDELL HOLMES.

Thou infinite Spirit of Life, in Thy sight, there is no old age. The step may grow feeble, the hair may whiten, the eye may grow dim, but each human soul is still Thy child. We gather about the tables of earth, families of children, some older, some younger, but all young in Thy sight. We pause for a moment this morning to pray for the spirit of youth. Let us cherish the power of hoping and of believing. Let us have that fine quality of the child life which keeps it facing the future with glad expectancy. Let us not give over our toils till we must. Let us not relinquish our interest in life till the evening shadows fall, and even at the last, let us lie down like the child who sleeps with his hand in the hand of his mother. Amen.

GEORGE L. PERIN.

O toiling hands of mortals!   O unwearied feet, travelling we know not whither! Soon, soon, it seems to you, you must come forth on some conspicuous hilltop, and but a little way further, against the setting sun, descry the spires of El Dorado.   Little do ye know your own blessedness; for to travel hopefully is a better thing than to arrive, and the true success is to labor.

ROBERT LOUIS STEVENSON.

Our Father, we thank Thee for the work that Thou givest us to do; for its joy, for its zest, even for its very task and weariness. We would interpret our labor by the highest good it brings us; through our brave and cheerful doing Thy heaven of peace is found. We thank Thee for our diviner hopes, and for the Spirit that would complete them. They light our days with gladness, and set our feet in large places, and though the higher hill-tops seem far away, yet meeting our duties faithfully, we do see them, and looking back we find the places of our departure lying far below. O blessed tasks! O blessed hopes! That lead us ever to our Father's love. Amen.

ALBERT J. COLEMAN.

God speaks to hearts of men in many ways:
Some the red banner of the rising sun,
Spread o'er the snow-clad hills, has taught his praise,
Some the sweet silence when the day is done;
Some, after loveless lives, at length have won
His word in children's hearts and children's gaze;
And some have found him where low rafters ring
To greet the hand that helps, the heart that cheers;
And some in prayer, and some in perfecting
Of watchful toil through unrewarding years;
And some not less are his, who vainly sought
His voice, and with his silence have been taught,—
Who bore his chains who bade them to be bound,
And at the end in finding not have found.

ANONYMOUS.

O God, all voices of the earth are Thine, even when there is no speech or language, Thy messages have many ways to reach the listening heart. Give us this day to hear at least some whisper of Thy grace. If it may be, open our minds and attune our spirits to receive more than we could hitherto interpret of the assurances sent to us by elevated goodness and love. So let us be defended this day against wrong, and do our work in joy and peace through the knowledge that Thou art with us, our friend and helper even unto the end. Amen.

HOWARD N. BROWN.

Did you ever see a schoolboy tumble on the ice without stooping immediately to re-buckle the strap of his skates? And would not Ignotus have painted a masterpiece if he could have found good brushes and a proper canvas? Life's shortcomings would be bitter indeed if we could not find excuses for them outside of ourselves. And as for life's successes — well, it is certainly wholesome to remember how many of them are due to a fortunate position and the proper tools.

HENRY VAN DYKE.

Our Father, God, help us to begin this new day with the right spirit in our hearts, — the spirit of love toward Thee and our fellowmen. Help us to begin the day if possible without mistake. If, in our human weakness we find that we have not succeeded, that we have erred or gone astray, help us not to despair, not to be discouraged; help us to know and to seek and to love the right. Help us never to forget what we owe to Thee, to our friends, and the beautiful world Thou hast given us. Daily bread we have, opportunities open, like books on every hand. Greater than all life's bitter is its sweet. Ever ready is the Master to bless; ever ready is the spirit to comfort Thy children look up and praise the Father eternal. Amen.

RANSOM A. GREENE.

I love Thee, O Son of Man! for Thy strength and Thy sweetness, for Thy simplicity, Thy courage, Thine infinite tenderness, for Thy glance which strengthens and pardons us, quickens us and lifts us up; for all that Thou hast brought us of consolation, of peace and of warmth of heart. Abide Thou with us! Teach us to see the divine spark imprisoned in every stone of the highway.

CHARLES WAGNER.

O Lord, our Heavenly Father, we thank Thee for all Thy manifold mercies to us, for all Thy constant care and watchfulness over us from the beginning of our lives to this day, for the revelations of Thy presence in the world about us, in the shining sky, in the earth beneath our feet, and in the faces of our friends. Bless us, O Lord, this day, with health and strength and a good courage, and grant that we may show our gratitude for all Thy goodness not only with our lips but in our lives, through Jesus Christ, our Lord. Amen.

GEORGE HODGES.

In every " Oh my Father! "
Slumbers deep a " Here, my child."
THOLUCK.

*This world, with its wonderful creations, its beauties,
and mysteries may lead a child up to the father's throne,
if his heart and mind are open to it. Fill the heart with
goodness and there is no place for badness. Fill the
soul with heaven, and there is no hell. And this delightful time will come when " God is all and in all."*
ABBIE E. DANFORTH.

Our Father, who art in heaven; we know that
Thou hast been good to us. We thank Thee for the
daily witnesses of Thy love. And we would walk
worthily before Thee. But we are weak. Help us,
O Father to see clearly what Thou would'st have
us do! Give us strength. Fill us with Thy spirit,
that all the way we may be pure and patient. Help
us to walk aright. In the name of Jesus Christ. Amen.
CHARLES H. PUFFER.

Grand is the seen, the light, to me — grand are the sky and stars,
Grand is the earth, and grand are lasting time and space,
And grand their laws, so multiform, puzzling, evolutionary;
But grander far the unseen soul of me, comprehending, endowing all those,
Lighting the light, the sky and stars, delving the earth, sailing the sea,
(What were all those, indeed, without thee, unseen soul? of what amount without Thee?)
More evolutionary, vast, puzzling, O my soul!
More multiform far — more lasting Thou than they.
WALT WHITMAN.

O Thou, our Heavenly Father, in spirit we reach out to Thy great spirit. Quicken within us visions of what things we may do this day, with Thee at hand, Thy love abounding. Give us vision that we may rise to the opportunities of our daily task. Let Thy holy spirit bear witness to the reality of our dreams and aspirations, that we may look not idly upon our opportunities, but rather that each new opportunity shall challenge us to nobler effort. O keep us this day full of faith in ourselves and Thee, each obedient to our vision, until full purposed, winning Thine approval, we shall accomplish the thing for which Thou sendest us, and Thine be the glory. Amen.

JAMES D. TILLINGHAST.

I see the wrong that round me lies,
I feel the guilt within,
With groan and travail cries
I hear the world confess its sin.

Within the maddening maze of things,
And tossed by storm and flood,
To one fixed stake my spirit clings:
I know that God is good.

I know not where his islands lift
Their fronded palms in air;
I only know I cannot drift
Beyond His love and care.
                    JOHN GREENLEAF WHITTIER.

O Thou, without whose care a sparrow does not fall, who through the pathless sky dost guide the bird seeking its distant nest, Thy trusting children are safe in Thy dear love. We know not the way before us, but Thou dost know; our feet may stumble in rough paths, but Thou wilt hold us up. Glad in this confidence, may we begin the day with song and finish it, whatever may befall us, in the calm assurance that all things work for good. Give us patience in perplexity, hope amid our fears, and faith to trust Thy holy will as best. Thus walking in Thy love may we reach home at last to see our Saviour's face. Amen.
STEPHEN A. NORTON.

Wouldst make thy life go fair and square?
Thou must not for the past feel care;
Whatever thy loss, thou must not mourn;
Must ever act as if new-born.
What each day wants of thee, that ask;
What each day tells thee, that make thy task;
With pride thine own performance viewing,
With heart to admire another's doing;
Above all, hate no human being,
And all the future leave to the All-Seeing.

GOETHE.

Dear Father, grateful for another new-born day, myself new-born, I greet Thee! Yesterday and all other yesterdays are in Thy keeping. *This day is mine!* For the failures of the past I care not, nor do I mourn the losses of the days gone by. *Today I am new-born!* Indeed, aspiring to Thy comprehensive wisdom, I may see my past and my present as one, and out of that past I may select — even from failures and losses — such experiences and lessons as will help me live the present — at least this one day which is mine! — more nobly, more fully, more usefully, more beautifully. May I, knowing myself to be Thy Child, respect myself as a creative spirit able to look upon its own work and to say: "Behold, it is good!" And above all, I pray: that, to-day and always, I may grow in grace and loving-kindness, — hating no one, but feeling, thinking, speaking, acting with good will towards all Thy creatures! *This day is mine!* The future I leave to Thee, All-Seeing Father! but feel myself Thy **open-eyed and confident** child. Amen.

CHARLES FLEISCHER.

'Mid pleasures and palaces though we may roam,
Be it ever so humble, there's no place like home;
A charm from the skies seems to hallow us there,
Which sought through the world is ne'er met with
    elsewhere.

An exile from home splendor dazzles in vain,
Oh give me my lowly thatched cottage again;
The birds singing gaily, that came at my call,
Give me them, and that peace of mind dearer than
    all.

J. HOWARD PAYNE.

O God, our Heavenly Father, we thank thee for the blessings of home; for the shelter, safety, and hallowed associations of our domestic habitation; for the sympathy and helpfulness of family relationship. Help us we pray thee to make ours an ideal household, bright with cheerfulness, an exemplification of Christian faith and hope. May the happiness of all be the object of each. To that end help us to be patient toward one another, kind and forgiving. May we realize by many beatific experiences that it is better to give than to receive, better to serve than to be served. May we be disposed, as occasion may arise, to share, for a season, the comfort and inspiration of our home with those who are homeless. We thank Thee for the bright assurance that beyond the fading scenes and transitory experiences of this life, there is, awaiting us, an eternal abiding place in " a continuing city " whose maker and builder is God, where there shall be no more parting, and where the shadows of our present life shall forever flee away. Amen.

CHARLES CONKLIN.

That ever-vivid scene of Bethlehem. . . . A father, a mother, and a child are there. No religion which began like that could ever lose its character. The first unit of human life, the soul, is there, in the new-born personality of the childhood. But the second unit of human life, the family, is just as truly there in the familiar relation of husband and wife and the sacred, eternal mystery of motherhood.

PHILLIPS BROOKS.

" Glory to God in the highest, and on earth Peace." We take up the angel symphony and give it new breath, this gladsome day of days. Thou who didst send Thy Son in the likeness of a little child, that by His life of increase in love and beauty and wisdom and power He might give us courage to begin as children the obedience that alone leads at last to the measure of the stature of His fulness, accept our un-utterable gratitude for all that gift. And oh, may He be born in us and formed in us, the hope of glory, that so we may share His peace, His victory, His exaltation, His union with Thee. Amen.

C. ELLWOOD NASH.

Two are the pathways by which mankind can to
virtue mount upward;
If thou shouldst find the one barr'd, open the other
will lie.
'Tis by exertion the Happy obtain her, the Suffering
by patience,
Blest is the man whose kind fate guides him along
upon both!

SCHILLER.

O Thou who hast kept us safely during the uncon-
sciousness of our slumbering hours, and brought us
refreshed to this morning light, prepare us for the
duties of this day by filling us with the assurance that
we are Thine, and that Thou lovest us. Help us to
be more like Thee, to love Thee more and serve Thee
better. May we manifest our love to Thee by our
willingness to be of service to our fellowmen. Make
us warm-hearted and true, helpful and kind, reflecting
Thy love and doing Thy will. We are glad to live in
this beautiful world. And we pray that we may be
faithful co-laborers with Jesus Christ, in being light,
love and joy to all lives. Amen.

CHARLES R. TENNEY.

Stronger, and more frequently, comes the temptation to stop singing, and let discord do its own wild work. But blessed are they that endure to the end, — singing patiently and sweetly, till all join in with loving acquiescence, and universal harmony prevails, without forcing into submission the free discord of a single voice.

This is the hardest and the bravest task which a true soul has to perform amid the clashing elements of time. But once has it been done perfectly unto the end; and that voice — so clear in its meekness — is heard above all the din of a tumultuous world: one after another chimes in with its patient sweetness; and, through infinite discords, the listening soul can perceive that the great tune is slowly coming into harmony.

LYDIA MARIA CHILD.

Our Father, who art in heaven! We thank Thee that we are permitted to see the light, engage in the duties and enter into the experiences of this new day. We thank Thee for the order and harmony of this wonderful universe; that every force and law and being supports and balances every other force, law and being; that every life contributes to or may contribute to the welfare of every other life, and we pray, that each one of us may come into such relations with Thee, the great harmonizing soul of things, as to add our little note to the full anthem of perpetual and adorable praise. In Christ's dear name, we ask and offer all. Amen.

A. J. PATTERSON.

It is said that a friend once asked the great composer, Haydn, why his church music was always so full of gladness. He answered, " I cannot make it otherwise; I write according to the thoughts I feel; when I think upon my God, my heart is so full of joy that the notes dance and leap from my pen; and since God has given me a cheerful heart, it will be pardoned me that I serve Him with a cheerful spirit."

Pardoned? Nay, it will be praised and rewarded. For God looks with approval and man turns with gratitude to everyone who shows by a cheerful life that religion is a blessing for this world and the next.

HENRY VAN DYKE.

Our Father in Heaven, we awake this morning with a sense of thankfulness for the beauty and glory of Thy creation. We praise Thee that as Thy children we can be conscious of the kingdom of heaven always about us. So we pray for that attitude of mind and spirit of soul that will unlock for us the divine life. Help us to be conscious of Thee in all the varied experiences of this day. If it shall be a day of burdens, give us strength to play our part uncomplainingly, if a day of joy to accept it with true gratitude; and when the shades of night shall call us to our rest, may our memory of the day bring us peace. Amen.

EDWARD C. DOWNEY.

Ah, don't be sorrowful, darling,
And don't be sorrowful, pray;
Taking the year together, my dear,
There isn't more night than day.

'Tis rainy weather, my darling;
Time's waves they heavily run;
But taking the year together, my dear,
There isn't more cloud than sun.

ALICE CARY.

We thank Thee, heavenly Father, for the days just
as they come. Nor would we measure the sunshine
against the storm as if to test Thy goodness by some
petty form of bookkeeping. Thou presidest over all
our days, and whatever may be the face of nature we
trust Thy love. Let us go forth today, not in critical
mood nor despondent mood but in the mood of high
Christian faith, anxious, not to test Thy providence,
but ready to do our own part, taking care to hold our
cup of blessing open-side up; so shall it catch the
manna when it falls. Then shall each passing day
be full of blessing. Amen.

GEORGE L. PERIN.

Fades the rose; the year grows old;
The tale is told;
Youth doth depart —
Only stays the heart.

Ah, no! if stays the heart,
Youth can ne'er depart,
Nor the sweet tale be told —
Never the rose fade, nor the year grow old.
RICHARD WATSON GILDER.

Dear Father, we thank Thee for the year now coming to its close, and for all that has blessed us in it. Help us to keep the good wherewith it has done us good in lasting memory. By the flight of time which its passing emphasizes move us to earnestness in the labors committed to our hands. Beyond this help us that we may be undisturbed, remembering that Thou art our dwelling place, and that we are the children of Thy love and the sharers of Thy everlastingness. So may we keep the vision of youth, the vision to which endings are but beginnings, the good leading to the better, and the best forever more. May Thy blessing be upon all whom we love and should pray for in this and every day, in Jesus' name. Amen.

CHARLES R. TENNEY

Be not afraid, dear friend. What of sickness! What of sorrow! What of failure! What of misfortune! What of death! Is not this God's world? Are not you God's child? Go forth into the New Year with brave heart. When fortune smiles, smile with her. When fortune frowns, smile the more, and trust in God.

GEORGE L. PERIN.

Our Heavenly Father, we stand upon the utmost verge of the old year. Forgetting the things that are behind, we stand with our faces looking earnestly into the future. We do not despise the past, we do not forget its manifold blessings. We do not forget that Thou hast been with us in the old year; for all this we would be grateful. With clear vision and earnestness of purpose, we would stand looking into the future expectantly, ready for its duties and its responsibilities; yet not ostentatiously nor with over-confidence, for we know our own infirmities, our own weaknesses. We would enter upon the New Year with confidence, not because of our own strength, but because of Thy living presence. Thou art always with us, Thou art pouring out Thy spirit upon us. O Lord, let us believe in Thee, and believing, let us have a heart for any fate. Amen.

GEORGE L. PERIN.

Services for Special Days

Good Friday
Easter
Thanksgiving Day
Birth of a Baby
Child's Birthday
Father's Birthday
Mother's Birthday
General Birthday

Why dost thou glare so fierce
O Death, as thou wouldst pierce,
With thine uplifted dart,
My sinking heart?

Yet though men fear thee so
Wherever thou dost go,
And tremble at thy feet,
Thou art a cheat!

Though men thy pity crave,
Though naught from thee can save,
Thy Master rules above,
Thou servest Love.

HENRY NEHEMIAH DODGE.

O Thou, who didst not spare Thine own Son, but didst deliver Him up for us all, we cannot ask Thee to withhold us from our Gethsemane nor even from our Calvary. But when Thou callest us to go down into the gloom or up to the cross, remember, O God, that we are dust. Might we so dwell with Thee in Thy secret place, as to abide under Thy shadow! There, sheltered and unafraid, we should sustain the rod as eager for its chastening stroke, praying only for wisdom to learn its lesson and acquire its discipline. With the picture of the crucified Savior before us, we only cry this day as He taught us, Thy will be done. Amen.

C. ELLWOOD NASH.

See, in that rock-hewn garden sepulchre,
The Holy One of God, despised and slain,
With nail-torn hands and feet, and spear-pierced side,
His gentle brow by mocking thorns defaced;
See where He lies, obedient unto death.
Into that pallid face the glow of life
Begins to steal, while silent and in awe
The heavenly watchers stand.   Now they with haste
Unwind the scented wrappings from His form
That fill the place with rich aromas rare,
Perfume of spicery and sweet spikenard's breath
Lingering since Love her alabastron broke,
And with her tresses wiped these tear-bathed feet.
And then, their joyful faces all aglow
Like flashing sunbeams, quickly by a touch
They roll away the stone with jarring shock,
As if an earthquake passed, and sitting there
Behold their Lord go forth, Death's Conqueror!

HENRY NEHEMIAH DODGE.

O Thou Eternal One, who gatherest our fleeting moments into Thy permanence, when we draw close to Thee the terrors of change and vicissitude pass away, and a sense of the stability and security of all that is good brings us peace. We rejoice to know through Thy gospel that " life is ever lord of death." " Thou didst not suffer Thy Holy One to see corruption," and we trust that because He lives we shall live also. O grant that, believing in Him, we may not see death save as a door to more abounding life, and so realize our privilege daily to be risen with Him in the newness and power of an endless life. Amen.

C. ELLWOOD NASH.

Make a joyful noise unto the Lord, all ye lands.

Serve the Lord with gladness: come before His presence with singing.

Know ye that the Lord He is God; it is He that hath made us, and not we ourselves; we are His people, and the sheep of His pasture.

Enter into His gates with thanksgiving, and into His courts with praise: be thankful unto Him, and bless His name.

For the Lord is good; His mercy is everlasting; and His truth endureth to all generations.

PSALM 100.

For days of health, for nights of quiet sleep; for seasons of bounty and of beauty, for all earth's contributions to our need through this past year: Good Lord, we thank Thee. For our country's shelter; for our homes; for the joy of faces, and the joy of hearts that love: for the power of great examples; for holy ones who lead us in the ways of life and love: for our powers of growth; for longings to be better and do more; for Ideals that ever rise above our real: for opportunities well used; for opportunities unused, and even those misused: Good Lord, we humbly thank Thee! For our temptations, and for any victory over sins that close beset us; for the gladness that abides with loyalty and the peace of the return: for the blessedness of service and the power to fit ourselves to others' needs: for our necessities to work; for burdens, pain, and disappointments, means of growth; for sorrow; for death: for all that brings us nearer to each other, nearer to ourselves, near to Thee; for Life: We thank Thee, O our Father!

WILLIAM C. GANNETT.

Where did you come from, baby dear?
Out of the everywhere into the here.

Where did you get your eyes so blue?
Out of the sky as I came through.

What makes the light in them sparkle and spin?
Some of the starry spikes left in.

Where did you get that little tear?
I found it waiting when I got here.

What makes your forehead so smooth and high?
A soft hand stroked it as I went by.

What makes your cheek like a warm white rose?
Something better than anyone knows.

Whence that three-cornered smile of bliss?
Three angels gave me at once a kiss.

Where did you get those arms and hands?
Love made itself into hooks and bands.

Feet, whence did you come, you darling things?
From the same box as the cherub's wings.

How did they all just come to be you?
God thought about me, and so I grew.

But how did you come to us, you dear?
God thought of You, and so I am here.

GEORGE MacDONALD

Fresh from the Gates of Heaven, our Father, this dear child has come, opening in our hearts springs of new and deeper affection. We thank Thee for this life whose coming has filled our lives with sunshine. Teach us how to live that we may guide it aright, so that as the years pass more and more sunlight shall be radiated. Even as Thine angels kissed the sweet rosebud lips and left a smile thereon, so may we kiss away the tears of life. Heavenly Father, we consecrate this child to Thy service. We pray that the ears may learn to listen for Thy voice, speaking in truth and purity. May the tiny hands be ever ready to do a service of love and may the feet be swift to do Thy bidding. Tenderly guide this precious child, for it needs Thy guidance, and safely guard it through all the years, lest it go astray. This we ask in the name of Him who took little children in His arms and blessed them, saying — "Suffer little children to come unto me, and forbid them not, for of such is the kingdom of Heaven." Amen.

FLORENCE H. PERIN.

*A dreary place would be this **earth**,*
   Were there no little people in it:
The song of life would lose its mirth,
   Were there no children to begin it:

No little forms, like buds to grow,
   And make the admiring heart surrender:
No little hands on breast and brow,
   To keep the thrilling love-chords tender.

*The sterner souls would grow more **stern**,*
   Unfeeling nature more inhuman,
And man to stoic coldness turn,
   *And woman would be less than **woman**.*

***Life's** song, indeed, would lose its charm,*
   Were there no babies to begin it;
A doleful place this world would be,
   Were there no little people in it.

JOHN GREENLEAF WHITTIER.

Our dear Heavenly Father, Thou lookest upon us all as Thy children, — whether our hair be flaxen or brown or white with age. We thank Thee today for the children of our own household, for our children, and all the children, and especially do we thank Thee for the one whose birthday we celebrate here to-day. May Thy blessing be upon him (her), may the skies be bright over his (her) head, — may the birds sing to him (her). May the flowers blossom around his (her) pathway. Thro' all the journey of this life let him (her) have the guidance of Thy Father hand. Amen.

GEORGE L. PERIN.

The boy enjoyed this kind of a father at the time, and later he came to understand, with a grateful heart, that there is no richer inheritance in all the treasury of unearned blessings. For, after all, the love, the patience, the kindly wisdom of a grown man who can enter into the perplexities and turbulent impulses of a boy's heart, and give him cheerful companionship, and lead him on by free and joyful ways to know and choose the things that are pure and lovely and of good report, make as fair an image as we can find of that loving, patient Wisdom which must be above us all if any good is to come out of our childish race.

HENRY VAN DYKE.

By Thy very name, our Father, Thou hast ennobled and sanctified the office of parenthood and attracted to it our respect and love. Thou hast commanded us to honor father and mother, that our days may be lengthened. Assured thus of Thy approval, O God, we call upon Thee to hallow our joy and gratitude on this anniversary day. We thank Thee for him whom we honor as " Father in the flesh " and pray Thee to grant him yet many days with health and strength to minister and to be ministered unto, to grow in grace and in favor with God and man, and to taste the sweet tributes of love and the rewards of good deeds finely done. Amen.

C. ELLWOOD NASH.

Blessings on the hand of woman!
  Angels guard her strength and grace;
In the cottage, palace, hovel, —
  O! no matter where the place.
Would that never storms assailed it,
  Rainbows ever gently curled;
For the hand that rocks the cradle
  Is the hand that rules the world.

Blessings on the hand of woman!
  Fathers, sons and daughters cry;
And the sacred song is mingled
  With the worship in the sky, —
Mingles where no tempest darkens,
  Rainbows evermore are curled;
For the hand that rocks the cradle
  Is the hand that rules the world.

JOHN GRAY.

Heavenly Father, Thou plantest anew Thine own love in the hearts of Thy children and so multipliest Thyself on the earth. We thank Thee today for the manifold incarnation of Thyself in the hearts of all true mothers. We have known the magic charm of mother love and it relates us anew to Thee. Here we celebrate the birthday of one who has honored us and blessed us by a sacred ministry. We thank Thee, our Father, for all the sweet memories of the past, for all the joy of the present relation with her, and for the hope that these sacred associations may long continue. Wilt Thou bless her whose birthday we honor here. Crown her with long life and happy days and the sweet consciousness of having ministered in love. Amen.

GEORGE L. PERIN.

Birthdays, what are they? One will say they are mileposts on the highway of life, marking the distance already traveled and suggesting what yet remains of the journey. Another looking into the deeper meaning of the years will suggest that they are memorial tablets recording the service of a passing life. But no matter under what figure you think of them, the coming into this world of a human life with all the magic powers of thought and love and faith and service is a thing of such transcendent moment, as to make it well worth while to mark the passing of the years.

GEORGE L. PERIN.

Father of all, it is Thou who hast made us and given us all things richly to enjoy; we thank Thee, therefore, for the birthday to which we have come. We thank Thee for the physical life, and all that makes it glad; for the power of intellect, and all the wealth it feeds upon; for love, and all the forms of love which answer to it; for faith which looks on Thee and heaven; for service, the exercise and opportunity of every gift and grace. Help us to be faithful that our felicity may be secure in Thee, and that we may ever recall the day of our birth with rejoicing. This we ask in Jesus' name. Amen.

CHARLES R. TENNEY.